Anonymous

The Influence of the Septuagint Upon the Peschita Psalter

Anonymous

The Influence of the Septuagint Upon the Peschita Psalter

ISBN/EAN: 9783337377724

Printed in Europe, USA, Canada, Australia, Japan

Cover: Foto ©Lupo / pixelio.de

More available books at **www.hansebooks.com**

THE
INFLUENCE OF THE SEPTUAGINT

UPON THE

PEŠIṬTÂ PSALTER

DISSERTATION

SUBMITTED IN PARTIAL FULFILLMENT OF THE REQUIREMENTS
FOR THE DEGREE OF DOCTOR OF PHILOSOPHY IN THE
UNIVERSITY FACULTY OF PHILOSOPHY
COLUMBIA COLLEGE

BY

J. FREDERIC BERG

NEW-YORK

PRINTED BY W. DRUGULIN, LEIPZIG, GERMANY

1895

PREFACE

The striking agreement between many variants of the Pᵉšiṭtâ and Septuagint from the Massoretic Text has long been noticed and commented upon by scholars such as Cornill,[1] Ryssel,[2] Perles[3] and Baethgen.[4] In addition to the occasional remarks in articles bearing upon the textual criticism of the Old Testament, many writers have given special attention to this subject.[5] Its very nature, however, does not permit of its being exhausted by any one scholar, however eminent. Though

---

[1] Cornill, *Das Buch des Propheten Ezechiel*, Leipzig, 1886, p. 153 seq.

[2] Ryssel, *Untersuchungen über die Textgestalt und die Echtheit des Buches Micha*, Leipzig, 1887, p. 169.

[3] Perles, *Meletemata Peschitthoniana*, p. 4.

[4] Baethgen, *Untersuchungen über die Psalmen nach der Peschita*, p. 25.

[5] Sebök, *Die syrische Uebersetzung der 12 kleinen Propheten*, p. 7. R. J. Gottheil, *Zur Textkritik der Pᵉšiṭtâ*, Mitteilungen des Akademisch-Orientalischen Vereins, Berlin 1887, p. 25. Friedrich Baethgen, *Der textkritische Werth d. alten Uebersetzungen zu d. Psalmen*. Jahrbücher für Protestantische Theologie 1882, No. 3, p. 448. Berthold Oppenheim, *Die Syrische Uebersetzung des fünften Buches der Psalmen und ihr Verhältniss zu dem Massoretischen Texte und den älteren Uebersetzungen, namentlich den LXX Targ.*, Leipzig, 1891, p. 3. William Wright, *Syriac literature*, Encycl. Brit. in loco.

we may accept Cornill's results as conclusive for Ezechiel, and Ryssel's for Micha, the question still remains open as regards the remaining thirty-seven books. Much has been done in the way of enlarging and improving the apparatus criticus of the Old Testament; so that a part of the laborious work done by Cornill is now rendered unnecessary. For example, the *Hagiographa Chaldaice* of Paul de Lagarde, Leipzig, 1873; the new critical Baer-Delitzsch Hebrew text, and *The Old Testament in Greek according to the Septuagint* by Swete, render much of the laborious comparison of Mss. unnecessary. It is rather a remarkable fact that the facilities for the critical study of the Pᵉšiṭṭâ are still so meagre and insufficient.[1] Not only are there no critical texts, but even the lexicographical work

---

[1] This fact has been remarked and commented upon by Prof. Gottheil (*Mitteilungen des Akademisch-Orientalischen Vereins*, Berlin, 1889, No. 2, p. 21). He says: "Wenig Mühe ist bis jetzt auf die Textkritik der Pᵉšiṭṭâ verwendet worden. Selbst die HSS., die in den verschiedenen Bibliotheken ruhen, harren noch immer einer genaueren Collation.... Ein ausgezeichneter Gelehrter hat auch jüngst erklärt, dass L. (Ausgabe von Lee) eine durchaus brauchbare und selbst für die textkritische Verwerthung von S im Grossen und Ganzen genügende Ausgabe ist" (Cornill, *Das Buch des Propheten Esechiel*, p. 140). Selbst wenn dieses Urteil für alle Bücher des alten Testaments sich als wahr herausstellen sollte, ist ein in der Weise hergestellter Text ungenügend für einen so wichtigen Bestandteil der syrischen Literatur. Dass der Text der Pᵉšiṭṭâ so "feststehend" gewesen ist, wie Cornill (ibid. p. 138) meint, glaube ich nicht." Also Prager, *De Veteris Testamenti Versione Syriaca quam Peschittho vocant Questiones Criticae*, p. 1: "Plerique viri docti in LXX interpp. versione, et Targumis pertractandis consumpserunt operam. Versio autem, quae illis non inferior mihi videtur dignitate et aetate—Peschittho (ܦܫܝܛܬܐ i. e. "Simplicem") dico—immerito adhuc est neglecta".

on these texts is still in its infancy. Payne-Smith's large *Thesaurus Syriacus*, which is beyond the means of most students, has now been happily supplemented by Brockelmann's handy *Lexicon Syriacum* (Berlin 1895). Yet the value of the Pᵉšiṭtâ for the purposes of lower criticism is being more and more appreciated; and with added appreciation will doubtless, in time, come additional facilities for studying it.

In Part I, under "External Proof of Septuagint Influence", much material interesting both in itself and in connection with the present subject, has been simply referred to, or relegated to a foot note; because it is of a kind easily accessible to students.

The variants of the Greek and Syriac, which largely constitute Part II, are arranged in the following order 1. Hebrew, 2. Syriac, 3. Greek, 4. Aramaic. For the rest, it seemed best to give them in the order in which they appear in the Psalter, following the Hebrew divisions; leaving their classification according to agreement or disagreement with both Hebrew and Aramaic for separate tabulation. In places where the variants seem explicable by a slight alteration of the Hebrew letters, such changes have been suggested in foot notes. These suggestions are entirely subjective; and are simply offered as a plausible, never as an authoritative, solution.

I desire to take this opportunity of acknowledging my deep indebtedness to my instructor, Prof. Richard J. H. Gottheil; not only for many valuable suggestions, but also for his generous loan of books and other material, which were inaccessible to me.

CONTENTS

	page
Preface	III—V

Part I. External evidence of a LXX influence upon the Pᵉšiṭtâ
Psalter .... 1—66
    Ch. I. Introduction .... 1—17
        § 1. General history of the question concerning
            a LXX influence upon the Pᵉšiṭtâ .... 1—10
        § 2. Importance of the question in its relation to
            lower Biblical Criticism .... 11—13
        § 3. Reasons for selecting the Psalter .... 13—17
    Ch. II. The Pᵉšiṭtâ Version .... 18—35
        § 1. Origin of the Pᵉšiṭtâ .... 18—22
        § 2. Authorship of the Pᵉšiṭtâ .... 22—28
        § 3. Characteristics of the Pᵉšiṭtâ Psalter ... 28—35
    Ch. III. Literary and ecclesiastical standing of the LXX
        during the early centuries A. D. .... 35—65
        § 1. New Testament quotations from the LXX . 35—48
        § 2. Quotations from the LXX by later sacred and
            profane writers .... 48—56
        § 3. Characteristics of the LXX Psalter .... 56—63
        § 4. Summary of the external evidence .... 64—65

Part II. Internal evidence of a LXX influence upon the Pᵉšiṭtâ
Psalter .... 66—136
    Ch. IV. Texts and text-criticism .... 66—136
        § 1. The superscriptions of the Psalms .... 66—68
        § 2. Texts used in collecting Greek and Syriac
            variants .... 69—94
        § 3. Greek and Syriac variants compared ... 95—135
        § 4. Summary of the internal evidence .... 134—136

Appendix I. Quotations in the Syriac New Testament from the
        Pᵉšiṭtâ Old Testament .... 137—150
Appendix II. Tabulation of the variants of the several Mss. from
        the text of Lee .... 151—157
Appendix III. Literature consulted .... 158—160

PART I

EXTERNAL EVIDENCE OF A SEPTUAGINT INFLUENCE UPON THE PᵉŠIṬṬÂ PSALTER

Chapter I

INTRODUCTION

§ 1. *General history of the question regarding a Septuagint influence upon the Pᵉšiṭṭâ*

That there exists a similarity between many portions of the Pᵉšiṭṭâ and Septuagint has long been known, yet it is not until comparatively recent times that the subject has received any particularly careful or systematic attention. Indeed it is one which involves so many other intricate problems, the solution of which for years seemed well-nigh hopeless, that its final settlement could only come through a long and tedious process of evolution. Ignorance as to the origin, precise date and authorship of the Pᵉšiṭṭa; misapprehension as to the authority, the literary and ecclesiastical standing of the Septuagint as well as uncertainty as to the original reading of the several texts, had first to be largely removed before any statement could authoratatively be made.

A.—Among the earliest works bearing directly upon our subject, is a book by Joseph Perles, published in 1859 entitled "Meletemata Peschitthoniana". Herein is suggested the probability of interpolations in the Syriac from the Septuagint in Genesis and Jeremiah but "Multo etiam evidentior est interpolatio e LXX petita Proverbiorum loco 11:29, qui locus duas exhibet interpretationes quarum quae alteram sequitur e versione τῶν LXX sumpta est, quod idem de Prov. xiv: 23 observari potest". He also states, that while Ezechiel and especially Proverbs show an affinity to the Targum, yet "In Jesaia et xii minoribus prophetis multa e versione τῶν LXX petita sint".[1]

Again Perles calls attention[2] to the foreign words in the Syriac Pentateuch many of which he refers directly to the Greek.[3] But even if such is the case, we can find in this fact no proof of any direct influence of the Septuagint. The power of the Greek language was felt among all civilized nations during the early centuries of our era, and doubtless many of the Greek words had been simply transliterated and incorporated in the language. That such was the case is evidenced by the large number of Greek words in the Syriac Version of the New Testament. Perles inclines to the opinion that the Septuagint had but little influence upon the Syriac Pentateuch, compared with that exerted by the Targumim. This relative degree of influence, however, is of com-

---

[1] *Meletemata Peschitthoniana*, p. 11, 14.   [2] Ibid, p. 27.

[3] A few examples of such words are Gen. xxi: 23 ܐܣܘܡܐ δῶμα (cf. Arab. ܣܛܚ), xxiv: 22 ܩܕܫܐ σειρά V. 14 (cf. i Kings xvii: 12), ܟܠܐܐ κάλαθος; xxxvii: 25 (Ez. xxvii:17) ܪܝܬܢܐ ῥητίνη (Eng. resin); vi:14 ܩܐܒܘܬܐ κιβωτός; Ex. xvi: 33 ܩܣܛܐ κίστη; xxv: 29 ܦܝܠܐ φιάλη; xxxv: 11 ܒܙܝܐ πόρπη (Onk & Psdjon. פורים); Lev. xx: 23 ܢܡܘܣܐ νόμος; ii: 5 ܡܢ ܠܓܢܐ ἀπὸ τηγάνου; Nu. xviii: 7 ܐܣܟܡܐ σχῆμα; Deut. vii: 4 ܓܠܝܦܐ γλυφή; xx: 20 ܩܪܩܘܡܐ χαράκωμα (Onk & Psdjon. כרכומא).

paratively little importance at present. It is sufficient that the influence exists, a fact which is confirmed by numerous examples in the Commentaries of Ephrem which agree with the Greek Version. Thus e. g. Gen. viii: 7 ויצא יצוא ושוב ܘܢܦܩ ܘܟܕ ܢܦܩ ܗܘܐ ܘܠܐ ܗܦܟ καὶ ἐξελθὼν οὐκ ἀνέστρεψεν— Gen. xiv: 7 ויכו את־כל שדה העמלקי ܠܟܠ ܪܘܪܒܢܐ ܕܥܡܠܩܝܐ πάντας τοὺς ἄρχοντας 'Αμαλήκ—Gen. 47: 31 על ראש המטה ܥܠ ܪܝܫ ܚܘܛܪܗ ἐπὶ τὸ ἄκρον τῆς ῥάβδου αὐτοῦ—Ex. xix: 13 במשך היובל ܘܡܐ ܕܢܬܩ ܩܪܢܐ ὅταν αἱ φωναί.... ἀπέλθῃ and many[1] others. In addition to this direct witness to a Septuagint influence upon the Pᵉšiṭtâ, Perles gives much valuable material for determining the origin and authorship of this Version which will be referred to in that connection.

B.—The next real advance in determining the extent of Septuagint influence was made by Isaac Prager in a work entitled "De Veteris Testamenti Versione Syriaca quam Peschittho vocant questiones criticae" published in 1875. Prager treats chiefly of two things: 1st, the origin and authorship of the Pᵉšiṭtâ; 2nd, the superscriptions of the Psalms. The former is undoubtedly of the utmost importance in connection with the question of a Septuagint influence upon the Pᵉšiṭtâ; for only in proportion as we have accurate information concerning the authorship and circumstances attending the origin of the Syriac Version, can we arrive at any definite conclusions concerning the various influences which have determined its character.[2] Prager gives but little direct testimony to Septuagint influence. In one place[3]

---

[1] e. g. Gen. ii: 4, 23, 24; iii: 2, 7, 9, 11, 16; iv: 8, 10, 15, 17, 25; v: 23, 29; vi: 10; vii: 8, 20; viii: 7, 17, 22; ix: 2, 5, 7, 20; xi: 27; xii: 3; xiv: 20; xv: 5; xvi: 6; xvii: 16; xviii: 5, etc.

[2] Further reference is made to this work in Ch. ii, § 1.

[3] *Loc. Cit.*, p. 28.

he somewhat casually remarks: "Occurunt nobis interdum loci, ubi ad litteram fere vocabula singula et in Peschittho et in LXX Versione inter se conveniunt", but he also adds: "neque tamen eandem efficiunt vim sententiarum".

C. The next work which comes under our consideration bears directly upon the subject under discussion—The Septuagint influence upon the Pᵉšiṭta Psalter—"Untersuchungen über die Psalmen nach der Peschita" *Part I* (published in 1878) by Friedrich Baethgen. After treating slightly of the origin and name of the Syriac Canon, the superscription of the Psalms and the history of the printed text, he makes a valuable contribution[1] in the tabulation of a list of variants collected from three Berlin Mss.[2] With three exceptions he seems to have accepted the text of Lee as sufficiently critical for his purposes. Baethgen's method of classification of the Greek and Syriac variants may be best discribed in his own words: "Ich gebe zu diesem Zweck im folgenden zunächst ein Verzeichniss derjenigen Stellen, in welchen der Syrer vom Hebraeer abweicht und zwar in vier Abtheilungen; die erste umfasst die Stellen, in welchen LXX, Hieronymus und Chaldaeer auf Seiten des Syrers stehen; die beiden folgenden die, in welchen zwei oder einer dieser Zeugen sich ihm anschliessen, und die vierte endlich die, mit welchen der Syrer allein steht."[3]

---

[1] P. 21—22, 23.

[2] "Ms. orient. Diez A octav 160 vollendet A. D. 1507 enthält die Psalmen nach der Peschita mit arabischer Interlinearversion; ebenso Ms. Diez quart 118 geschrieben A. D. 1515, beide in melkitischer Schrift. Ms. orient. quart 374, den Schriftzügen nach aus dem 17. oder 18. Jahrhundert, enthält die Psalmen von 26, 9 ܕܘܝܕ ܒܪܝܟ an; die Schrift ist Jacobitisch." For a tabulation of these variants, see ch. iv § 2.

[3] The last two divisions, at least in the form proposed, did not appear—leaving the work incomplete.

In this treatise Baethgen gives about one hundred variants, which is about one quarter the entire number. Very probably the article to which he refers when he says:[1] "Aeussere Gründe veranlassen mich augenblicklich nur dieses Bruchstück meiner Arbeit in dem für Habilitationsschriften vorgeschriebenen Format zu veröffentlichen. Das Ganze soll wie ich hoffe in kurzer Zeit erscheinen" is that which appeared in 1882 in the "Jahrbücher für Protestantische Theologie"[2] entitled "Der textkritische Werth der alten Uebersetzungen zu den Psalmen". This last gives only about seventy-five Greek and Syriac variants, which, though containing much valuable and excellent material, must yet be considered unsatisfactory so far as the question of a Septuagint influence upon the Peŝiṭtâ is concerned for the following reasons.

1) The variants of the different Syriac Mss. are not noted, leaving it uncertain what the correct reading is or possibly might be.

2) The number of the Greek and Syriac variants which agree with each other against the Massoretic text is small; and selected, as it were, at random, from the whole Psalter, give no suggestion as to the probable entire number of variants.

3) The variants tabulated are not compared with the Aramaic, leaving it questionable whether both the Greek and Syriac variants may not find their true explanation in the Targumim.

4) The Latin translation, substituted to a large extent for the Syriac text, must necessarily be unsatisfactory and insufficient for the present discussion.

5) There is no complete summary or tabulation of results. Of the list of variants[3] taken from the Septuagint, Syriac

---

[1] p. 30. [2] No. 3, p. 405—459 and No. 4, p. 593—667.
[3] *Loc. Cit.* No. 4, p. 593 seq.

Hieronymus and Targum, many are open to criticism as representing mistranslations of Hebrew tenses. Possibly a few rules may be laid down with moderate certainty subject always to exceptions; but the fact that the Hebrew Text which formed the basis of the Septuagint was undoubtedly without vowel points, as well as the fact that many vowel letters were not written,[1] make it a very delicate task to alter the translations of the Hebrew tenses upon the basis of Septuagint readings;[2] for, in any case, translation and exegesis must be closely interwoven. Baethgen himself says regarding these variants: "Der Werth oder Unwerth dieser Varianten ist nur vereinzelt angedeutet, denn es sollte ein kritischer Apparat, nicht ein Kommentar geliefert werden".[3]

D. In the year 1886 appeared that masterpiece of modern textual criticism "Das Buch des Propheten Ezechiel" by Dr. Carl Heinrich Cornill. An entire chapter is here devoted to the Syriac text of Ezechiel; and Dr. Cornill conclusively proves a

---

[1] On quiescent vowel letters cf. Chowlson *Hebraica*, Vol vi; Paul de Lagarde, *Anmerkungen zur griech. Uebersetz. d. Prov.* (p. 4); and Driver, *Notes on the Hebrew Text of Samuel*, p. lxix.

[2] A few examples are ψ iv: 2 עֲנֵנִי] O (= Sept.) εἰσήκουσε μου = עֲנָנִי, ם (= Syriac) exaudisti me. ψ ix: 10 ויהי] O Praeterit Hι כם (כ = Targ) fut.—Yet the future is common as a past in the language of poetry, cf. Driver, *Hebrew Tenses*. Ch. iii, § 27 a and f. V. 14 חנני] O ם ἐλέησόν με = חנני; ψ x: 14 יעזב] O ם יעוב; ψ xxvii: 8 בקשו] O ם as praet. = בקשו; ψ xxix: 10 ישב ם as praet. = ישב; ψ xxxiii: 17 ימלט] O ם ימלט; ψ xlix: 20 יראו] O ם ὄψεται = יראה; ψ lvi: 2 שאפני] O ם conculcavit me = שאפני V. 9. שמה] O ἔθου = שמת; ψ lix: 16 וילני] O murmurabunt = וילינו; ψ lxiv: 5 יראו ם = יראו; ψ lxv: 3 שמע] O ם שָׁמַע ψ lxxix: 7 אכל] O ם אכלו By omitting the vowel signs and letters, it is readily seen that any such emendation is very arbitrary.

[3] *Jahrbücher für Protestantische Theologie* No. 3, p. 406.

Septuagint influence upon the Pᵉšiṭta text of that book. He says[1]: "ᵓ ist nämlich keine reine Recension sondern eine gemischte. Zunächst hat LXX bedeutend auf sie eingewirkt". While the list of variants noted is confessedly incomplete, they are sufficient to bear out his statement that "ᵓ offenbar LXX, welche auf eine ganz andere Lesart zurückgeht, mit dem massorethischen Texte combiniert hat"[2]. Some of the agreements between Syriac and Greek against the Hebrew are noted below.[3]

E. In the following year 1887 Dr. Ryssel published his "Untersuchungen über die Textgestalt und die Echtheit des Buches Micha". For purposes of determining the precise relation of the Septuagint to the Pᵉšiṭtâ the work is not as conveniently, perhaps scientifically, arranged as that of Cornill. In a chapter on the Pᵉšiṭtâ[4] he says: "Besondere Erwähnung verdient noch die Abhängigkeit der Pesch. von den LXX. Mögen einzelne Uebereinstimmungen auch in der nämlichen Textvorlage und mehr noch in der gemeinsam ihnen zu Gebote stehenden exegetischen Tradition ihren Grund haben, immerhin müssen die meisten dieser *Uebereinstimmungen auf directe Benutzung der*

---

[1] *Das Buch des Propheten Ezechiel*, p. 153.   [2] Ibid., p. 154.

[3] p 153—viii: 5 המזבח την προς ανατολας ܚܕܒܫܢܐ; xi: 7 הוציא ἐξάξω ܐܢܐ ܐܦܩ; xxx: 9 בצים להחריד σπευδοντες αφανισαι ܚܣܝܡܝܢ ܠܡܚܒܠܘ. Dagegen scheint mir directe Abhängigkeit von LXX vorzuliegen in Fällen wie—xvi: 54 בנחמך אתן εν τῷ παροργισαι (σε) με ܒܪܘܓܙܟܝ; xvii: 3, 22. את צמרת τα επιλεκτα ܓܒܝܬܐ; xvii: 22 מראש ינקותיו רך אקטף εκ κορυφης καρδιας αυτων αποκνιω ܠܒܗ ܐܩܛܘܦ ܡܢܗ; xxiv: 4 מבחר עצמים מלא] εκσεσαρκισμενα απο των ορων ܒܬܕܟܐ ܢܕ̈ܒܚܝܢ; xxvii: 11 ונמדים και φυλακες ܘܩܠܝܢ V. 20 בבגדי חפש μετα κτηνων εκλεκτων ܒܩܠܝܢ ܕܟܒܘܕ̈ܐ; xxviii: 13 תפך ונקבך τους θησαυρους σου και τας αποθηκας σου ܡܓܫܠܬܟ ܚܕ ܬܥܠܝ ܚܕ et al.   [4] Ibid., p. 171.

LXX zurückgehen". He remarks further on that: "Die Syrische Uebersetzung wenigstens in ihrer gegenwärtigen Gestalt vielfach von der LXX abhängig ist". "Ihre gegenwärtige Gestalt" would of course include many interpolations. While Dr. Ryssel does not enter into any very elaborate proof of a Septuagint influence, yet his frequent reference[1] of Syriac variants to that source leaves us no doubt that such an influence exists to a large extent in the Book of Micha.

F.—As has already been stated, one of the difficulties in the way of an ultimate adjustment of the relations of Septuagint and Pešiṭtâ, is to obtain the original text of the Syriac. That there were subsequent Syriac translations made directly from the LXX we know. Some fragments are still preserved of the translation of Jacob of Edessa, which represents a commingling of the old Pešiṭtâ and the Alexandrine version. Another translation of this nature is that of Polycarp, made in the beginning of the sixth century, largely after the recension of Lucian. Of more importance yet is the Syriac reissue of the Hexapla cited by Eusebius and Pamphilius, and made in Alexandria by Bishop Paul of Tella.[2] How far, then, the text of the old Pešiṭtâ was altered in conformity with these translations in its subsequent reissues, is a question of considerable importance. Prof. Richard Gottheil is of the opinion that the Ms. used by Bar 'Ebrâyâ had been modified in

---

[1] Thus for example i: 5, 6, 8, 11; ii: 4, 6; vii: 8 (in part); xi: 12 (compare ἐν θλίψει) iii: 7; iv: 1, 12; vi: 2, 8, 9; vii: 3, 4a, 12. Also i: 13a "ist vielleicht ܐ vor ܪܟܫܐ eine spätere Correctur nach dem Griech. ἱππευόντων—i: 2 (durch πάντες οἱ ἐν αὐτῇ der LXX bedingt sein". cf. furthur ii: 1; ii: 6, 7, 12; iii: 1; vi: 10 et al.

[2] Cf. Buhl, *Old Testament Canon*, p. 145; De Sacy, *Notices et Extraits des Mss. de la Bibl. Nation.* iv, 648 seq.; Field, *Hexapla* i. p. lxvii.

accordance with the Syriac Hexapla.¹ He says, in commenting upon the text of Bar ʿEbrâyâ: "Es sind nicht nur die mâsôretischen Bemerkungen für die Geschichte des Pešittâ-Textes von Belang. Der Text selbst, den ʿEbrâjâ citiert, weicht öfters von dem ab, der uns gewöhnlich vorliegt und es ist die Frage nicht unberechtigt, woher diese Verschiedenheit stamme. Dass ein Mann wie Bar ʿEbrâjâ, wenn er sich vornimmt einen Text zu kommentieren — ja sogar *festzustellen* — rein aus dem Gedächtnis diesen Text citieren sollte, scheint mir höchst unwahrscheinlich. Dass er verschiedene Codices benutzt hat, deutet er selbst an — einige sollen sogar wegen ihrer Correctheit berühmt gewesen sein. Dass auch er selbst — trotz seiner Vorliebe für die hexaplarische Uebersetzung — solche hexaplarische Lesarten an Stelle der der Peʿittâ gesetzt haben soll, klingt mir gleichfalls unwahrscheinlich. Es müssen solche schon in seiner Vorlage gestanden haben".² In consequence, the variants of the text of Bar ʿEbrâyâ are of considerable importance since they may represent the original readings. In connection with the question of a Septuagint influence upon the original Pešittâ text, Prof. Gottheil remarks:³ "Dass der ursprüngliche Text der Pešittâ unter dem Einfluss der LXX gestanden hat, ist bekannte Thatsache.... Bemerkenswert ist es auch, dass die Hs. Sachau 215, die Excerpte aus dem Commentar des Theodor von Mopsuestia enthält, im Text mehr Berührungen mit den LXX zeigt als der von Lee".

G. One of the most recent articles bearing upon the present subject is "Die Syrische Uebersetzung des fünften Buches der

---

[1] *Mittheilungen des Akademisch-Orient. Vereins;* Berlin 1889, No. 2 pp. 22—28.

[2] P. 25; cf. also Rahlfs, *Zeitschrift für Alttest. Wissenschaft* ix, p. 161 seq.

[3] P. 25 note 14.

Psalmen (107—150) und ihr Verhältnis zu den Massoretischen Texte und den älteren Uebersetzungen"[1] by Berthold Oppenheim. In his preface he tabulates about forty or fifty places where a Septuagint influence upon the Pᵉšiṭṭâ may be observed, but does not give the text. Throughout his work he makes frequent reference to the LXX, and plainly states:[2] "Das Verhältnis der Peschitta zu den LXX und Targ. ist hiernach derartig, dass sie selbständig und frei übersetzt hat, jedoch auch vielfach durch LXX beeinflusst wurde". This work must be considered unsatisfactory for several reasons, chiefly the following 1) It is extremely cumbersome and, as there is neither final tabulation of results nor systematic classification of the variants, is of little practical use. 2) There is no intimation upon what Syriac or Septuagint text the author bases his conclusions, and it is therefore unscientific.

Such are some of the principle works bearing directly upon the question of the Septuagint influence upon the Pᵉšiṭṭâ. Many others[3] might be mentioned, but without materially adding to the data already obtained. As the question thus stands, we must consider a Septuagint influence as certain in Ezechiel and Micha, and probable in the Psalter.

[1] Leipzig, 1891.   [2] Ibid., p. 4.
[3] Hertzel, *De Pent. Ver. Syr. quam P. vocant*, 1825; Credner, *De Prophetarum minor. versionis Syr.*; Stenij, *De Syriaca libri Yobi interp.* Helsingfors, 1887; Fränkel, *Animadversiones Criticae in Ver. Syr. Pesch. librorum Koheleth et Ruth*, 1871; Baethgen, *Deutsche Literatur-Zeitung*, Oct. 13, 1894. col. 1284 seq; König, *Einleitung*, p. 124 seq; Nestle, *Hertzog's Real-Encycl.* XV, 192 seq.; Wright, *Syriac Literature*, Ency. Brit. *in loco*.

§ 2. *The importance of the question of a LXX influence upon the Pᵉšiṭtâ in relation to lower Biblical criticism*

In matters relating to the textual criticism of the Old Testament, because of the greater age of the Septuagint, the Pᵉšiṭtâ has always been obliged to take a subordinate place. The inevitable result of this tendency has been to curtail the critical authority of the Pᵉšiṭtâ when it differs from both Septuagint and Massoretic text. But while the Syriac rendering is seldom, if ever, adopted against both Greek and Hebrew, it is yet somewhat inconsistently considered a strong confirmation of the version with which it agrees. If we are to lay down the general a priori rule that the Pᵉšiṭtâ is in error when it stands alone, it must follow that its agreement with either or all of the other versions is a matter of no consequence. Such a conclusion no one will admit; but the question still remains open: *How much* importance shall be attached to the Syriac variants which are against the other authorities? The answer to this question must largely depend upon the answer to another: Is the Pᵉšiṭtâ an independent translation? If it is, its critical value is greater then that now ascribed to it; but if not—if it has been influenced by other translations, as the Septuagint and Targum—it must ever content itself with a rank subordinate to these two.

In consequence of this uncertainty as to the true position of the Pᵉšiṭtâ, the work of textual criticism is at present largely subjective; the student weighing the evidence upon his own intellectual scales, and deciding by no other index than his own judgement, guided by the following rules[1] each of which may be subject to exception:

[1] Merx, *Das Gedicht von Hiob*, Introduction, p. lxxiii.

I. Stimmt Peschita und Septuaginta gegen den masorethischen Text, so enthalten sie das Aeltere.

II. Stimmt Peschita und Masora gegen Septuaginta, so hat letztere das Präjudiz, aber nicht die Gewissheit, das Echte zu bieten.

III. Stimmt Masora und Septuaginta gegen Peschita, so können nur die gewichtigsten inneren Gründe die Entscheidung auf die Seite der Peschita lenken. Die drei soeben angeführten Reihen von Stellen werden dies belegen.

Such are the rules which are followed in the main by textual critics.

To demonstrate that the Peširtâ is not an independent translation it will not be sufficient simply to discern traces of Septuagint influence in the rendering of individual words. We must determine, if possible, how that influence was brought to bear upon the text; whether the LXX was the original text or a critical commentary, only such renderings being accepted as in the judgement of the Syriac translators best expressed the meaning of the original; or, whether there was a still greater dependence, the LXX being employed as a translation in a language more familiar than the Hebrew, and as such being often bodily substituted in phrases, and even whole verses, when the original was difficult or unintelligible. Nor must we fail to ascertain whether the readings of both LXX and Peširtâ, when they agree, may not be traced to a common source in the Aramaic Targum.

If as the result of these investigations the Peširtâ displays a marked conformity to many LXX variants from the Massoretic Text, we must conclude it to be in a measure dependent upon that version; and, in consequence, its conformities to that text will be of less importance than its deviations; especially if such variants cannot be directly ascribed to the Targum or to translators' errors (both of which explanations, however, are often entirely satisfactory)[1]. Moreover if the Pešittâ be proved to be a dependent translation, the foregoing rules for textual criticism must be modified as follows:

I. When the Pešittâ and Septuagint agree against the Massoretic text, there is a probability, but not an absolute certainty, in favor of the latter.

II. When the Pešittâ and Massoretic Text agree against the Septuagint, only the weightiest internal reasons can decide in favor of the latter.

III. When the Pešittâ is against both Septuagint and Massoretic Text, the latter is to be preferred.[2]

§ 3. *Reasons for selecting the Book of Psalms*

A.—The first reason which makes the Psalter especially desirable as the basis of an investigation as to the mutual relation of Septuagint and Pešittâ, is the fact that the texts of the Hebrew, Greek and Syriac Psalters are in good condition. While the Hebrew presents many passages difficult of interpretation, yet there are few unintelligible, a statement which could not be made regarding other books, e. g. Job.

Of the 70 Qerês in the Book of Psalms, 49 concern simply the omission of a ו or a י, or the substitution of one of these letters for the other.[3] Occasionally we meet with instances where another reading might be substituted[4] as

[1] On the relation of the Pešittâ to the Targum, cf. Cornill, *Das Buch des Propheten Ezechiel*, p. 154—5; Ryssel, *Micha*, p. 170; Baethgen, *Jahrbücher für Protestantische Theologie* 1882, No. 3, p. 448.

[2] The variants of the Pešittâ would be of greater value if it were not for the undoubted ignorance of Hebrew shown by some of its translators. See ch. II, § 3.

[3] Baer-Delitzsch Ed. of The Psalms p. 155.

[4] cf. Capellus, *Critica Sacra*, lib. iv. ch. ii. and v. viii; Cornill,

ψ xviii: 11 וידא על־כנפי־רוח with which cf. ii Sam. xxii: 11 וירא על־כנפי־רוח. More numerous are the variants in vocalization as ψ lxxv: 7 מִדְבָּר and מְמַדְבָּר, or between the Massora and old translations as ψ ii: 9. תִּרְעֵם LXX, Syr. Jerome. תְּרֹעֵם; ψ x: 17 תָּכִין LXX Syr. Sym. תָּבִין; ψ xi: 3 הַשָּׁתוֹת LXX, Syr. הָשֵׁת; ψ xv: 4 לְהָרַע LXX, Syr. לְהָרֵעַ; ψ ci: 5 אֹתוֹ לֹא אוּכָל LXX אֹתוֹ לֹא אֹכַל. Examples might be multiplied; but it is evident that such variant readings are of little importance, since they do not materially affect the sense.

While the Greek text varies widely in many places from the Massoretic Text, yet the Mss. are remarkably consistent with each other. The vast majority of variants[1] is made up either of different spellings of the same words, or of synonymous words; thus ψ xvii: 38 B ἐκλίπωσιν, AU ἐκλείπωσιν, ψ xxii: 4 B κακα, R πονηρα. The result is that in those instances where a Greek variant can be made to agree with the Hebrew by substituting a different reading the presumption is in favor of the variant.

Among the Syriac Mss. we find still fewer variants than among the Hebrew Mss. Of these some are errors in spelling; a few are really different readings; but the large majority are

---

Ezechiel, p. 127; Wellhausen-Bleek, *Einleitung* p. 616; Buhl, *Old Test. Canon*, p. 237; The variants shown by the different Mss. have been most completely collated by J. B. De Rossi, *Variae Lectiones Vet. Test.* 4 vols. Parma 1784—98. But little help in restoring the original passages can be obtained from these variants of the Mss., since all belong to the same recension and are all descended from the same archetype. cf. Lagarde, *Proverbien*, p. 2; Olshausen, *Die Psalmen* (1883), p. 17 seq; Driver, *Notes on the Heb. Text of Samuel*, p. xxxvii.

[1] Old Test. in Greek, ed. by Swete, with appendix; also *Quinquagena prima Ps.* ed. by Lagarde.

simply the omission or addition of a ܘ[1]. In regard to the Pᵉšittâ text Buhl remarks:[2] "Although the critical establishment of the Peshito text is indeed still in its infancy, it is even already clear that no important results are to be expected from any future criticism of the text"[3]. Certainly we must get far back of existing codices, if we wish to find any very important variants from the commonly accepted text.[4]

B.—A second reason for selecting the Psalter is found in the fact that while Greek and Syriac variants are to be found in every book of the Old Testament, they are especially numerous in the Book of Psalms. Prager[5] in commenting upon the agreement of words in the Septuagint and Pᵉšittâ says: "Eiusmodi exempla quae plus minusve in omnibus Scripturae Sacrae libris maximeque in Psalmis exstant". Driver also[6] refers to the Psalms as affording the most numerous illustrations of variants of the Septuagint from the Hebrew. We may therefore confidently expect that if a Septuagint influence upon the Pᵉšittâ is to be found in any or every book, it will at least be most evident in the Psalter.

C.—A third reason lies in the fact that no other book of the Old Testament is more frequently quoted by New Testament and other sacred writers[7] than this book of Psalms, nor

---

[1] See Appendix ii.

[2] *Old Testament Canon*, p. 192.

[3] This is perhaps a sweeping assertion and can only apply to the known Mss. Nor is much to be hoped for from the quotations of Ephrem and Aphraates.

[4] See Appendix ii.

[5] *De Vet. Text. Syr. Quaest. Crit.*, p. 28.

[6] *Notes on Heb. Text of Sam.* Introduction, p. lxv.

[7] Toy, *Quotations in the New Testament*. Introduction. "Early Quotations from LXX"; Hatch, *Essays in Biblical Greek*, p. 172; Perles, *Melet. Pesch.*, p. 53—54; Staerk, *Alttestament. Citate bei*

has any other book obtained such extensive ecclesiastical use. Baethgen[1] declares: "Neben und vor dem Pentateuch ist bei Syrern wie in allen Kirchengemeinschaften, der Psalter das vorzüglichste alttestamentliche Erbauungsbuch gewesen, und man ist von vorn herein geneigt anzunehmen, dass er der Gemeinde besonders früh zugänglich gemacht sei". Owing to this extensive liturgical use of the Psalter, its language has become interwoven with world history and fairly moulded into the minds of men. Even He who "spake as never man spake" found in the songs of David the fittest expression of his feelings, and at last breathed out his soul in the words of the "Sweet Psalmist of Israel". To this fact are likewise to be attributed many of the Greek and Syriac variants: but they are of a nature easily detected, consisting chiefly in the repetition of certain set words or phrases intended either to enhance the sacredness of the passage or, as is equally probable in consideration of their musical use, to fill out the metre.[2]

den Schriftstellern des Neuen Test. Zeit. für Wissenschaft. Theologie. vol. 38, p. 218.

[1] *Untersuchungen über d. Psalmen nach d. Pesch.*, p. 6.

[2] e. g. ψ iii:8 ὁ θεός μου; ψ 4:8 καὶ οἴνου καὶ ἐλαίου αὐτῶν; ψ v:11 Κύριε; ψ vii:12 καὶ ἰσχυρὸς καὶ μακρόθυμος; ψ x:5 τὸν δίκαιον καὶ τὸν ἀσεβῆ; ψ xvii:7 ἐκ ναοῦ ἁγίου; xvii:31 ὁ θεός μου (the poss. pronoun μου is thus frequently added especially in connection with the name of God) cf. V. 47; ψ xxiv:5; xxvii:1; xliii:5 but seldom is it omitted as xlii:2; ψ xliv:6 Δύνατε; ψ lix:12 ὁ θεος; ψ lxiii:2 ἐν τῷ δέεσθαί με πρός σέ; ψ lxvii:6 ταραχθήσονται ἀπὸ προσώπου αὐτοῦ; ψ lxvii:34 ψάλατε τῷ θεῷ; ψ lxxxiv:9 ἐν ἐμοί (making the appeal more personal); ψ xciv:4 ὅτι οὐκ ἀπώσεται Κύριος τὸν λαὸν αὐτοῦ; ψ cxiii:25 αἰνέσουσίν σε Κύριε; ψ cxliv:14 πιστὸς Κύριος ἐν τοῖς λόγοις αὐτοῦ καὶ ὅσιος ἐν πᾶσι τοῖς ἔργοις αὐτοῦ. For further examples see ch. iii, § 3.

D.—Again, in the variety of thought and language of the Psalms is given the largest scope for the P[e]šiṭṭâ translators to display their knowledge of Hebrew, and their ability to render it in their own language, idiom for idiom; for in its songs of triumph, in its confessions of sin, in its prayers of thanksgiving and its outbursts of grief, in its prophetic utterances as well as historical reminiscenses, the Psalter adapts itself to every emotion and requirement of man. Furthermore, the book is not exposed to those modifications by historians and theologians to which are liable such books as Kings, Chronicles, Samuel and the Prophetical writings.

We come now to the main discussion of the question of the Septuagint influence upon the P[e]šiṭṭâ, which naturally falls into two chief divisions.

I. The external evidence of such an influence, obtained from facts connected with the origin, authorship and character of the P[e]šiṭṭâ version, as well as from the contemporaneous literary and ecclesiastical standing of the Septuagint and the most striking characteristics of that version.

II. The comparison of the Greek and Syriac variants which agree with each other against the Massoretic Text and the Targum.

The Syriac additions are of a precisely similar nature; as ψ xvii : 1 ܫܡܥ ܡܪܝܐ ܙܕܝܩܐ; ψ xxiv : 2 ܘܥܠܗܘܢ; V. 5 ܐܠܗܐ ܦܪܘܩܢ; ψ xxviii : 1 ܐܠܗܝ (cf. ὁ θεός μου in the preceding) and ψ lxxx : 3 ܐܠܗܐ ܚܝܠܬܢܐ; ψ cxlii : 8, 9 ܡܪܝܐ; ψ xlii : 6 ܡܛܠ ܕܬܘܒ ܐܘܕܐ ܠܗ ܠܦܪܘܩܐ ܕܐܦ̈ܝ ܘܐܠܗܝ; ψ xlvii : 9 ܥܡ ܐܠܗܗ ܕܐܒܪܗܡ. Also, by an insertion of the pronoun ܠܟ (cf. Grk. σοι and σε) the appeal is made personal, ψ lvi : 12; ψ lxxiv : 18; ψ cx : 2; ψ lxxxiv : 9 ܐܠܗܐ ܐܠܗܘ̈ܬܢ; ψ lxxxvi : 11 ܢܚܕܐ ܠܒܝ ܟܐܝܠܝܢ ܕܕܚܠܝܢ ܠܫܡܟ; ψ cxxxi : 5 ܠܐܠܗܗ ܕܝܥܩܘܒ. Further examples are given in ch. ii : § 3.

Chapter II

THE P^ešIṬTÂ VERSION

§ 1. *Origin of the P^ešiṭtâ*

Concerning the origin of the P^ešiṭtâ much has been written, but little is certainly known. Tradition, it is true, supplies us with some information; but it is difficult to know just how to separate that which is historic from that which is purely legendary, the true from the false. Bar 'Ebrâyâ in the preface to his book ܐܘܨܪ ܐܪ̈ܙܐ[1] says ܟܠܗ ܕܝܢ ܗܕܐ ܡܦܫܩܢܘܬܐ (ܡܦܩܬܐ ܦܫܝܛܬܐ) ܬܠܬ ܡܦܫܩܢ̈ܘܬܐ ܗܘܝ. ܚܕܐ ܡܢ ܕܒܝܘܡܘܗܝ ܕܫܠܝܡܘܢ ܘܕܚܝܪܡ ܡܠܟܐ ܐܬܦܫܩܬ ܕܬܪ̈ܬܝܢ ܕܐܣܝܐ ܟܗܢܐ ܟܕ ܫܕܪܗ ܐܬܘܪܝܐ ܠܫܡܪܝܢ ܐܥܒܪܗ ܕܬܠܬ ܕܒܝܘܡܝ ܐܕܝ ܫܠܝܚܐ ܘܐܒܓܪ ܡܠܟܐ ܕܐܘܪܗܝ ܐܬܦܫܩܬ. ܐܡܬܝ ܕܐܦ ܠܕܝܬܩܐ ܚܕܬܐ ܗܘ ܒܡܕܒܪܢܘܬܐ ܦܫܝܛܬܐ ܐܥܒܪܘ. But all of these theories bear a very suspicious resemblance to the traditional sending of "The Seventy", and no reliance can be placed upon them. That it could not have been composed later than the time of Ephrem has been successfully demonstrated by Wiseman;[2] and that Ephrem himself is not the author is sufficiently evidenced by the fact that he quotes from it, calling it ܡܦܩܬܢ "Our Version". Modern scholars agree that it was in common canonical use at his time. This is inferred from the words of Ephrem who speaks of the P^ešiṭtâ[3] as "The Scriptures" thus: ܢܒܝܐ ܕܗܪܟܐ ܐܡܪ ܟܬܒܐ ܥܒܪܝܐ ܗܘ ܕܝܢ ܒܪܢܫܐ ܢܚܘܗ; also as "Inter-

[1] Assemani, *Bibliotheca Orientalis*, vol. ii, pp. 24, 279.

[2] *Horae Syriacae*, pp. 107—108.

[3] The name P^ešiṭtâ does not occur in any of the early writings,

pres" ܕܝܘ ܕܡܠ ܡܢ ܕܝܠܬܗ ܗܘ ܕܣܘܪܝܐ ܐܝܟ ܕܥܒܕ ܐܢܐ.[1] These words Ephrem would probably not have used had not the version been commonly accepted.[2] Furthermore, in view of the fact that Ephrem was ignorant of the meaning of many words used in the Old Testament Pešiṭtâ, and taking into consideration the long lapse of time necessary for words to become obsolete, it may very properly be concluded that the Pešiṭtâ was written long before the time of Ephrem, when intermixed with the so-called Chaldee it resembled

and is only first met with in Mss. of the ninth and tenth centuries (Buhl, *Old Testament Canon*, p. 185). The precise meaning of the name is somewhat doubtful. Prager (*De Vet. Test. Syr.*, p. 1) says "De nomine "Peschittho" multum est disceptatum. Alii ducunt ܦܫܝܛܬܐ a ܦܫܝܛ vocabulo, voluntque esse "vulgatam, vulgo acceptam, canonicam"; alii statuunt Peschittho significare "Simplicem" i. e. quae ad verbum exemplo adstipulatur, vocemque opponunt "versionibus paraphrasticis" (ut apud Judaeos על דרך הפשט opponitur הדרוש). Hanc vero sententiam refutare studuit Geiger (Verhand.[d. erst. Versam. deut. u. ausländ. Orient., p. 9) qui, ratus, פשט vocabulum proprie respondere verbo "explicandi", "Peschittho" esse "explicatam" "conversam" voluit". Abul-Pharaj (Bar 'Ebrâyâ) goes so far as to refer the name to the Arab. بسيطة. The most probable explanation is that suggested by Field and Nöldeke: ἁπλᾶ, by way of contrast to the Syro-Hexapla translation which had obtained a wide circulation among the Syrians. The designation was at first only applied to the Old Testament, but later included the New Testament as well. (Buhl, *O. T. Canon*, p. 185.)

[1] *Opera* i, 498 comment. to i Kings xviii : 44.
[2] Prager (p. 4) cites Ephrem (opp. 1 : 380 ad i Sam. 24 : 4) ܥܠ ܕܝܢ ܗܕܐ ܐܡܪ ܥܒܕܐ ܕܒܥܠܕܒܒܐ ܗܘ ܕܠܟܠܗܘܢ and says "ܡܦܩܬܐ igitur opponitur voci ܦܫܝܛܬܐ, idcirco intellegendum est: versio quam nos, i. e. scriptor, pro fundamento iecimus, quam nos sequimur".

the language of the Targum. Thus Wichelhaus[1] states "Num inde conjecturam faceret de Pesch. aetate et patria nescius ut rem expediret, nomina quae Ephraem interpretatur spectare ad res raras remotasque a communi vitae usu statuit; at virum doctissimum fugit res maximi momenti; nam quamvis verba plebs nesciret, tamen novisse debebat Ephraem vir sermonis Syriaci peritissimus."[2]

We have moreover the statement of Jacob of Edessa[3] that certain scribes were sent by the Apostle Adai and by Abgar, King of Edessa into Palestine to translate the Scriptures; a statement which Išoʻdad, bishop of Hadatha, partially corroborates when he says[4] (referring to Chronicles and the Prophetical Books) ܐܬܗܐ݂݂ ܕܚܕܚܕܢܐ ܕܟܬܒܐ ܕܕܘ̈ܒܐ ܟܬܒ̈ܗܐ ܡܛܠ ܐܝܘܪ̈. ܚܝܡܥܩ̈ܗܐ ܕܐܬܝ.݁݁ ܘܒܟܬܐ ܕܥܠܬܢ̈. Of a similar nature is the account given by Abul Pharaj[5]
وهذا النقل السبعينى هو المعتبر عند علمائنا وهو الذى بايدى الروم وباقى فوق النصارى حلا السريان وخصوصا المشارقة فان نسختهم المسماة بسيطة (الترك البلاغة فى نقلها) تطابق نسخة اليهود واما المغاربة فلهم النقلان البسيط المنقول من العبرانى الى السريانى بعد مجىء السيد المسيح فى زمان ادى السليح وقيل قبله فى زمان سليمان بن داود وحيرم.

The first reliable witness to the existence of the Pᵉšittâ is Athanasius (about A.D. 350); but as Christianity had undoubtedly found a foothold in Syria by the middle of the second century, Greek not being generally known, of necessity there must have been some translation of the Scriptures into the Syriac language long before the time of Athanasius.

---

[1] *De Novi Test. Versione Syriaca Antiqua.*
[2] cf. Perles *Melet. Pesch.*, p. 4, nt. h.
[3] Bar ʻEbrâyâ to ψ x; Wiseman, p. 103.
[4] Assemani, *Bibliotheca Orientalis*, iii, 1, p. 212.
[5] Pococke, *Historia Dynastiarum*, p. 100.

We should be furnished with a conclusive proof of the early existence of the Pᵉšiṭtâ if the ὁ Σύρος cited by Melito Sardensis[1] could be proved to be identical with it. But unfortunately it is very uncertain exactly to what this ὁ Συρος, often quoted by early church fathers,[2] refers. Field has suggested that this ὁ Συρος was a translation of the Old Testament into Greek which circulated in Syria.[3] This is quite probable. Even if it be assumed that ὁ Συρος was a Syriac translation existing in the second century, it is yet impossible, without further evidence, to prove its identity with the Pᵉšiṭtâ. Certainly the passage quoted by Melito κρεμαμενος ἐν σαβεκ (Gen. xxii : 13) does not agree with our present text. Theodore of Mopsuestia gives us little hope of establishing any identity between the two when he states:[4] ἡρμήνευται δὲ ταῦτα εἰς μὲν τὴν Σύρων παρ' ὅτου δήποτε οὐδὲ γὰρ ἔγνωσται μέχρι τῆς τήμερον ὅστις ποτὲ οὗτός ἐστίν.

A final witness to the early existence of the Pᵉšiṭtâ Old Testament is the Syriac New Testament. While it is for the most part slavishly faithful to the Greek, yet, in quoting from the Old Testament in a number of instances, it follows the Pᵉšiṭtâ against both Hebrew and Septuagint[5]. As the Syriac

[1] on Κατεχόμενος τῶν κεράτων, he says ὁ Σύρος καὶ ὁ Ἑβραῖος κρεμάμενός φασιν κτλ. Scholia ad Gen. xxii : 13.

[2] Diodorus, Gen. xxii : 13 (בסבך אחז) τὸ ἐν φυτῷ οὐκ ἔχει ὁ Σύρος μόνον δὲ τὸ Σαβέκ (ܣܒܟܐ) τοῦτο δὲ τὸ ὄνομα τοῦ φυτοῦ εἶναι νομίζω τοῖς δὲ Ἑβραίοις δοκεῖ τὸ Σαβὲκ (סבך) ἄφεσιν σημαίνειν. Similar references are made by Eusebius, Hieronymus, Theodoret et al. See also Perles, *Melet. Pesch.* Annot. i, p. 49—51.

[3] See Buhl, *Old Testament Canon*, p. 187.

[4] *Scriptorum veterum nova collectio e Vat. codd.* edita ab Ang. Maio. Romae 1832. tom. vi, p. 194: Theodor. Mopsuest. in Sophoniam C. i, 6.

[5] See Appendix i.

New Testament was completed by the latter part of the first century[1] or towards the end of the second,[2] the Pᵉšiṭtâ Old Testament must have existed at or before this time.

§ 7. *Authorship of the Pᵉsiṭtâ*

A.—Proof of a plurality of authors

A question of equal importance to that of the precise or approximate date of composition, and of equal difficulty in determining satisfactorily, relates to the authorship of the Pᵉšiṭtâ. That this version is the work of many hands is well known.[3] Passing over the tradition of the sending of a *number of scribes* by Abgar, it is only necessary to glance at the character of the various books to find positive evidence of several or many authors. Thus, while the Pentateuch is very literally translated, modified slightly by the influence of the Septuagint and to a larger degree by the Targum, the book of Chronicles[4] possesses all the peculiarities of a Jewish Targum.[5] As a matter of fact this book did not originally belong to the Syriac canon;[6] and Fränkel, who has examined it carefully, conjectures that it was composed by Jews of Edessa in the third century.[5] Proverbs likewise resembles the Aramaic Targum;[7] while the Psalms

---

[1] Wichelhaus, p. 120.

[2] Hug, *Einleitung in d. Schrift d. N. T.*, i, p. 366 seq. Prager, *De Vet. Test. Syr.*, pp. 12, 32.

[3] Perles, *Melet. Pesch.*, p. 6—8. Prager, *De Vet. Test. Syr.*, pp. 13 seq.

[4] Howorth, *The true Sept. Version of Chronicles-Esra-Nehemiah*. Academy July 22, 1893, pp. 73, 74.

[5] Buhl, *Old Testament Canon*, p. 191.

[6] Ibid. p. 53. It is noteworthy that this book is not interpolated on the basis of the LXX. *Jahrbücher für Protest. Theologie* v. 758.

[7] Perles, *Melet. Pesch.*, p. 14.

although a free translation, bear no such resemblance. The text of Job is in parts unintelligible, due partly to corruption from external causes, partly to the influence of other translations.¹ The Minor Prophets are for the most part well, although freely, translated.²

If further proof of a plurality of authors is needed, it may be found in the statement of Ephrem who refers to them in the plural ܗܠܝܢ ܡܦܫܩܢܐ ܣܘܪܝܝܐ. The precise number being of no importance, (nor could it possibly be ascertained) the next question which naturally arises is: were the translators Jews, or Christians, or both? Supporting a solely Jewish authorship may be mentioned Simon;³ a solely Christian origin Hirtzel,⁴ Kirsch⁵ and Gesenius.⁶ More numerous are those supporting a Jewish-Christian authorship, among whom are Perles,⁷ Dathe,⁸ Noeldeke⁹ and Wichelhaus(?)¹⁰

---

[1] Stenij, *De Syriaca libri Jobi interpret.* i.

[2] cf. Credner, *De Proph. minor. versionis Syr.*, Sebök, *Die syrische Uebersetzung der 12 kleinen Proph. und ihr Verhältniss zu dem Mass. Text.* cf. Perles, p. 14.

[3] *Histoire critique du vieux Text*, p. 305.

[4] *De Pent. Syr. Vers.*, p. 129.   [5] *Pent. Syr.*, p. xiv.

[6] *Commentar über den Jesaja*, vol. i, p. 85 seq.

[7] *Melet. Pesch.*, p. 21.   [8] *Praef. in Ps. Syr.*, p. xxiii seq.

[9] *Die Alttestamentliche Literatur*, p. 263.

[10] It is doubtful which opinion Wichelhaus favors, since he is not consistent in his statements. Perles calls attention to this fact: "Uno loco (p. 73) dicit se vix credere, versionem Simplicem a Judaeis scriptam esse quia "in Talmude proculdubio hujus versionis mentio exstaret, si hominis Judaei esset opus. Neque ea simplicitate gaudebant Judaei qua versio Syrorum nitet et emicat" alio vero loco (p. 119) auctore rege Izate in Palaestina factum esse censet. Sed vir in Syriacis doctissimus non satis traditionum Palaestinensium notitia imbutus fuit, ut earum vestigia in Pesch.

B.—Arguments for Jewish Authorship

One of the strongest arguments for a Jewish authorship of the Pešiṭtâ is the familiarity, not to say dependence, which its authors place upon Jewish tradition.[1] The resemblance which many of the books bear to the Aramaic Targum has already been referred to. That these could have been the work of a Syrian Christian is not only highly improbable; but, taken into consideration with the complete absence of any motive for such work, wellnigh impossible. A further argument is found in the fact that the Apocrypha was wanting in the original Syriac canon.[2] Perles, in opposition to the theory of Wichelhaus says: "Nos statuimus, originem Judaïcam versionis Simplicis ex interna eius indole satis demonstrari aliterque eius locus difficillimus omnino non explicari posse".[3] In support of this statement there follow numerous examples from the Prophets, Hagiographa etc. One or two of these will suffice: ii Sam. xxiv: 15 ויתן ה' דבר בישראל מהבקר ועד עת מועד ܒܐ ܓܝܪ ܀ ܘܡܛܬ݀ ܠܥܕܢ ܚܬܡ. Syrus in eandem sententiam de verbis עד עת מועד abit quam de illis Rabbini statuerunt, Berach. 62 b. מהבקר ועד עת מועד מאי עת מועד אמר שמואל סבא התניא דר' חנינא משמיה דר' חנינא משעת שחיטת התמיד עד שעת זריקתו ר' יוחנן אמר עד חצות ממש. Also ii Kings xxv: 3. Hebrew reads simply בתשעה לחדש the Pešiṭtâ ܘܐܬܚܣܢ ܟܦܢܐ ܠܡܕܝܢ̄ܬܐ ܕܡܢ ܘܠܝܬ ܗܘܐ ܠܚܡܐ ܕܢܐܟܠܘܢ ܥܡܐ ܕܐܪܥܐ, with which cf. Jer. xxxix: 2 and lii: 2.[4]

invenire portuisset" (*Melet. Pesch.*, p. 15). Cf. also the statement of Prager, *De Ver. Syr.*, p. 19.

[1] Schönfelder, *Onkelos und Pesch.* 1869. Berliner, *Targ. Onkelos* ii: 126; Sebök, *Die Syr. Uebersetz. d. 12 kl. Proph.*, p. 7; Cornill, *Esechiel*, p. 154 seq.

[2] Buhl, *Old Testament Canon* § 69, p. 187—8.

[3] *Melet. Pesch.*, p. 16.

[4] Many more examples are given by Perles, *Melet. Pesch.*, p. 17 seq.

While these and numerous other examples drawn from the Pentateuch leave little room to doubt that the authors of these books were Jews, at least so far as birth and education are concerned; yet there is nothing to warrant the additional inference that they were likewise Jews in faith; and it is difficult to see with what motive a Jew of the first or second century would have produced a version of the Scriptures like the Pᵉšiṭtâ. Moreover, none of the Jewish writings make mention of any such translation of the Syrian Jews; though frequently referring to the Septuagint, Aquila and the Targumim.[1] Prager says:[2] "Quod vero aiunt versiones non ita ad litteram factas ut Aquilae, nec tam paraphrasticas quam Targumim, propter eam ipsam causam non a Judaeis esse profectas: haec argumentatio absurdissima mihi videtur". But since nationality depends upon birth, education and character, while religion is simply a conviction, it may be expected that the former will leave plainer traces than the latter. The one is easily seen in the authorities consulted, the style and form of composition; the other more subtly discerned in—the motive.[3]

C.—Arguments for Christian Authorship

From the earliest times of which we have record the Pᵉšiṭtâ has been claimed by the Syrian Christians as their Bible trans-

[1] Buhl, *Old Testament Canon*, p. 186.
[2] *De Vet. Test. Syr.*, p. 17.
[3] Buhl (*Old Testament Canon*, p. 185) suggests the possibility of the Jews residing in the border lands between the Roman and Parthian empires being in need of a translation of the Old Testament into their own language. But this is improbable, in view of the familiarity with Jewish tradition, and therefore presumably with the Hebrew language, upon which the main argument for Jewish authorship is largely based.

lation[1], and it is referred to frequently by Ephrem as ܡܦܩܬܐ "Our Version". Whatever of truth there may be in tradition is on the side of Christian authorship. The negative argument advanced by Noeldeke: "Ferner ist die Peš̄ittâ so weit wir wissen nie von Juden gebraucht", is rather weak. Nothing can be argued from the fact that the name ܦܫܝܛܬܐ does not appear in the Talmud, since it is only first employed by Bar 'Ebrâyâ. But certain words, as תרגום and מתרגמין[2], make it uncertain whether or not a Syriac Version is quoted in the Talmud; in all probability it is not.[3] The dialect, according to Noeldeke, is the same as that of the New Testament; but this fact proves little. The strongest argument in favor of a purely Christian authorship is derived from the many passages which bear a Christian coloring. Thus, for example, Is. vii : 14 הנה העלמה הרה the Peš̄ittâ renders ܗܐ ܒܬܘܠܬܐ ܒܛܢܐ which makes the passage a direct references to the birth of the Messiah from the womb of the virgin.[4] Evidently a Jew would not have rendered עלמה by ܒܬܘܠܬܐ. Is. ix : 5 ויקרא שמו....אל גבור ܘܐܬܩܪܝ... ܐܠܗܐ ܓܢܒܪܐ; Is. liii : 8 כי נגע למו ܡܛܠ ܕܡܚܐ; Is. lii : 15 כן יזה ܗܟܢܐ ܢܕܟܐ; Ps. xix : 5 בכל הארץ יצא קום ובקצה תבל מליהם לשמש שם־אהל בהם ܐܪܥܐ ܢܦܩܬ ܡܠܬܗܘܢ ܘܒܣܘܦܝܗ̇ ܕܬܒܝܠ; Ps. cx : 3 עמך נדבת ביום חילך ܕܥܡܟ ܡܫܒܚܐ ܒܝܘܡܐ; also Zach. xii : 10 והביטו את אשר דקרו ܘܢܚܘܪܘܢ ܠܗܘ ܕܕܩܪܘ. These and other similar passages would give us pretty sure

---

[1] Buhl, *Old Testament Canon*, p. 186.
[2] cf. Talmud of Palestine, Sabbath c. 16, § 1; Megilla 3 a.
[3] Prager, *De Vet. Text. Syr.*, p. 18, also p. 19 note 3.
[4] The common Syriac equivalent for עלמה is ܥܠܝܡܬܐ, cf. Prager, p. 19.

proof of Christian authorship, provided we could be certain that these passages were a part of the original translation, and not subsequent modifications. Unfortunately this cannot at present be demonstrated; and therefore the only verdict which can be pronounced upon the arguments for Christian authorship[1] is "not proven".

D.—Argument for Jewish-Christian authorship

The theory which embraces whatever is plausible in both of the preceding opinions, and is open to none of the objections to either, is the one which has obtained the largest number of adherents, i. e. that the authors of the Pešittâ were proselyte Jews, viz. Jewish Christians. The view that they were both Jews and Christians does not seem plausible; for it is extremely doubtful if they could have engaged harmoniously in such a work. Buhl[2] says: "The probability is strongly in favor of the idea that it (Pešittâ) owed its origin to Christian effort, while, to some extent, fragments of older Jewish translations[3] have been made use of in it; and for the rest, the translation was made by Jewish Christians". Since we have no means of definitely discriminating, there can be no valid objection to extending the Jewish-Christian authorship over the whole

[1] cf. Wiseman, *Horae Syriacae*, p. 100 seq.
[2] *Old Testament Canon*, p. 186.
[3] Prager advances the theory that the Pešittâ was translated by Jews and handed down by them to the Christians; who, either from ignorance of the Hebrew language or from dissatisfaction with some of its doctrines, changed many of the passages. In this way were added some of the "later messianic superscriptions" to the Psalms. There is, however, nothing to warrant any such an assumption; and the undisputed fact that some passages were changed by later Christians does not militate in the least against an early Christian origin.

Old Testament. While, like the others, this theory cannot be stringently demonstrated, its plausibility is sufficient excuse for resting it upon the impossibility of its being disproved.

§ 3. *Characteristics of the Pᵉšiṭtâ*

We have already seen how varied is the character of the Pᵉšiṭtâ in individual books. Let us now particularize and inquire concerning the most marked characteristics of the Syriac version of the Book of Psalms. The Pᵉšiṭtâ Psalter bears the superscription ܟܬܒܐ ܕܡܙܡܘܪܐ ܕܕܘܝܕ ܡܠܟܐ ܘܢܒܝܐ.[1] Its division into books is the same as the Hebrew[2]; but the enumeration of the Psalms is slightly different. Ps. cxiv is combined with Ps. cxv (as in the LXX), while Ps. cxlvii is divided at verse 12.[3] A striking feature of the Syriac Psalter is the freedom with which the Hebrew superscriptions are omitted. This was first done, according to the statements of Syriac writers, through the influence of Theodore of Mopsuestia.[4] The superscriptions[5] which exist in the various Mss. are a later addition taken from the commentaries of the

---

[1] The Hebrew is simply ספר תהלות. The Ceriani text bears the superscription ܬܫܒܚܬܐ ܕܡܙܡܘܪܐ ܕܕܘܝܕ.

[2] BK. i: ψ 1—41; BK. ii: 42—72; BK. iii: 73—89; BK. iv: 90—106; BK. v: 107—150.

[3] This is also the case in the LXX; but the P. does not unite ψ ix and x.

[4] Baethgen, *Z. A. W.* 1885, p. 66 seq., and *Untersuchung über d. Ps. nach d. Pesch.*, p. 10 seq.; Prager, *De Vet. Test. Syr.*, p. 49 seq.; Wright, *Catalogue of Syr. Mss. in Brit. Museum*, i, 116 seq.; Buhl, *Old Testament Canon*, p. 190.

[5] The authenticity of the superscriptions is discussed in Part ii.

Church Fathers, and especially from Theodore.[1] The general style of the Pᵉšiṭṭâ Psalter is by no means uniform. In some places it is faithful to the original, in others irreconcilable with it both from a grammatical and lexicographical point of view. Sometimes it gives a literal rendering, again proceeds with the greatest freedom, at times bordering on incoherency. This statement finds its illustration in many of the Psalms.[2]

One of the most noticeable characteristics of this translation is the frequency with which personal pronouns are supplied or interchanged:—ψ xxii : 5 בטחו] ܣܒܪܘ ܒܟ; ψ ii : 12 דרך] ܐܘܪܚܗ; ψ iv : 2 בצר] ܒܐܘܠܨܢ; ψ xviii : 15 וברקים] ܘܒܪܩܘܗܝ; ψ xxiii : 3 שמו] ܫܡܟ; ψ xxvii : 7 אקרא] ܕܩܪܝܬܟ; ψ xxix : 2 קדש] ܕܩܘܕܫܗ; ψ xli : 6 לבו] ܒܠܒܗܘܢ; ψ xlix : 18 לך] ܠܗ; ψ l : 21 והחרשתי] Pesch. + ܠܟ; ψ li : 10 תכבסני] ܫܠܠܝܢ ܗܘ; ψ lii : 8 אל] ܐܠܗܘܢ (Ceriani); ψ lix : 4 ורצון] Peš. + ܥܠܝ; ibid. ויכוננו] Peš. + ܥܠܝ; ψ lxiv : 1 בשיחי] ܟܕ ܐܬܟܫܦܬ ܠܟ; ψ lxxii : 3 בצדקה] ܒܙܕܝܩܘܬܟ; ψ xcvi : 4 יהוה] ܡܪܢ; ψ ciii : 4 הגואל] ܦܪܩ ܠܟ; ψ cxvi : 16 פתחת] ܫܪܝܬ ܐܢܬ; ψ cxix : 7 לבב] ܠܟ; V. 18 גל] Peš. + ܠܝ; ψ cxxxvii : 4 נשיר] Peš. + ܠܗܘܢ; cf. also ψ xxii : 5; ψ xxxii : 5; ψ xlix : 13; ψ l : 21; ψ cxv : 14; ψ cxvi : 18; ψ cxvii : 16; ψ cxviii : 26; ψ cxxxix : 11; ψ cxxvi : 4; ψ c : 3; ψ cxvii : 7; ψ lxxxviii : 66; ψ cx : 2.

Much less common is the omission of a pronoun; a few examples are ψ xxvi : 3 באמתך] ܒܗܝܡܢܘܬܐ; ψ xl : 3 לאלהינו] ܠܐܠܗܐ; ψ xlix : 12 בשמותם] ܫܡܗܐ; ψ lxxxv : 13 וארצנו] ܘܐܪܥܐ; ψ cxv : 14 עמו] ܥܡܐ; ibid. v. 18 עמו] ܥܡܐ;

[1] cf. *Studia Biblica* vol ii: Neubauer, *Authorship and Titles of the Psalms according to Eearly Jewish Authorities.*

[2] e. g. ψ xxxv; ψ xl; ψ xlv; ψ xli; ψ lxxxix; ψ cxxxix; ψ cxl.

ψ cxlvii : 17 קרחו] ܓܠܝܕܐ; cf. also ψ xvii : 14; ψ xxiv : 6; ψ xxviii : 1, 7; ψ xxxi : 16; ψ lxxxv : 3; ψ cix : 5.

Sometimes words and phrases are added with a view to supplementing or continuing the thought:—ψ xvi : 11 שבע שמחות את־פניך ܐܣܒܥ ܡܢ ܚܕܘܬܗ ܕܦܪܨܘܦܟ ܘܡܢ ܒܣܝܡܘܬܐ נעמות בימינך ܕܙܟܘܬܐ ܕܝܡܝܢܟ; ψ xxii : 31 זרע יעבדנו יספר לאדני לדור ܘܙܪܥܐ ܕܢܦܠܚܘܢܗ. ܢܫܬܥܐ ܕܡܪܗ ܠܕܪܐ; ψ xxviii : 8 עז־למו ܚܝܠܐ ܗܘ ܕܦܘܪܩܢܗ; ψ xxxv : 12 שכול לנפשי ܘܐܘܒܕܘ ܢܦܫ ܐܒܠ ܠܚܡܝ ܕܐܬܚܠܦܐ; ψ xli : 9 אוכל לחמי ܡܢ ܒܢ̈ܝܢܫܐ; ψ xlv : 2 יפיפית ܫܦܝܪ ܒܚܙܘܗ; ibid. 13 ממשבצות זהב לבושה ܘܡܨܒܬܐ ܠܒܘܫܗ ܕܕܗܒܐ ܠܓܠܐ; ψ lii : 6 ועליו ישחקו ܘܢܫܒܚܘܢ ܒܡܪܝܐ ܘܢܐܡܪܘܢ; ψ lvii : 17 ואזמרה ܘܐܙܡܪ ܘܬܫܒܚܢ ܢܫܒܚܘܢ; ψ lxv : 11 ומעגליך ירעפון. דשן ܒܐܝܡܪ̈ܝ ܬܕܐܪܐ; ψ lxvi : 6 שמך ܠܫܡܟ ܠܥܠܡ̈ܝܢ; ibid. 4 לכו ܘܢܐܡܪ̈ܘܢ ܬܘ; ibid. 16 קראתי ܩܪܝܬܗ ܘܫܒܚܬ; ψ lxxviii : 44 בל־ ישתיון ܕܠܐ ܢܫܬܘܢ ܡ̈ܝܐ; ψ xc : 2 ותחולל ארץ ותבל ܘܥܕܠܐ ܬܬܚܠܠ ܐܪܥܐ ܘܥܕܠܐ ܬܬܬܩܢ ܬܐܒܝܠ; cf. also ψ l : 21; ψ lii : 10; ψ lxxii : 10; ψ lxviii : 9, 17; ψ cvii · 3.

Frequently several Hebrew words are rendered either by one of the same words, or by a different word conveying a similar idea:—ψ xxxi : 3 תנחני ותנהלני ܬܕܒܪܢܝ; ibid. 19 פעלת לחוסים ܠܕܡܣܬܒܪܝܢ; ψ xxxiii : 2 בנבל עשור ܒܩܝܬܪܐ ܕܥܣܪ̈ ܢܒ̈ܝܢ; ibid. 14 ממכון שבתו ܘܡܢ ܡܬܩܢ ܡܘܬܒܗ; ψ xxxvii : 20 כיקר כרים ܡܩ̈ܠܡܐ; ψ xxxviii : 22 אדני תשועתי ܦܪܘܩܢܝ; ψ xlii : 4 ואשפכה עלי נפשי ܘܐܬܦܠܓܬ ܢܦܫܝ; ψ lxiv : 1 תצר חיי ܢܛܪܢܝ; ψ lxviii : 15 הר־אלהים הר־בשן הר גבננים הר־בשן ܠܛܘܪܐ ܕܓܒܢܐ ܠܛܘܪܐ ܕܒܫܢ; ψ lxxi : 13 חרפה וכלמה ܒܗܬܬܐ ψ lxxvii : 11 אזכיר מעללי־יה כי־אזכרה מקדם פלאך ܡܛܠ ܕܐܬܕܟܪܬ

ܠܟܠܗܘܢ ‎; ψ cxviii : 66 טוב טעם ܟܠܗܘܢ
ܘܡܘܠܟܢܝܗܘܢ.

The word ܟܠ or ܟܠܗ is frequently added; this is significant when compared to the similarly frequent occurrence of the Greek πάντες (see below). Examples of such instances may be found in ψ xiii:3; ψ xxii:18; ψ xxiv:2; ψ xxvi:7; ψ xxxii:5; ψ xxxvi:12; ψ xlv:12; ψ xliii:4; ψ lvi:4; ψ lviii:2; ψ lxii:9; ψ lxix:19; ψ lxxv:5; ψ lxxviii:51; ψ lxxxix:47, 50; ψ xcvii:6; ψ ciii:22; ψ cvii:3; ψ cxi:2; ψ cxviii:35, 119; ψ cxxxviii:4.

A Hebrew singular, especially where it has a collective signification, is frequently rendered by the plural:—ψ xix:7 פתי ܠܫܒܪܐ (This is an invariable rendering; cf. also ψ cxv:6, ψ cxviii:130); ψ xxvii:14 לבך ܠܠܒܘܬܗ; ψ xlv:3 חן ܛܝܒܘܬܐ; ψ xlvi:4 נהר ܢܗܪܘܬܐ; ψ lxxiv:15 ונחל ܘܢܚܠܐ; ψ lxxvi:6 ܘܟܠ ܢܡܐ ; ψ lxxx:11 ואל-נהר ܘܠܢܗܪܘܬܐ ;ܘܐܒܕ ܕܐܒܐ ורכב וסוס; ψ lxxxix:15 תרועה ܚܓܘܫܬܢܐ; v. 19 וחסיד ܘܡܣܦܣܐ.ܘ; v. 44 מטהרו ܡܕܟܝܢܘܗܝ; ψ cxviii:36 אל-בצע ܠܒܨܬܐ; v. 109 ܒܟܦܝ ܒܐܝ̈ܕܝ; ψ cxxxviii:15 עצמי ܓܪܡܝ̈; v. 17 מה עצמו ܡܠܐ. ܘܫܠܛܝܢ ܘܐܢܐ ܚܫܒܬ ܪܐܫיהם. Very seldom, on the contrary, is a Hebrew plural rendered by a singular. A few instances may be cited, as ψ x:5 משפטיך ܕܝܢܟ; ψ xlv:9 בגות ܒܪܬ; ψ lii:4 דברי-בלע ܡܠܬܐ ܕܡܒܠܠܝܢ; ψ cxxxi:1 ענותו ܡܘܟܟܗ; ψ cl:2 בגבורתיו ܒܚܝܠܬܢܘܬܗ.[1]

Some of the variants in the Pᵉšiṭṭâ can be traced directly to carelessness, the author translating a word similar in appearance or sound. ψ xiii:3 עצות ܚܛܗܐ – עצבת; ψ lix:4 הגה ܕܗܡܣ – המה; ψ lxix:5 מצמתי ܥܡ ܣܢܐܝ̈ –

---

[1] cf. Baethgen, *J. P. T.* 1882, No. 3, p. 427.

מעצמותי; ψ lxxxiv:7 אל־אלהים ܐܠܗܐ ܐܠܗ̈ܝܢ — אֱל־אלהים; ψ lxxxvii:7 ושרים ܘܪ̈ܘܙܒܢܐ — ושׂרים; ψ lxxxix:47 זכר־אני מהחלד ܐܬܕܟܪܝܢ ܡܢ ܫܘܝܐ — זכרני מחלד (?); ψ xc:15 כימות עניתנו ܡܛܠ ܕܡܝܬܘ ܚܘܒܝܢ — כי מתו עונותנו; ψ xci:3 מדבר ܡܢ ܡܡܠܠܐ — מדבר (cf. LXX ἀπὸ λόγου); ψ xcviii:7 ירעם ܢܘܥ — ירעם; ψ cii:8 מהוללי ܘܡܫܒܚܢܝ — מהללי; ψ civ:12 מבין עפאים ܡܢ ܒܝܢܬ ܟܐܦ̈ܐ — כיפאים; ψ cvii:8 חסדו ܘܚܣܝ̈ܕܘܗܝ — חסידיו; ψ cxviii:116 כאמרתך ܒܡܠܬܟ — באמרתך. Throughout the entire Syriac Psalter the Hebrew כ is rendered ܒ. Carelessness is also shown in the inversion of two words connected by the simple copula:— ψ xxxii:4 יומם ולילה ܒܠܠܝܐ ܘܐܝܡܡܐ; ψ xliv:5 מלכי אלהים ܐܠܗܐ ܡܠܟܝ; ψ lxxiv:20 נאות חמס ܚܛܘܦܐ ܘܥܘܠܐ; ψ lxxxii:3 פלטו־דל ואביון מיד רשעים הצילו ܦܨܘ ܠܡܣܟܢܐ ܘܠܒܨ̈ܝܪܐ ܘܠܡܣܟܢܐ ܘܠܡܚܝ̈ܠܐ ܦܨܘ; ψ cxxxix:10 גם־שם ידך תנחני ותאחזני ימינך ܐܦ ܬܡܢ ܐܝܕܟ ܬܐܚܕܢܝ ܘܬܕܒܪܢܝ ܝܡܝܢܟ.

A striking characteristic of the Syriac, for which it is difficult to account, is its invariable rendering of a rhetorical question by a negative sentence. As this rule is without exception, a few examples will suffice:—ψ xviii:32 etc. כי מי אלוה ܡܛܠ ܕܠܝܬ ܐܠܗܐ; ψ xxx:9 היודך עפר היגיד אמתך ܠܐ ܡܘܕܐ ܠܟ ܥܦܪܐ ܘܠܐ ܡܚܘܐ ܗܝܡܢܘܬܟ; ψ lvi:8 על־און פלט־למו ܘܐܡܪܘ ܕܠܝܬ ܠܗ ܡܦܨܝܢܐ; ψ xlix:6 למה אירא בימי ܠܐ ܕܚܠ ܐܢܐ; ψ l:13 האוכל ܠܐ ܐܟܠ ܐܢܐ; ψ lxxxv:7 הלא אתה תשוב ܐܠܐ ܐܢܬ ܐܗܦܟ; ψ lxxxix:47 על־מה־שוא ܡܛܠ ܕܠܐ ܣܘܦܐ.

Sometimes the abstract is rendered in Syriac by the concrete, possibly through carelessness or ignorance, but most

probably intentionally, with a view to imparting additional vividness of expression. So also the symbol is sometimes put for the thing symbolised,—ψ vii: 14 הנה יחבל־און ܡܛܠ
ܕܚܒܠ ܥܘܠܐ; ψ ix: 6 תמו חֳרָבוֹת ܚܪܒܘܗ ܒܣܝܦܐ, here the sword is regarded as the symbol of destruction (another explanation is that the Syriac translator read חֲרָבוֹת); ψ xvii: 7 חסדיך ܬܕܡܘܪ̈ܬܐ; ψ xxv: 21 תם־וישר ܬܡ̈ܝܡܐ ܘܬܪ̈ܝܨܐ (cf. LXX ἄκακοι καὶ εὐθεῖς); ψ xxvi: 6 בנקיון ܕܒܟܐܢܘܬ; ψ xxxvi: 1 נאם־פשע לרשע ܡܬܚܫܒ ܥܘܠܐ ܪܘܫܥܐ; ψ xxxvii: 37 שמר־תם וראה ישר ܛܪ ܬܡܝܡܘܬܐ ܘܚܙܝ ܬܪܝܨܘܬܐ (with this cf. LXX Φύλασσε ἀκακίαν καὶ ἴδε εὐθύτητα); ψ lii: 1 חסד אל ܘܥܠ ܡܣܟܢܐ v. 4 דברי־בלע ܕܡܡܠܠܝܢ ܥܘܠܐ; ψ lv: 4 עלי און ܡܛܠ ܕܢܓܠܗ ܥܠ ܥܘܠܐ; ψ lix: 3 עזים ܒܥܘܫܢܗܘܢ; ψ lxxii: 3 בצדקה ܘܙܕܝܩܘܬܟ; ψ lxxvii: 13 בקדש ܡܩܕܫܐ ܗܘ; ψ lxxxv: 13 צֶדֶק ܘܙܕܝܩܘܬܐ; ψ cvii: 42 ישרים ܘܙ̈ܕܝܩܐ; ψ cxviii: 29 שֶׁקֶר ܕܥܘ̈ܠܐ v. 113 סעפים ܠܥܘ̈ܠܐ v. 133 כל־און ܥܘܠܐ; ψ cxix: 2 משפת־שקר ܡܢ ܣܦ̈ܘܬܐ ܕܥܘ̈ܠܐ; ψ cxliv: 4 וגבורתיך ܘܓܢܒܪܘܬܟ cf. ψ cl: 2.

The name of God is frequently supplied; sometimes the word ܐܠܗܐ, but more usually ܡܪܝܐ. This characteristic finds its probable explanation in the excessive liturgical use of the Psalter, and is further significant when taken in connection with the still more frequent occurrence in the Septuagint of ὁ θεός. Examples of additions of this word may be found in ψ xxviii: 1; ψ xxxi: 4; ψ li: 14; ψ cxi: 9; ψ cxviii: 68; ψ cxlii: 9; ψ cxxxi: 2, 5, ψ cxliv: 13; ψ cxlvi: 9. Strangely enough the Syriac falls nowhere more lamentably short than in its rendering of tropes applied to the name of God. This can hardly be due either to misapprehension or lack of appreciation of rhetorical figures, since they are freely employed in other instances as we have seen above. The only explanation I can offer is of an exceedingly speculative nature. At all times and among all nations the majority of religious people have been the laboring class, the "common people", the poor who, as a rule, are also the ignorant. To such, a metaphor or a trope, except of the most commonplace nature, is as the language of the sphinx. In order therefore to prevent any possible misconception, where God himself is concerned, only figures of the simplest kind, such as could be apprehended by even the most ignorant, were employed. Such was the plan adopted by Luther; except that he sought in his use of language not only to accomodate but also to elevate. So, the fewer the tropes, the more readily would those employed associate themselves with the sacred name. Thus סלעי and צור and מגן are alike usually translated by one word ܚܝܠܐ ܡܥܕܪܢܐ cf. ψ xviii:2; ψ xxii:10; ψ xxxi:3; ψ xl:2; ψ xlii:9; ψ lxxi:3; ψ lxxviii:16; ψ civ:18; ψ xci:3; ψ cxviii:114; ψ cxliii:2; et al. מגן however, unlike סלעי and צור, is sometimes rendered by other words as ܡܣܥܪܢܐ; ψ iii:3; ψ xxxiii:20; ψ lxxxiv:9; ψ cxv:9, 10, 11; ψ cxliii:2; by ܡܚܣܝܐ as ψ xviii:35; ψ xxxi:6; ψ xxxv:2; by ܡܣܝܥܐ; ψ lxxxiv:11; by ܡܣܬܘܪܐ ψ xlvii:9; by ܬܘܟܠܢܐ ψ lix:11; and by ܡܠܟܐ ψ lxxvi:3. בידך is often rendered simply by ܠܝ ψ xxxi:5; ψ lxxxix:12. These peculiarities meet with no explanation in the Septuagint.

The Syriac shows a fondness for long sentences; frequently combining two short sentences by means of causal or final particles. ψ ix:21, ܕܓܒܪܐ; ψ xxxiii:20 ܡܛܠ ܕܗܘ; ψ xxxvii:35 ܠܓܒܪܐ ܕܐܬܝ; ψ lxxii:4 ܕܒܗܘܢ. At other times the Syriac resorts to paraphrases which bear little or no resemblance to the Hebrew; ψ cxxxix:16 גלמי ראו עיניך ועל־ספרך כלם יכתבו ימים יצרו ולא אחד בהם ܘܥܠ ܣܦܪܟ ܟܠܗܘܢ ܢܬܟܬܒܘܢ ܒܐܝܡܡܐ ܢܬܓܒܠܘܢ ܘܠܐ; ψ lxxiv:5, 6, ועת קדמות ואת יודע במעלה למעלה בסבך־עץ

ܘܐܡܪ ܐܝܟ ܗܠܝܢ ܓܠܐ ܦܬܚܗ ܝܚܕ ܒܡܫܠ ܬܗܠܬܗ ܘܬܫܒܚܬܗ ܢܐܡܪܘܢ
ܐܝܟ ܗܢܐ ܐܡܘܢ܀ ܘܡܪܝܐ ܒܛܠ ܐܢܘܢ ܥܕܡܐ ܠܥܠܡ ܥܠܡܝܢ
ܘܬܘܒ ܥܒܘܕܐ ܘܩܒܘܠܐ cf. also ψ lxv: 8, 11; ψ cix: 17;
ψ cxxxix: 4; ψ clxv: 14; ψ cii: 5.

From these main characteristic features of the Pᵉšittâ Psalter, three facts may be inferred concerning the translator or translators.

I. Their knowledge of Hebrew was imperfect as evidenced by the numerous mistakes and departures from that text which can only be attributed to ignorance.

II. Their motive, more religious than scholarly, was to secure a readable translation, not a critical version.

III. In the diversity of style, part literal, part free, there is suggested a dependence upon other translations, possibly the Septuagint and Targum.

Chapter III

LITERARY AND ECCLESIASTICAL STANDING OF THE SEPTUAGINT DURING THE 1ˢᵗ AND 2ᵈ CENTURIES A. D.

§ 3. *New Testament quotations from the LXX*

In considering the character of the Syriac Version, we have learned enough concerning its authors to be certain that they would employ any translation of recognised authority which would assist them in their own work. The question now to be considered is: was the literary and ecclesiastical standing of the Septuagint during the first and second centuries A. D., at which time the Pᵉšittâ was probably made, sufficiently high to warrant its being employed as a legitimate aid in translating the Hebrew?

As witness to the high authority which the LXX had obtained among Christians as early as the beginning of the first century, we may cite the attitude displayed toward it by New Testament writers. Scholars to-day are nearly all agreed that none of the quotations in the gospels were made directly from the Hebrew,[1] but either from the Septuagint or an unwritten vernacular Targum, which would account for many of the differences in reading.

The most natural classification of these quotations is that made by Toy[2] into four groups[3].

I. Those agreeing with the Hebrew and Septuagint (to this group belong a large number of the quotations).

II. Those agreeing with the Septuagint against the Hebrew. (As this group is by far the largest of all, it would seem to warrant our including within it the quotations of the first class).

III. Those agreeing with the Hebrew against the Septuagint.

IV. Those agreeing with neither; the number of quotations in these last two groups being very small.

Since this whole subject has been fully and ably discussed by Prof. Crawford H. Toy in his work entitled "Quotations in the New Testament" and equally fully, although somewhat less scientifically, by Dr. Mc.Turpie under the title of "The Old Testament in the New",[4] it will only be necessary here to consider in detail the quotations belonging to the second group which bear directly upon our subject.

The facts concerning the quotations in general in which all authorities agree are briefly the following: the quotations made by the Synoptics are all from the Prophets and Psalms,

[1] cf. Toy, *Quotations in the N. T.*, p. ix; Turpie, *The Old Testament in the New*, p. xv; Neubauer, *The Dialects spoken in Palest. in the Time of Christ.* Studia Biblica vol. 1, p. 67.

[2] Ibid. p. ix.

[3] Turpie makes five classes (p. xvi), as does Gray, *Journal of Sacred Literature.* No. iv, Oct. 1848.

[4] cf. also Staerk, *Zeitschrift für Wissenschaft. Theologie* vol. 38.

excepting Luke ii:23, 24 from Ex. xiii:2, Lev. xii:8, and possibly John xix:36 from Ex. xii:46. They agree in the majority of cases with the LXX. Acts takes its quotations, with a single exception (xiii:47[1]), from the Septuagint. The catholic and pastoral Epistles make their quotations with greater or less freedom from the same source. In the Epistle to the Hebrews alone, fifteen quotations agree with the Hebrew and Septuagint, eight with the Septuagint against the Hebrew and three with neither[2]. In the book of Revelation there are no direct quotations.

By comparing these quotations with the Pešiṭtâ, we find that in these instances the Syriac O. T. follows the Hebrew; while the Syriac New Testament (except in six instances) follows the Septuagint in preference to either the Hebrew or Pešiṭtâ Old Testament. These six instances, however[3], together with numerous others, not to be mentioned in this connection[4], show that in all probability the Syriac translators of the New Testament consulted, and often quoted, the Syriac Old

[1] If this quotation is from the LXX, it is from a text very different from any known. The Hebrew reads ונתתיך לאור גוים להיות ישועתי עד־קצה הארץ LXX Ἰδοὺ δέδωκά σε εἰς διαθήκην γένους εἰς φῶς ἐθνῶν τοῦ εἶναί σε εἰς σωτηρίαν ἕως ἐσχάτου τῆς γῆς. Acts. Τέθεικά σε εἰς φῶς ἐθνῶν τοῦ εἶναί σε εἰς σωτηρίαν ἕως ἐσχάτου τῆς γῆς. The insertion of διαθήκην γένους may be from Is. xlix:8 or xlii:6 by a scribal error. In Acts a messianic interpretation is put on the words "Servant of Yahve".

[2] Westcott, *Epistle to the Hebrews*, p. 479.

[3] Math. xiii:14, 15 from Is. vi:9, 10; Rom. ix:29 from Is. 1:9; Rom. x:18 from Ps. xix:5; Heb. ii:13 from Is. viii:17, 18; Heb. x:5—7 from Ps. xl:7—9; and Heb. xiii:6 from ψ cxviii:6.

[4] See Appendix I.

Testament.[1] This is especially true of the Psalter. The quotations are arranged[2] according to the order in which they appear in the New Testament.[3]

Math. iv : 7; *Lk.* iv : 12; *Deut.* vi : 16

Deut. vi : 16 לא תנסו את יהוה אלהיכם.
LXX, Math., Lk. οὐκ ἐκπειράσεις κύριον τὸν θεόν σου.
P. ܠܐ ܬܢܣܘܢ ܠܡܪܝܐ ܐܠܗܟܘܢ.
S. ܠܐ ܬܢܣܐ ܠܡܪܝܐ ܐܠܗܟ.

Math. xiii : 14, 15; *Acts.* xxviii : 26, 27; *Is.* vi : 9—10.

H. ויאמר לך ואמרת לעם הזה שמעו שמוע ואל תבינו וראו ראו ואל־
תדעו השמן לב העם הזה ואזניו הכבד ועיניו השע כדיראה בעיניו ובאזניו
ישמע ולבבו יבין ושב ורפא לו:

LXX and G. Καὶ εἶπεν πορεύθητι καὶ εἰπὸν τῷ λαῷ τούτῳ ἀκοῇ ἀκούσετε καὶ οὐ μὴ συνῆτε καὶ βλέποντες βλέψετε καὶ οὐ μὴ ἴδητε ἐπαχύνθη γὰρ ἡ καρδία τοῦ λαοῦ τούτου καὶ τοῖς ὠσὶν αὐτῶν βαρέως ἤκουσαν καὶ τοὺς ὀφθαλμοὺς ἐκάμμυσαν μή ποτε ἴδωσιν τοῖς ὀφθαλμοῖς καὶ τοῖς ὠσὶν ἀκούσωσιν καὶ τῇ καρδίᾳ συνῶσιν καὶ ἐπιστρέψωσιν καὶ ἰάσομαι αὐτούς.[4]

P. ܘܐܡܪ ܕܙܠ ܘܐܡܪ ܠܥܡܐ ܗܢܐ ܕܫܡܥܐ ܬܫܡܥܘܢ ܘܠܐ ܬܣܬܟܠܘܢ ܘܡܚܙܐ ܬܚܙܘܢ ܘܠܐ ܬܕܥܘܢ.

---

[1] See ch. ii, § 1, p. 21.
[2] For the texts used see ch. iv, § 2.
[3] The following abbreviations are used, P. = Peš. O. T., S. = Peš. N. T., H. = Hebrew, G. = Greek New Testament.
[4] In v. 10 Math. and Acts have ὀφθαλμοὺς αὐτῶν; and Acts reverses the words of the introductory clause, reading πορεύθητι πρὸς τὸν λαὸν τοῦτον καὶ εἰπόν. The parallel readings in Mk. iv : 12; viii : 18; Lk. viii : 10; Jn. ix : 39; xii : 40 agree, with slight verbal differences, with the LXX.

ܐܘܩܪ ܘܥܝ̈ܢܘܗܝ܂ ܥܡܨ ܕܠܐ ܢܚܙܐ ܒܥܝ̈ܢܘܗܝ܂ ܘܢܫܡܥ
ܒܐܕ̈ܢܘܗܝ܂ ܘܢܣܬܟܠ ܒܠܒܗ ܘܢܬܘܒ ܘܢܫܬܒܩ ܠܗ.

S. ܕܫܡܥܐ ܬܫܡܥܘܢ ܘܠܐ ܬܣܬܟܠܘܢ ܘܡܚܙܐ ܬܚܙܘܢ
ܘܠܐ ܬܕܥܘܢ ܐܬܥܒܝ ܠܗ ܓܝܪ ܠܒܗ ܕܥܡܐ ܗܢܐ
ܘܒܐܕ̈ܢܝܗܘܢ ܝܩܝܪܐܝܬ ܫܡܥܘ ܘܥܝ̈ܢܝܗܘܢ ܥܡܨܘ ܕܠܐ
ܢܚܙܘܢ ܒܥܝ̈ܢܝܗܘܢ ܘܢܫܡܥܘܢ ܒܐܕ̈ܢܝܗܘܢ ܘܢܣܬܟܠܘܢ
ܒܠܒܗܘܢ ܘܢܬܘܒܘܢ ܘܐܐܣܐ ܐܢܘܢ.[1]

Math. xxi: 42; *Mk.* xii: 10, 11; ψ cxviii: 22, 23.

H. אבן מאסו הבונים היתה לראש פנה מאת יהוה היתה זאת היא נפלאת בעינינו

LXX and G. Λίθον ὃν ἀπεδοκίμασαν οἱ οἰκοδομοῦντες οὗτος ἐγενήθη εἰς κεφαλὴν γωνίας· παρὰ κυρίου ἐγένετο αὕτη καὶ ἔστι θαυμαστὴ ἐν ὀφθαλμοῖς ἡμῶν.[2]

P. and S. ܟܐܦܐ ܕܐܣܠܝܘ ܒ̈ܢܝܐ ܗܝ ܗܘܬ ܠܪܝܫܗ
ܕܒܢܝܢܐ ܡܢ ܩܕܡ ܡܪܝܐ ܗܘܬ ܗܕܐ ܘܐܝܬܝܗ̇
ܬܕܡܘܪܬܐ ܒܥܝ̈ܢܝܢ.[3]

Acts. vii: 49, 50; *Isa.* lxvi: 1, 2.

H. השמים כסאי והארץ הדם רגלי אי־זה בית אשר תבנו־לי ואי־זה מקום מנוחתי ואת־כל־אלה ידי עשתה:

LXX and G. Ὁ οὐρανός μου θρόνος καὶ ἡ γῆ ὑποπόδιον τῶν ποδῶν μου· ποῖον οἶκον οἰκοδομήσετέ μοι; καὶ ποῖος

[1] S is here substantially the same as P.

[2] Lk. xx: 17 and i Pet. ii: 7 likewise agree verbally with the LXX, but omit the last sentence. Acts iv: 11 agrees with neither LXX nor H.

[3] S differs in conformity to the LXX; reading for ܕܒܢܝܢܐ, ܕܙܘܝܬܐ; and for ܩܕܡ, ܠܘܬ.

τόπος τῆς καταπαύσεώς μου; πάντα γὰρ ταῦτα ἐποίησεν ἡ χείρ μου.[1]

P. ⟨Syriac⟩

S. ⟨Syriac⟩

Rom. iv: 3, 9; *Gal.* iii: 6; *Jas.* ii: 23; *Gen.* xv: 6.

H. ‏האמן ביהוה ויחשבה לו צדקה‎.
LXX and G. Ἐπίστευσεν Ἀβραμ[2] τῷ θεῷ καὶ ἐλογίσθη αὐτῷ εἰς δικαιοσύνην.

P. and S. ⟨Syriac⟩

Rom. iv: 7, 8; ψ xxxii: 1—2.

H. ‏אשרי נשוי־פשע כסוי חטאה אשרי־אדם לא יחשב יהוה לו עון‎.
LXX and G. Μακάριοι ὧν ἀφέθησαν αἱ ἀνομίαι καὶ ὧν ἐπεκαλύφθησαν αἱ ἁμαρτίαι μακάριος ἀνὴρ οὗ οὐ μὴ λογίσηται κύριος ἁμαρτίαν.

P. ⟨Syriac⟩

S. ⟨Syriac⟩

---

[1] Acts inserts λέγει Κύριος before καὶ ποῖος, reading ἢ τίς. In the last clause the order of the words is inverted.

[2] G. reads Ἀβραάμ.

John. xii: 38; *Rom*. x: 16; *Isa*. liii: 1.

H. מי האמין לשמעתנו וזרוע יהוה על־מי נגלתה׃

LXX and G. Κύριε τίς ἐπίστευσε τῇ ἀκοῇ ἡμῶν; καὶ ὁ βραχίων κυρίου τίνι ἀπεκαλύφθη.[1]

P. and S. ܡܢ ܗܝܡܢ ܠܫܡܥܢ ܘܕܪܥܗ ܕܡܪܝܐ ܠܡܢ ܐܬܓܠܝ.[2]

Acts. ii: 25—28, 31; xiii: 35; ψ xvi: 8—11.

H. שויתי יהוה לנגדי תמיד כי מימיני בל־אמוט׃ לכן שמח לבי ויגל כבודי אף־בשרי ישכן לבטח׃ כי לא־תעזב נפשי לשאול לא־תתן חסידך לראות שחת׃ תודיעני ארח חיים שבע שמחות את־פניך׃

LXX and G. Προωρώμην τὸν κύριον ἐνώπιόν μου διὰ παντός, ὅτι ἐκ δεξιῶν μού ἐστιν ἵνα μὴ σαλευθῶ· διὰ τοῦτο ηὐφράνθη ἡ καρδία μου καὶ ἠγαλλιάσατο ἡ γλῶσσά μου, ἔτι δὲ καὶ ἡ σάρξ μου κατασκηνώσει ἐπ' ἐλπίδι· ὅτι οὐκ ἐγκαταλείψεις τὴν ψυχήν μου εἰς ᾅδην, οὐδὲ δώσεις τὸν ὅσιόν σου ἰδεῖν διαφθοράν ἐγνώρισάς μοι ὁδοὺς ζωῆς· πληρώσεις με εὐφροσύνης μετὰ τοῦ προσώπου σου.[3]

P. ܚܙܝܬ ܠܡܪܝܐ ܠܘܩܒܠܝ ܒܟܠܙܒܢ ܘܗܘܐ ܡܢ ܝܡܝܢܝ
ܕܠܐ ܐܙܘܥ ܡܛܠ ܗܢܐ ܚܕܝ ܠܒܝ ܘܪܘܙ ܐܝܩܪܝ ܘܐܦ ܒܣܪܝ
ܢܫܪܐ ܥܠ ܣܒܪܐ ܡܛܠ ܕܠܐ ܫܒܩܬ ܠܢܦܫܝ ܒܫܝܘܠ ܘܠܐ ܝܗܒܬ
ܠܚܣܝܕܟ ܕܢܚܙܐ ܚܒܠܐ ܬܘܕܥܢܝ ܐܘܪܚܟ ܕܚܝܐ ܘܐܣܒܥ
ܡܢ ܚܕܘܬܗ ܕܦܪܨܘܦܟ.

S. ܡܩܕܡ ܗܘܝܬ ܚܙܐ ܠܡܪܝ ܒܟܠܙܒܢ ܕܥܠ ܝܡܝܢܝ
ܗܘ ܕܠܐ ܐܙܘܥ ܡܛܠ ܗܢܐ ܐܬܒܣܡ ܠܒܝ ܘܪܘܙܬ
ܫܘܒܚܝ ܘܐܦ ܦܓܪܝ ܢܫܪܐ ܥܠ ܣܒܪܐ ܕܠܐ ܫܒܩ

[1] Rom. has only the first clause.

[2] S. reads ܡܢܘ; and ܫܡܥܬܢ ܡܠܟ in Rom.

[3] Acts. xiii: 35 has only the clause οὐ δώσεις τὸν ὅσιόν σου ἰδεῖν διαφθοράν.

ܐܢܬ ܠܢܦܫ ܟܘܠ ܘܠܐ ܗܘ ܐܢܬ ܠܢܦܫܟ ܕܢܣܒܐ ܣܟܠܐ.
ܚܠܝܬ ܠܐ ܐܘܪܚܐ ܕܢܒ̈ܝܐ ܬܡܠܟܢ ܒܡܫܡܫܘܬܐ ܕܡ ܦܪܘܩܢ.

Acts. vii : 35; *Ex.* ii : 14

H. מי שמך לאיש שר ושפט עלינו׃

LXX and G. Τίς σε κατέστησεν ἄρχοντα καὶ δικαστὴν ἐφ' ἡμῶν.[1]

P. ܡܢܘ ܥܒܕܟ ܓܒܪ ܪܫ ܘܕܝܢ ܥܠܝܢ.

S. ܡܢܘ ܐܩܝܡܟ ܥܠܝܢ ܪܫܐ ܘܕܝܢܐ.

Rom. ix : 29; *Is.* i : 9.

H. לולי יהוה צבאות הותיר לנו שריד כמעט כסדם היינו לעמרה דמינו׃

LXX and G. Καὶ εἰ μὴ κύριος Σαβαώθ ἐγκατέλιπεν ἡμῖν σπέρμα ὡς Σόδομα ἂν ἐγενήθημεν καὶ ὡς Γόμορρα ἂν ὡμοιώθημεν.

P. and S. ܘܐܠܘܠܐ ܡܪܝܐ ܨܒܐܘܬ ܐܘܬܪ ܠܢ ܣܪܝܕܐ ܐܝܟ ܣܕܘܡ ܗܘܝܢ ܗܘܝܢ ܘܠܥܡܘܪܐ ܡܬܕܡܝܢ ܗܘܝܢ.

Rom. x : 18; ψ xix : 5.

H. בכל־הארץ יצא קום ובקצה תבל מליהם׃

LXX and G. Εἰς πᾶσαν τὴν γῆν ἐξῆλθεν ὁ φθόγγος αὐτῶν καὶ εἰς τὰ πέρατα τῆς οἰκουμένης τὰ ῥήματα αὐτῶν.

P. and S. ܒܟܠܗ ܐܪܥܐ ܢܦܩ ܣܒܪܬܗܘܢ ܘܒܣܘܦܗܐ ܕܬܐܒܝܠ ܡܠܝܗܘܢ.[2]

Rom. x : 20, 21; *Is.* lxv : 1, 2.

H. נדרשתי ללוא שאלו נמצאתי ללא בקשני ..... פרשתי ידי כל־היום אל־עם סורר׃

[1] G. omits ἐφ' ἡμῶν.

[2] S renders ܣܒܪܬܗܘܢ by ܢܦܩ ܩܠܗܘܢ, and also reads ܘܒܣܘ̈ܦܝܗ.

LXX. Ἐμφανὴς ἐγενήθην τοῖς ἐμὲ μὴ ἐπερωτῶσιν εὑρέθην τοῖς ἐμὲ μὴ ζητοῦσιν ... ἐξεπέτασα τὰς χεῖράς μου ὅλην τὴν ἡμέραν πρὸς λαὸν ἀπειθοῦντα καὶ ἀντιλέγοντα.

G. Εὑρέθην τοῖς ἐμὲ μὴ ζητοῦσιν ἐμφανὴς ἐγενόμην τοῖς ἐμὲ μὴ ἐπερωτῶσιν ... Ὅλην τὴν ἡμέραν ἐξεπέτασα τὰς χεῖράς μου πρὸς λαὸν ἀπειθοῦντα καὶ ἀντιλέγοντα.[1]

P. ܐܬܚܙܝܬ ܠܐܝܠܝܢ ܕܠܐ ܫܐܠܘܢܝ ܘܐܫܬܟܚܬ ܠܐܝܠܝܢ ܕܠܐ ܒܥܐܘܢܝ ... ܦܫܛܬ ܐܝܕܝ ܟܠܗ ܝܘܡܐ ܠܥܡܐ ܕܠܐ ܡܬܛܦܝܣ.

S. ܐܬܚܙܝܬ ܠܐܝܠܝܢ ܕܠܐ ܒܥܐܘܢܝ ܘܐܫܬܟܚܬ ܠܐܝܠܝܢ ܕܠܐ ܫܐܠܘܢܝ ... ܝܘܡܐ ܟܠܗ ܦܫܛܬ ܐܝܕܝ ܠܥܡܐ ܡܪܡܪܢܐ ܘܕܠܐ ܡܬܛܦܝܣ.

Rom. xi: 34; i *Cor.* ii: 16; *Is.* xl: 13.

H. מי תכן את־רוח יהוה ואיש עצתו יודיענו:

LXX. Τίς ἔγνω νοῦν κυρίου καὶ τίς αὐτοῦ σύμβουλος ἐγένετο ὃς συμβιβᾷ αὐτόν.

Rom. Τίς ἔγνω νοῦν κυρίου ἢ τίς σύμβουλος αὐτοῦ ἐγένετο.

Cor. Τίς ἔγνω νοῦν κυρίου ὃς συμβιβάσει αὐτόν.[2]

P. ܡܢܘ ܓܝܪ ܝܕܥ ܪܥܝܢܗ ܕܡܪܝܐ ܐܘ ܡܢܘ ܗܘܐ ܠܗ ܒܥܠ ܡܠܟܐ.

Rom. ܡܢܘ ܓܝܪ ܝܕܥ ܪܥܝܢܗ ܕܡܪܝܐ ܐܘ ܡܢܘ ܗܘܐ ܠܗ ܒܥܠ ܡܠܟܐ.

Cor. ܡܢܘ ܓܝܪ ܝܕܥ ܪܥܝܢܗ ܕܡܪܝܐ ܕܢܠܦܝܘܗܝ.

[1] The difference between the LXX and G. is not so great as it appears at first sight. They only differ in one word; the latter having ἐγενομην, the former ἐγενηθην. For the rest, the order of the words is simply inverted.

[2] The reading of Cor. is found in Codex Alexandrinus and Codex Sinaiticus; but it is uncertain whether this is a true LXX variant or an attempt to conform to the N. T. text.

Rom. xii : 20; *Prov.* xxv : 21, 22.

H. אם־רעב שנאך האכילהו לחם ואם צמא השקהו מים׃ כי גחלים אתה חתה על־ראשו׃

LXX and G. Ἐὰν πεινᾷ ὁ ἐχθρός σου ψώμιζε αὐτὸν ἐὰν διψᾷ πότιζε αὐτόν· τοῦτο γὰρ ποιῶν ἄνθρακας πυρὸς σωρεύσεις ἐπὶ τὴν κεφαλὴν αὐτοῦ.

P. and S. ܐܢ ܟܦܢ ܒܥܠܕܒܒܟ ܐܘܟܠܝܗܝ ܘܐܢ ܨܗܐ ܐܫܩܝܗܝ ܘܗܟܢ ܗܠܝܢ ܬܥܒܕ ܠܗ ܓܘܡܪ̈ܐ ܕܢܘܪܐ ܐܢܬ ܐܚܬ ܥܠ ܪܫܗ.[1]

Rom. xv : 10; *Deut.* xxxii : 43.

H. הרנינו גוים עמו׃

LXX and G. Εὐφράνθητε ἔθνη μετὰ τοῦ λαοῦ αὐτοῦ.[2]

P. ܫܒܚܘ ܥܡܘܗܝ ܥܡܡ̈ܐ ܥܡܗ.

S. ܐܬܒܣܡܘ ܥܡܡ̈ܐ ܥܡ ܥܡܗ.

Rom. xv : 12; *Is.* xi : 10.

H. והיה ביום ההוא שרש ישי אשר עמד לנס עמים אליו גוים ידרשו׃

LXX. Καὶ ἔσται ἐν τῇ ἡμέρᾳ ἐκείνῃ ἡ ῥίζα τοῦ Ἰεσσαὶ καὶ ὁ ἀνιστάμενος ἄρχειν ἐθνῶν ἐπ' αὐτῷ ἔθνη ἐλπιοῦσι.

Rom. Ἔσται ἡ ῥίζα τοῦ Ἰεσσαὶ καὶ ὁ ἀνιστάμενος ἄρχειν ἐθνῶν ἐπ' αὐτῷ ἔθνη ἐλπιοῦσιν.

P. ܘܢܗܘܐ ܒܝܘܡܐ ܗܘ ܥܩܪܗ ܕܐܝܫܝ ܕܩܐܡ ܐܬܐ ܠܥܡ̈ܡܐ ܘܥܠܘܗܝ ܥܡ̈ܡܐ ܢܣܒܪܘܢ ܘܬܗܘܐ ܢܝܚܬܗ ܐܝܩܪܐ.

S. ܕܢܗܘܐ ܥܩܪܐ ܠܐܝܫܝ ܘܗܘ ܕܢܩܘܡ ܢܗܘܐ ܪܫܐ ܠܥܡ̈ܡܐ.

[1] For ܘܗܟܢ S reads ܘܐܢ; and after ܕܢܘܪܐ reads ܬܟܢܫ ܥܠ ܪܝܫܗ.

[2] cf. Toy, *Quot. in the N. T.*, p. 165 seq.; Turpie, *The O. T. in the New*, p. 108.

Mk. x:8; i *Cor.* vi:16; *Math.* xix:5; *Eph.* v:31; *Gen.* ii:24.

H. והיו לבשר אחד׃
LXX and G. ἔσονται οἱ δύο εἰς σάρκα μίαν.
P. and S. ܘܢܗܘܘܢ ܬܪ̈ܝܗܘܢ ܚܕ ܒܣܪ.

i *Cor.* iii:20; ψ xciv:11.

H. כי־המה הבל׃
LXX and G. ὅτι εἰσὶ μάταιοι.
P. ܡܛܠ ܕܠܗܒܠܐ ܐܢܘܢ.
S. ܕܚܟܝ̈ܡܐ ܕܣܪ̈ܝܩܢ ܐܢܝ̈ܢ.

i *Cor.* ix:9; i *Tim.* v:18; *Deut.* xxv:4.

H. לא־תחסם שור בדישו׃
LXX and Cor. Οὐ φιμώσεις βοῦν ἀλοῶντα.[1]
Tim. βοῦν ἀλοῶντα οὐ φιμώσεις.
P. and S. ܠܐ ܬܒܠܘܡ ܬܘܪܐ ܒܕܝܫܬܐ.[2]

i *Cor.* xv:32; *Is.* xxii:13.

H. אכול ושתו כי מחר נמות׃
LXX and G. Φάγωμεν καὶ πίωμεν αὔριον γὰρ ἀποθνήσκομεν.
P. ܢܐܟܘܠ ܘܢܫܬܐ ܡܛܠ ܕܡܚܪ ܢܡܘܬ.
S. ܢܐܟܘܠ ܘܢܫܬܐ ܡܚܪ ܓܝܪ ܡܝܬܝܢܢ.

Gal. iv:27; *Isa.* liv:1.

H. רני עקרה לא ילדה פצחי רנה וצהלי לא־חלה כי־רבים בני־שוממה מבני בעולה׃

[1] Westcott and Hort read φιμώσεις, according to א A B³ of LXX. Tischendorf reads κημώσεις with B* D* F G etc.

[2] S. reads ܕܕܝܫ in Cor.

LXX and G. Εὐφράνθητι στεῖρα ἡ οὐ τίκτουσα ῥῆξον καὶ βόησον ἡ οὐκ ὠδίνουσα ὅτι πολλὰ τὰ τέκνα τῆς ἐρήμου μᾶλλον ἢ τῆς ἐχούσης τὸν ἄνδρα.

P. ܫܒܚܝ ܥܩܪܬܐ ܕܠܐ ܝܠܕܬ ܘܐܬܦܨܚܝ ܒܬܫܒܘܚܬܐ
ܘܩܥܝ ܕܠܐ ܚܒܠܬ ܡܛܠ ܕܣܓܝܐܝܢ ܒܢܝܗ ܕܨܕܝܬܐ ܝܬܝܪ
ܡܢ ܒܢܝܗ ܕܒܥܠܬܐ ܐܡܪ ܡܪܝܐ.

S. ܕܐܬܒܣܡܝ ܥܩܪܬܐ ܗܝ ܕܠܐ ܝܠܕܐ ܘܐܬܦܨܚܝ
ܘܩܥܝ ܗܝ ܕܠܐ ܡܚܒܠܐ ܡܛܠ ܕܣܓܝܐܝܢ ܒܢܝܗ ܕܨܕܝܬܐ
ܝܬܝܪ ܡܢ ܒܢܝܗ ܕܒܥܠܬܐ.

Heb. ii: 13; *Is.* viii: 17, 18.

H. וקויתי לו׃ הנה אנכי והילדים אשר נתן־לי יהוה׃

LXX. Καὶ πεποιθὼς ἔσομαι ἐπ᾽ αὐτῷ, ἰδοὺ ἐγὼ καὶ τὰ παιδία ἅ μοι ἔδωκεν ὁ θεός.[1]

G. Ἐγὼ ἔσομαι πεποιθὼς ἐπ᾽ αὐτῷ . . . ἰδοὺ ἐγὼ καὶ παιδία ἅ μοι ἔδωκεν ὁ θεός.

P. ܘܐܬܟܠ ܥܠܘܗܝ: ܗܐ ܐܢܐ ܘܒܢܝܐ ܕܝܗܒ ܠܝ ܡܪܝܐ.

S. ܐܢܐ ܐܗܘܐ ܬܟܝܠ ܥܠܘܗܝ... ܗܐ ܐܢܐ ܘܒܢܝܐ
ܕܝܗܒܬ ܠܝ ܐܠܗܐ.

Heb. x: 5—7; ψ xl: 7—9.

H. זבח ומנחה לא חפצת אזנים כרית לי עולה וחטאה לא שאלת׃
אז אמרתי הנה־באתי במגלת־ספר כתוב עלי׃ לעשות־רצונך אלהי חפצתי׃

LXX and G. Θυσίαν καὶ προσφορὰν οὐκ ἠθέλησας, σῶμα δὲ κατηρτίσω μοι· ὁλοκαύτωμα καὶ περὶ ἁμαρτίας οὐκ ᾔτησας τότε εἶπον Ἰδοὺ ἥκω ἐν κεφαλίδι βιβλίου γέγραπται περὶ ἐμοῦ τοῦ ποιῆσαι τὸ θέλημά σου ὁ θεός μου ἐβουλήθην.[2]

P. and S. ܕܒ̈ܚܐ ܘܩܘܪ̈ܒܢܐ ܠܐ ܨܒܝܬ ܐܕ̈ܢܐ ܕܝܢ ܢܩܒܬ

[1] LXX usually renders יהוה by Κύριος.

[2] G. differs slightly, reading ὁλοκαυτώματα (pl.) and ηὐδόκησας for ᾔτησας; also omitting ἐβουλήθην.

ܠܝ ܘܡܣܩ̈ܬܐ ܥܠܬ̈ܐ ܕܚܠܦ ܣܟܠܘ̈ܬܐ ܠܐ ܫܐܠܬ ܗܝܕܝܢ
ܐܡܪܬ ܗܐ ܐܬܝܬ ܕܒܪܝܫ ܟܬܒ̈ܐ ܟܬܝܒ ܥܠܝ ܠܡܥܒܕ
ܨܒܝܢܟ ܐܠܗܐ ܨܒܝܬ.[1]

Heb. x:37—38; *Hab.* ii:3—4.

H. כי בא יבא לא יאחר: הנה עפלה לא־ישרה נפשו בו וצדיק באמונתו יחיה:

LXX. Ὅτι ἐρχόμενος ἥξει καὶ οὐ μὴ χρονίσῃ· ἐὰν ὑποστείληται οὐκ εὐδοκεῖ ἡ ψυχή μου ἐν αὐτῷ ὁ δὲ δίκαιος ἐκ πίστεώς μου ζήσεται.

G. Ἔτι γὰρ μικρὸν ὅσον ὅσον ὁ ἐρχόμενος ἥξει καὶ οὐ χρονίσει· ὁ δὲ δίκαιός [μου] ἐκ πίστεως ζήσεται καὶ ἐὰν ὑποστείληται οὐκ εὐδοκεῖ ἡ ψυχή μου ἐν αὐτῷ.[2]

P. ܡܛܠ ܕܥܕܟܝܠ ܐܬܐ ܘܠܐ ܡܘܚܪ ܘܡܬܡܗܠܐ ܠܐ ܨܒܝܐ
ܢܦܫܗ ܘܙܕܝܩܐ ܒܗܝܡܢܘܬܐ ܢܚܐ.

S. ܕܢܐܬܐ ܗܘ ܕܐܬܐ ܘܠܐ ܢܘܚܪ ܒܐܝܢܐ ܕܐܡ ܡܢ
ܗܝܡܢܘܬܐ ܕܝܠܝ ܢܚܐ.

Heb. xi:21; *Gen.* xlvii:31.

H: וישתחו ישראל על ראש המטה:

LXX and G. Καὶ προσεκύνησεν Ἰσραὴλ ἐπὶ τὸ ἄκρον τῆς ῥάβδου αὐτοῦ.[3]

P. ܘܣܓܕ ܐܝܣܪܝܠ ܥܠ ܪܝܫ ܚܘܛܪܗ.
S. ܘܣܓܕ ܥܠ ܪܝܫ ܚܘܛܪܗ.

[1] S. reads ܨܒܝܢܐ ܕܝܢ ܐܠܗܝܬ.

[2] Toy, *Quotations in the N. T.*, p. 125; Turpie, *O. T. in the New*, p. 116.

[3] G. reads Ἰακωβ for Ἰσραηλ. Similarly the Syriac New Testament reads ܝܥܩܘܒ.

Heb. xiii: 6; ψ cxviii: 6.

H. יהוה לי לא אירא מה־יעשה לי אדם :

LXX and G. Κύριος ἐμοὶ βοηθός καὶ οὐ φοβηθήσομαι τί ποιήσει μοι ἄνθρωπος.

P. and S. ܡܢ ܡܕܡܢ ܠܐ ܐܕܚܠ ܡܪܝܐ ܠܝ ܥܕܘܪܐ ܕܢܥܒܕ ܠܝ ܒܪܢܫܐ.

From these quotations, thirty-six in all, two important facts concerning the Septuagint are revealed:

I. That the New Testament writers regarded it as of equal ecclesiastical authority with the Hebrew, i. e. as the word of God.

II. That "certain adaptations and combinations[1] of Scripture passed into current Scriptural[2] phraseology".

Such being the use of the Septuagint among church writers of the early part of the first century, let us next consider the attitude displayed toward it by later Christian and Jewish writers.

§ 2. *Quotations from the LXX by later Sacred and Profane writers*

While the Septuagint thus received its ecclesiastical endorsement by Apostolic writers, it was by no means universally recognized as an authority. For not until the Hebrew language had become wholly the language of the learned,[3] did the Septuagint gradually, not through merit but necessity, supplant both the use and, to a large extent, the authority of the Massoretic Text.[4] Much of the animosity on the part

---

[1] This is of special significance when we remember the power familiar language has over new translations, as illustrated in the popular rejection of the last revised English Version.

[2] Toy, *Quotations in the N. T.* Introduction.

[3] Neubauer, *Studia Biblica* i, p. 39 seq.

[4] "Dark as the Day on which the golden calf was made; for

of the Jews against the Septuagint, at first, was owing to
its prevalent use among, and consequently alleged corruption
by, the Christians; an antipathy which found its final vent in
the new translations by Aquila, Theodotion, Symmachus et al.[1]

a. Septuagint used in temple services

Very early among the Alexandrian Jews the Greek Version was
highly esteemed, and in later times was regarded as inspired.
Philo holds that inspiration was not limited to any one period. The
Septuagint was used in the synagogue services[2] wherever Greek
was spoken, and became the medium through which the ancient
civilized world became acquainted with the Scriptures. Schürer
states[3] that "Wherever Jews were found to be living, there
the law and the prophets were read and expounded every Sabbath,
and the religious ordinances observed. *The language employed
in public worship was, as a rule, undoubtedly the Greek*".[4]
Furthermore, since the use of Hebrew was only compulsory
in certain passages, as the priestly benediction for example,
it must have been considered legitimate to read the Scriptures
in the Synagogue service in some other language—as the
Greek. Kautzsch has shown[5] the improbability of any simul-

---

the law cannot be translated with impunity" (Massekhet Sopherim
i, p. 11) is the characterization of the birth-day of a translation
destined so largely to supercede its inspired original.

[1] For accounts of the origin etc. of the Sept. see Appendix iii.

[2] Buhl, *Old Testament Canon*, p. 15.

[3] *The Jewish People in the Time of Christ*, II:ii, p. 283.

[4] As opposed to this view, see Lightfoot, *Horae Hebraicae in
Epis I. ad Cor.* Addenda ad Cap. xiv (Opp. ii: 933—940) with
which cf. Hody, *De Bibliorum textibus originalibus*, pp. 224—228
(in answer to Lightfoot); also Waehner, *Antiquitates Ebraeorum*,
§ 253. Frankel, *Vorstudien zu der LXX*, p. 56.

[5] *De Veteris Testamenti locis a Paulo Apostolo allegatis*, Lips. 1869.

taneous use of the Hebrew and Greek Text, by demonstrating that the Apostle Paul was only familiar with the Greek translation of the Old Testament. That the Greek Version only was used in public worship is further corroborated by several of the Church Fathers as Justin,[1] ἔμειναν αἱ βίβλοι καὶ παρ' Αἰγυπτίοις μέχρι τοῦ δεῦρυ καὶ πανταχοῦ παρὰ πᾶσίν εἰσιν Ἰουδαίοις, οἳ καὶ ἀναγινώσκοντες οὐ συνιᾶσι τὰ εἰρημένα—with which compare further the statement of Tertullian:[2] Hodie apud Serapeum Ptolemaei bibliothecae cum ipsis Hebraicis litteris exhibentur. Sed et Judaei palam lectitant. Vectigalis libertas; vulgo aditur sabbatis omnibus. The statement is also made[3] Εἰ δέ τις φάσκοι.... μὴ ἡμῖν τὰς βίβλους ταύτας ἀλλὰ Ἰουδαίοις προσήκειν διὰ τὸ ἔτι καὶ νῦν ἐν ταῖς συναγωγαῖς[4] αὐτῶν σῴζεσθαι κ. τ. λ. In all these passages the Greek translation of the Old Testament is expressly referred to. In Palestine the Septuagint was by no means so highly esteemed; yet even here an exception must be made in favor of the LXX Psalter, which "was held in high esteem and used in the temple service".[5] Traces of its use in the Temple are still discernible in some of the subscriptions of the Psalms selected to be read on the several days of the week.[6] Gradually, however, the other books came into requisition; until at the time of the dispersion, all the several translations had

---

[1] *Apolog.* i : 31.
[2] cf. *Dial. c. Tryph.* c. lxxii. with Tertullian *Apolog.* c. xviii.
[3] Pseudo-Justin, *Coh. ad Graec.* c. xiii. (Third Cent. A. D.).
[4] On the preserving of the Scriptures in the Synagogues, cf. Josephus, *Antiquities*, xvi : 6, 2, and Chrysost. *Orat. adv. Jud.* i : 5.
[5] Buhl, *Old Testament Canon*, p. 15.
[6] ψ xxiv; ψ xlviii; ψ xciii; ψ xciv.

been combined into a whole and recognised by the Jews as their text of Scripture.[1]

b[1]. Josephus and the Septuagint[2]

A still higher tribute to the literary value of the Septuagint than its somewhat compulsory use in the Synagogues, is paid by the historian Josephus, who freely consults and quotes it in his great work, The History of the Jews. A native of Palestine, when still very young, Josephus had acquired a profound knowledge of Hebrew Law and Rabbinical Literature[3]; and in addition was so well versed in Greek, as to be counted among the classic writers in that language. St. Jerome styles him the "Graecus Livius", and Niebuhr pronounces him to be a Greek writer of singular purity.[4] As an historian he is not entirely accurate; but of especial significance is the fact that in compiling his History, notwithstanding his perfect familiarity with the Hebrew, he made extensive use of the Septuagint.[5] This is confirmed by the fact that he uses certain portions of Ezra and Esther which do not appear in the Hebrew text. Thus, for example, Ezra ch. iii—v:6 belongs solely to the Greek revision of the book[6]; and relates how Zerubbabel obtains the favor of Darius, and receives from him permission for the exiles' return. This stands in direct opposition to the rest of the narrative; for after the times of Darius (iii—v:6) Cyrus is subsequently mentioned (v. 7—70). Thus history is inverted, since first we have Artaxerxes (ii, 15—25), then Darius and Cyrus, and finally Zerubbabel who

---

[1] Schürer, *The Jewish People in the Time of Christ*, II, iii, p. 163.
[2] *Josephus und LXX*, ZAW. 1890. 242; also Jacob, *Das Buch Esther bei den LXX*, ibid. p. 280.
[3] Schürer, *History of the Jews in the Time of Christ*, I, i, p. 85 seq.
[4] *Anc. Hist.* iii, p. 455.
[5] Schürer, Ibid., Div. ii, vol. iii, p. 179.   [6] Ibid., p. 179.

having obtained permission from Darius for the exiles to return, goes back with them in the time of Cyrus. From this it is quite evident that Josephus used the Septuagint Version of Ezra, interpolating ch. iii—v, 6 from another source.[1]

From Esther he quotes[2] Ch. ii: 21—23 which reads quite differently from the Hebrew.[3] Καὶ ἐλυπήθησαν οἱ δύο εὐνοῦχοι τοῦ βασιλέως οἱ ἀρχισωματοφύλακες ὅτι προήχθη Μαρδοχαῖος καὶ ἐζήτουν ἀποκτεῖναι Ἀρταξέρξην τὸν βασιλέα καὶ ἐδηλώθη Μαρδοχαίῳ ὁ λόγος καὶ ἐσήμανεν Ἐσθὴρ καὶ αὐτὴ ἐνεφάνισεν τῷ βασιλεῖ τὰ τῆς ἐπιβουλῆς· ὁ δὲ βασιλεὺς ἤτασεν τοὺς δύο εὐνούχους καὶ ἐκρέμασεν αὐτοὺς καὶ προσέταξεν ὁ βασιλεὺς καταχωρίσαι εἰς μνημόσυνον ἐν τῇ βασιλικῇ βιβλιοθήκῃ ὑπὲρ τῆς εὐνοίας Μαρδοχαίου ἐν ἐγκωμίῳ.

b². Other Jewish historians

Among other Jewish historians who chronologically precede Josephus, but whose works are of less importance, may be mentioned Demetrius, a Jewish Hellenist who compiled a short history of Israel. His work was intitled περὶ τῶν ἐν τῇ Ἰουδαίᾳ βασιλέων, and is chiefly of importance in the present connection because of his undisputed use of the Septuagint[4]; which fact must place the origin of that Version early

---

[1] cf. Keil, *Einleitung*, 3rd ed., p. 704 seq.

[2] Ant. xi, 1—5; cf. Schürer, *The Jewish People* etc. Div. ii vol iii, p. 179.

[3] The Hebrew reads: בימים ההם ומרדכי ישב בשער־המלך קצף בגתן ותרש שני־סריסי המלך משמרי הסף ויבקשו לשלח יד במלך אחשורש ויודע הדבר למרדכי ויגד לאסתר המלכה ותאמר אסתר למלך בשם מרדכי ויבקש הדבר וימצא ויתלו שניהם על־עץ ויכתב בספר דברי הימים לפני המלך:

[4] Hody, *De biblior. textibus*, p. 107; Bloch, *Die Quellen des Flavius Josephus* (1879), p. 56, seq.

in the second century B. C. That the works of Demetrius were consulted, if not quoted, by Josephus is pretty certain; though Josephus confounded him[2] with Demetrius Phalerus.[1] One other historian must here be mentioned, Aristeus[2], of whose works nothing is known excepting a fragment on Job of which he is the author. Aristeus affirms that Ιωβ is identical with 'Ιωβαβ Gen. xxxvi: 33, and that he is therefore a grandson of Esau. There is no doubt that Aristeus made use of the LXX in his translation of Job; and it is a noteworthy fact that in the supplement to Job in the LXX, the personal affairs of Job are recounted exactly after the manner of Aristeus.[3]

c. Philo and the Septuagint

The works of Philo abound with quotations from the Septuagint, which so nearly correspond to our present text as to make it certain that that version was used. Thus Gen. i: 31 LXX. Καὶ εἶδεν ὁ θεὸς τὰ πάντα ὅσα ἐποίησε καὶ ἰδοὺ καλὰ λίαν. Philo[4] εἶδεν ὁ θεὸς τὰ πάντα ὅσα ἐποίησεν καὶ ἰδοὺ ἀγαθὰ σφόδρα.[5] Gen. ii: 1 Καὶ συνετελέσθησαν ὁ οὐρανὸς καὶ ἡ γῆ καὶ πᾶς ὁ κόσμος αὐτῶν. Philo. Καὶ ἐτελέσθησαν οἱ οὐρανοὶ καὶ ἡ γῆ καὶ πᾶς ὁ κόσμος αὐτῶν. But more interesting yet in the present connection are his quotations from the Psalms. ψ xxxvi: 4 in *De Plantatione Noe* 7 (i:335)

---

[1] Freudenthal, *Alexander Polyhistor*, p. 170, note; Müller, *Fragm.* ii: 369ª.

[2] Schürer, *The Jewish People in the Time of Christ*, II. iii: 200—208.

[3] Freudenthal, *Alexander Polyhistor*, pp. 136—143 and 231.

[4] *Quis rer. divin. heres* 32 (i, 495). On the quotations of Philo et al. from the LXX, see Hatch, *Essays in Biblical Greek*, Oxford 1889. "Early quotations from the LXX", p. 131 seq.

[5] σφόδρα is the reading of Aquila and Symmachus.

and *De Somniis*[1] ii: 37 (: 690) κατεστύφησαν τοῦ Κυρίου καὶ δώσει σοι τὰ αἰτήματα τῆς καρδίας σου. Also ψ lxxiv: 5[2] εἶπα τοῖς παρανομοῦσιν μὴ παρανομεῖν καὶ τοῖς ἁμαρτάνουσιν. Μὴ ὑψοῦτε κέρας;. ψ lxxix: 5[3] Κύριε ὁ θεὸς τῶν δυνάμεων ἕως πότε ὀργίζῃ ἐπὶ τὴν προσευχὴν τοῦ δούλου σου; ψ c: 1[4] Ἔλεος καὶ κρίσιν ᾄσομαί σοι Κύριε. Sometimes there are variants; but these are unimportant[5]. For example, ψ xlv: 5 τοῦ ποταμοῦ τὰ ὁρμήματα εὐφραίνουσι τὴν πόλιν τοῦ θεου. Philo quotes[6] τὸ ὅρμημα τοῦ ποταμοῦ εὐφραίνει. Many other quotations might be given[7]; but these suffice to show the relation of Philo to the LXX; his entire dependence upon it being proven by the frequency and accuracy of his quotations.

d. Early Church Fathers and the Septuagint

Among the early Church Fathers whose works abound with Septuagint quotations, may be mentioned chiefly Clement of Rome, Barnabas and Justin Martyr. Thus Clement quotes ψ xxxi: 1, 2 (in C. 50) μακάριοι ὧν ἀφέθησαν αἱ ἀνομίαι καὶ ὧν ἐπεκαλύφθησαν αἱ ἁμαρτίαι, μακάριος ἀνὴρ οὗ μὴ λογίσηται Κύριος ἁμαρτίαν οὐδέ ἐστιν ἐν τῷ στόματι αὐτοῦ δόλος[8]. Also ψ lxii: 5 οὕτως εὐλογήσω σε ἐν τῇ ζωῇ μου ἐν τῷ ὀνόματί σου ἀρῶ σὰς χεῖρός μου. Hatch[9] says: "The general fidelity of Clement to the text of the LXX is sometimes shown

---

[1] Schürer, *The Jewish People etc.* Div. ii, vol. iii, p. 337.
[2] *Quot Deus immut.* 17 (i, 284).
[3] *De Migrat. Abraham* 28 (i, 460); Schürer, *ibid* Div ii, vol. iii, p. 335.
[4] *Quot Deus immut.* 16 (i, 284).
[5] Hatch, *Essays in Biblical Greek*, p. 172.
[6] *De Somniis* ii: 38 (i, 691).   [7] Hatch, *ibid.*, p. 174.
[8] Clement reads οὗ οὐ μὴ λογίσηται, as אc.aRa.
[9] *Ibid.*, p. 176.

by his reproduction of its mistranslation. For example in ψ 50 (51) 8 the Hebrew clearly means (as it is translated in the English Revised Version) 'Behold thou desirest truth in the inward parts; and in the hidden part thou shalt make me to know wisdom', but the LXX, which is followed by Clement c. 18, 6, translates ninbɔ by τὰ ἄδηλα and destroys the parallelism of the verse by joining it to the second member, viz., ἰδοὺ γὰρ ἀλήθειαν ἠγάπησας τὰ ἄδηλα καὶ τὰ κρύφια τῆς σοφίας σου ἐδήλωσάς μοι." Clement also has many quotations from Isaiah, which are for the most part faithful reproductions of the LXX text.[1]

Equally numerous and faithful are the quotations of Barnabas 1, 9; ψ i:5 (in c. ii) διὰ τοῦτο οὐκ ἀναστήσονται (οἱ) ἀσεβεῖς ἐν κρίσει οὐδὲ ἁμαρτωλοὶ ἐν βουλῇ δικαίων. ψ xxii: 17 ὅτι ἐκύκλωσάν με κύνες πολλοὶ συναγωγὴ πονηρευομένων περιέσχον με ὤρυξαν χεῖράς μου καὶ πόδας. Barnabas' quotations from Isaiah exist with such variations as are found in known Mss. of the LXX.[2]

The Text of Justin Martyr rests practically upon only one Ms., the Cod. Paris 450, (A. D. 1364). From this there is a copy known as Codex Claromontanus, now in the Middlehill collection at Cheltenham[3]; also two Mss. containing fragments of Justin's works, one in the Vatican Library[4], and the other in the National Library at Paris[5]. Therefore the longer quotations in the Paris Ms. of Justin are untrustworthy; since the scribe

[1] cf. Is. i: 16—20; xxix: 13; lii; lx: 17; see Hatch, *Essays in Biblical Greek*, p. 177—179.

[2] *Ibid.*, p. 182, where other examples are given.

[3] See Harnack, *Die Ueberlieferung d. griech. Apolog. d. II. Jahrh. in der alten Kirche u. im Mittelalter* in the *Stud. und Untersuch. s. Gesch. d. altchrist. Lit.* Bd. I, Leipzig 1882; cf. Hatch, *Essays in Biblical Greek*, p. 187.

[4] Cod. Ottobonianus.   [5] Cod. Supplem. Gr. 190.

copied them for himself from some other Ms.[1] But the shorter quotations form an integral part of Justin's own text e. g.:—
ψ xxi: 3 τὴν ἐπιθυμίαν τῆς ψυχῆς αὐτοῦ ἔδωκας αὐτῷ καὶ τὴν δέησιν τῶν χειλέων αὐτοῦ οὐκ ἐστέρησας αὐτόν[2]. Also ψ xxiv: 7 ἄρατε πύλας οἱ ἄρχοντες ὑμῶν καὶ ἐπάρθητε πύλαι αἰώνιοι καὶ εἰσελεύσεται (Justin ἵνα εἰσέλθῃ) ὁ βασιλεὺς τῆς δόξης[3]; ψ lxxxi: 7 ὑμεῖς δὲ ἂν ὡς ἄνθρωποι ἀποθνήσκετε καὶ ὡς εἰς τῶν ἀρχόντων πίπτετε.[4] As would be expected from the character of Justin's writings, dealing chiefly in controversions concerning Messianic prophecy, the quotations are most numerous in the Book of Isaiah, and are very valuable for purposes of textual criticism.[5]

From this survey of the attitude of Jewish and Christian writers toward the Septuagint, two facts are plainly revealed.

I. That the Septuagint was used by the *Jews* in temple worship, and by *Jewish historians* and writers in preference to the Hebrew.

II. That the Septuagint was freely quoted by New Testament and later *Christian writers*; and finally adopted by the Early *Christian Church* as their standard Scripture text.

§ 3. *Characteristics of the Septuagint Psalter*

In general it must be said of the Greek Version of the Psalter that it is not a free translation. Luther's characterization of the whole translation, while in general too severe, yet applies with considerable justice to the Psalms. "The Seventy Greek translators have so translated the Hebrew Bible into the Greek language as to show themselves inexperienced in, and unacquainted with, the Hebrew. Their translation is very

---

[1] *Ibid.* 189—190. [2] *Tryph.* 98 and 99.
[3] *Tryph.* 85, Apol. 1151. [4] *Tryph.* 124.
[5] Hatch, *Essays in Biblical Greek*, p. 197 seq.

trifling and absurd, for they have disdained to speak the letters, words and style". This last is an excellent summary of three noticeable characteristics of the Septuagint, viz—a tendency to mistake and interchange letters, to misinterpret words, and to alter the construction of sentences. In considering the following main characteristics of the Septuagint Psalter, those of the Pᵉšittâ already noted[1] must be borne in mind, in order that resemblances may be noted and differences marked.[2]

As was the case with the Pᵉšittâ, several peculiarities of the Greek can be directly traced to the extensive use of the Psalter for liturgical purposes. For this reason the name of God is frequently supplied, both in the vocative (Κύριε) to make the prayer a more direct appeal to God, and in the nominative (Κύριος or ὁ θεός) to lend additional sacredness to the passage. Examples of instances where the word Κύριε is added are:—ψ v:6, 12; ψ vii:7; ψ xxiv:21; ψ xxx:23; ψ xxxiv:18; ψ xliii:24; ψ xlvii:12; ψ l:17, 20; ψ liv:24; ψ lxxxiii:6; ψ lxxxiv:8; ψ lxxxvii:2; ψ xciii:19; ψ ciii:1; ψ cxviii:85, 93, 94, 97, 169; ψ cxxxviii:13; ψ cxli:8; ψ cxlii:8. Instances where Κύριος and θεός are supplied are:—ψ ii:6, 12; ψ iii:8; ψ xli:6; ψ lv:8; ψ lxvii:12, 34; ψ xcvii:1; ψ cii:11; ψ cxiv:5. Very seldom, however, is the name omitted; a few examples are: ψ xxv:6; ψ xli:3; ψ lxvii:21; ψ lxviii:7, 30; ψ lxxii:28; ψ lxxxix:2; ψ xci:10; ψ cxii:1.

Similarly to the Syriac ܟܠ, the word πάντες is frequently supplied: ψ ii:10 שפטי] πάντες οἱ κρίνοντες; ψ xxiv:1 וישבי] πάντες οἱ κατοικοῦντες; ψ xxxv:5 עליהן] πάσῃ ὁδῷ; v 13 פעלי] πάντες οἱ ἐργαζόμενοι (cf. ψ lii:5); ψ lxi:9 עם] πᾶσα συναγωγὴ λαοῦ; ψ xcviii:3 יודו שמך] ἐξομολογησάσθωσαν

---

[1] Ch II, § 3, p. 28.
[2] In referring to the Greek Psalms, I have used the LXX enumeration.

πάντες; ψ ciii : 20 [מלאכיו] πάντες οἱ ἄγγελοι αὐτοῦ. The Hebrew תמיד is also sometimes rendered by διὰ παντός, e. g. ψ xviii : 15; where the word is supplied; also ψ xxxix : 17 [אהבי תשועתך] οἱ ἀγαπῶντες τὸ σωτήριόν σου διὰ παντός; ψ cxviii : 119 [אהבתי עדתיך] ἠγάπησα τὰ μαρτύριά σου διὰ παντός. In other forms of πας, ψ cxviii : 64 [הארץ] πᾶσα ἡ γῆ; ψ cxxxviii : 2 [בנתה לרעי] σὺ συνῆκας πάντας τοὺς διαλογισμούς μου; ψ cxxxvii : 4 [כי שמעו אמרי] ὅτι ἤκουσαν πάντα τὰ ῥήματα.

Again like the Pᵉšiṭṭâ, personal pronouns are frequently supplied both in the singular and plural; which, while not materially changing the sense of the passage, change a general prayer into a particular petition, enabling the individual to personally appropriate the words of the Psalmist, and clothing them with additional meaning and sacredness e. g.; ψ iii : 3 [באלהים] ἐν θεῷ αὐτοῦ; ψ xi : 2 [הושיעה] σῶσόν με; ψ xvi : 1 [צדק] τῆς δικαιοσύνης μου; V. 13 [קדמה] πρόφθασον αὐτούς; V. 14 [בחיים] ἐν τῇ ζωῇ αὐτῶν; ψ xvii : 31 [האל] ὁ θεός μου; ψ xxi : 25 [שמע] εἰσήκουσέν μου; ψ xxvi : 5 [רעה] κακῶν μου; ψ xxxvii : 20 [עצמו] κεκρατίωνται ὑπὲρ ἐμέ; ψ xxxviii : 10 [עשׂתה] ποιήσας με; ψ xlii : 5 [אלהים] ὁ θεός μου; ψ xlix : 7 [ואדברה] καὶ λαλήσω σοι; ψ lviii : 11 [אלהים] ὁ θεός μου; ψ lxii : 7 [באשמרות] ἐν τῷ ὄρθρῳ μου; ψ lxxvi : 14, 15 [אלהים] ὁ θεὸς ἡμῶν; ψ lxxvii : 38 [און] ταῖς ἁμαρτίαις αὐτῶν; ψ xxii : 6; ψ xlvi : 7; ψ lxxx : 8; ψ lxxxiv : 9; ψ xcv : 9; ψ cvi : 20; ψ cxii : 1; ψ cxiii : 20; ψ cxvii : 16; ψ cxviii : 58; ψ cxxv : 6; ψ cxxxiii : 1; ψ cxxxviii : 7; ψ cxl : 9. Occasionally the pronoun referrs to God; ψ xxi : 3 [אקרא] κεκράξομαι . . . πρὸς σέ; ψ xxviii : 2 [בהדרת־קדש] ἐν αὐλῇ ἁγίᾳ αὐτοῦ; ψ lxiii : 2 [קולי] ἐν τῷ δέεσθαί με πρὸς σέ; ψ lxxiii : 23 [תמיד] διὰ παντὸς πρὸς σέ; ψ cxvii : 28 [אלהי] θεός μου εἶ σύ. Less frequent is the omission of a pronoun; but examples are not so rare as in the Pᵉšiṭṭâ: ψ v : 12 [ויעלצו בך] ἀγαλλιάσονται; ψ xii : 4 [עיני] τοὺς ὀφθαλμούς; ψ xxxi : 5 [אודיעך] ἐγνώρισα; ψ xxxiv : 22 [אדני]

Κύριε; ψ xl : 13 [עוגתי] ἀκακίαν; ψ xlii : 2 [אלהי] ὁ θεός; ψ lxvii : 29 [אלהיך] θεός; ψ lxviii : 14 [עני] ἐπάκουσον; ψ lxx : 16 [אדני] Κυρίου; ψ lxxii : 2 [רגלי] οἱ πόδες; ψ lxxxviii : 19 [מנגני] ἀντίλημψις; ψ xc : 3 [ויצלך] ῥύσεται; ψ xciv : 9 בחנוני ... נסוני ἐπείρασαν ... ἐδοκίμασαν (א*T + με); ψ cv : 34 [אמר יהוה להם] εἶπεν Κύριος; V. 44 [ויזכר להם] καὶ ἐμνήσθη; ψ cix : 2 [עוד] δυνάμεως; ψ cxviii : 79 [ישובו לי] ἐπιστρεψάτωσαν; V. 88 [חיני] ζήσομαι; V. 173 [לעזרני] τοῦ σῶσαι; ψ cxxxviii : 20 [ימרך] ἐρεῖς.

Just as in the Peshittâ, words and sometimes sentences are added in the Septuagint with a view to amplifying or explaining the original meaning. In this case, likewise, it may easily be conceived that the concise, often abrupt and eliptical expressions of the Hebrew, would grate harshly on the critical ear of the Greek, a perfect metre or rhythm requiring additional syllables. Some such explanation seems to be required, since the additions are not contained in the Targum. Thus ψ i : 4 [אשר־תרדפני רוח] + LXX + ἀπὸ προσώπου τῆς γῆς; ψ vii : 12 [אלהים שופט צדיק] + καὶ ἰσχυρὸς καὶ μακρόθυμος; ψ xiii : 5 [פחדו פחד] + οὗ οὐκ ἦν φόβος; ψ xxiii : 4 [נשבע למרמה] + τῷ πλησίον αὐτοῦ; ψ xxx : 2 [פלטני] + καὶ ἐξελοῦ με; ψ xxxii : 10 [מחשבות עמים] + καὶ ἀθετεῖ βουλὰς ἀρχόντων; ψ xxxvi : 20 [ואיבי יהוה] + ἅμα τῷ δοξασθῆναι αὐτοὺς καὶ ὑψωθῆναι; V. 36 [ולא נמצא] + ὁ τόπος αὐτοῦ; ψ xl : 2 [אל־דל] + καὶ πένητα; ψ lv : 3 [כל־היום] + ἀπὸ ὕψους ἡμέρας; ψ lxvii : 34 [לרכב] ψάλατε τῷ θεῷ τῷ ἐπιβεβηκότι; ψ lxx : 21 [קדוש ישראל] + καὶ ἐκ τῶν ἀβύσσων πάλιν ἀνήγαγές με; ψ xciv : 4 [אשר בידו] ὅτι οὐκ ἀπώσεται Κύριος τὸν λαὸν αὐτοῦ; ψ cvii : 2 [נכון לבי אלהים] + ἑτοίμη ἡ καρδία μου; ψ cxviii : 103 [מדבש] + καὶ κηρίον; ψ cxxxvii : 1 [אודך בכל־לבי] + ὅτι ἤκουσας τὰ ῥήματα τοῦ στόματός μου.

Very frequently a Hebrew singular is translated by a plural. This is especially true of words which have a collective signification, as דבר, אמרה and יד. But instances are not as frequent as in the Pᵉšiṭtâ; ψ xvi:6 [אמרתי] τῶν ῥημάτων μου; ψ xxi:17 [ידי ורגלי] χεῖράς μου καὶ πόδας; ψ xxx:9 [ביד] εἰς χεῖρας; ψ xxxi:1 [פשע] αἱ ἀνομίαι; ψ lxxi:14 [מחמס] ἐξ ἀδικίας; V. 15 [ויתפלל] προσεύξονται; ψ lxxvi:3 [ידי] ταῖς χερσίν μου; ψ cxviii:172 [אמרתך] τὰ λόγια (אᶜᵃ R T); ψ cxix:2 [משפת־שקר] χειλέων ἀδίκων. Very seldom do we find a Hebrew plural rendered by a Greek singular; ψ lxv:9 [נפשנו] τὴν ψυχήν μου; ψ lxvii:15 [מלכים] βασιλεὺς τῶν δυναμῶν.

Unlike the Pᵉšiṭtâ, the Septuagint is guilty of no errors which may be ascribed to ignorance. Real lexicographical errors are never found; although some words are curiously interpreted. Thus אלהים, when the context would demand its translation as a plural οἱ θεοί, the LXX, unwilling to commit itself to an even apparent concession to polytheism, avoided the difficulty by translating ἄγγελλοι; cf. ψ viii:6; ψ xcv:7; ψ cxxxviii:1. So also the word צלמות is fancifully derived from צֶלֶם מות, and rendered σκία θανάτου, an example which all other translations have followed[1]; cf. ψ xxii:4; ψ xliii:19; ψ cvi:10; ψ cvi:14. על־פני is usually rendered simply by ἐνώπιον; and the particle את is more often translated as a preposition by σύν, than as a sign of the accusative. It is difficult to affirm with any certainty that the LXX ever errs in its rendering of the Hebrew tenses, for to lay down any invariable rule for translation is impossible.[2] Generally speaking, the Hebrew perfect is translated by the Greek Aorist, as in ψ i:1 [הלך ... עמד ... ישב] ἐπορεύθη ... ἔστη ... ἐκάθισεν; the Imperfect by the future, ψ i:2 [יהגה] μελετήσει; and the Imperative mood frequently by the

---

[1] More probably the word should be read צַלְמוּת; cf. Arab. ظلمة or ظلمات as Qu'rân Sur. ii:v 19, signifying "intense darkness".

[2] Driver, "*A Treatise on the Use of the Tenses in Hebrew*", p. vi—vii.

Aorist, ψ xv: 11 תודעני] ἐγνώρισάς μοι, but there are many exceptions.[1]

Grammatical errors, however, are not infrequent, e. g. ψ xxi: 22 עניתני] τὴν ταπείνωσίν μου; ψ cxviii: 133 ואל תשלט] καὶ μὴ κατακυριευσάτω (Syr. ܘܠܐ ܢܫܠܛ); ψ cix: 6 רבה] πολλῶν; ψ xcvi: 6 הוד] ἐξομολόγησις. Only once is a negative sentence changed into an affirmative, ψ civ: 28 ולא־מרו את־דבריו] καὶ παρεπίκραναν τοὺς λόγους αὐτοῦ. The reason for this change was probably the wish to secure historic accuracy; since the statement of the Hebrew does not agree with tradition. (Cf. Ex. x: 21.) Possibly for לא the reading should be לו; but the construction would hardly bear such a change. In many Psalms the concluding הללויה is removed to the beginnig of the following Psalm, as ψ cxiii; ψ cxlv—cxlix.

Frequently also the LXX is guilty of carelessness. ψ iv: 3 אלהים [כבדי לב למה = βαρυκάρδιοι ἵνα τί – כבדי לב למה; ψ xliii: 5 צוה] ὁ θεός μου ὁ ἐντελλόμενος – אלהי צוה; ψ lvii: 12 שפטם] ὁ θεός κρίνων αὐτοὺς – שפטם; ψ ciii: 17 ברושים] ἡγεῖται αὐτῶν – בראשם; ψ cv: 7 עלים] ἀναβαίνοντες – עלים. But more frequent instances of evident carelessness are where a י has been mistaken for ו, and vice-versa. Still, even here it must be remembered that the introduction of the vowel letters in the middle of the word belongs to comparatively recent times, often depending upon the mere volition of the scribes. Also at the end of a word, the vowel letters י, ו, ה, א were frequently not written[2]. Furthermore, according to Lagarde[3], the same is likewise true of the two letters ם, ן; their omission being simply marked by the

---

[1] Baethgen, *Jahrbücher für Protestantische Theologie* No. 4, 1882, p. 593, seq.

[2] Chwolson, *The quiescent letters* הוי; *Hebraica*, vi, p. 89—108.

[3] *Anmerkungen zur griechischen Uebersetzung der Proverbien*, p. 4.

diacritical¹ sign ('). In the same manner, that which seems to be carelessness on the part of the Septuagint in exchanging the ו and י, may in fact have been a simple matter of exegesis. Thus ψ ii: 6 [נסכתי מלכי] κατεστάθην βασιλεὺς ὑπ' αὐτοῦ — נסכתי מלכו; ψ xv: 3 [כל חפצי] πάντα τὰ θελήματα αὐτοῦ — כל־חפצו; ψ xvi: 11 [אשורנו] ἐκβαλόντες με — אשורני; V. 12 [דמינו] ὑπέλαβόν με — דמוני; ψ xxi: 30 [ונפשו לא חיה] καὶ ἡ ψυχή μου αὐτῷ ζῇ — ונפשי לו חיה; ψ xxxiv: 19 [ויקרצו עין] καὶ διανεύοντες ὀφθαλμοῖς — יקרצו עין; ψ xxxv: 2 [בקרב לבי] ἐν ἑαυτῷ — בקרב לבו; ψ xxxvii: 12 [נגעו] ἤγγισαν — נגעי; ψ xlv: 5 [קדש משכני] ἡγίασε τὸ σκήνωμα αὐτοῦ — קדש משכנו; ψ lxiii: 7 [וקרב] προσελεύσεται — יקרב (following the general rule of an impserfect by a future); ψ lxxii: 10 [עמו] ὁ λαός μου — עמי; ibid. [ומי מלא] καὶ ἡμέραι πλήρεις — ימי מלא (possibly here a י was simply omitted); ψ lxxxix: 16 [יראה] καὶ ἴδε — וראה; ψ cviii: 28 [קמו] οἱ ἐπανιστάμενοί μοι — קמי; ψ cxviii: 3 [פעלו עולה] οἱ ἐργαζόμενοι τὴν ἀνομίαν — פעלי עולה; ψ cxliii: 15 [אשרי] ἐμακάρισαν — אשרו; ψ cxliv: 5 [ודברי] λαλήσουσι — ידברו.

In the Septuagint, as in the Pᵉšiṭtâ, there are instances where several words connected by the simple copula are inverted. ψ lxxii: 26 [שארי ולבבי] ἐξέλιπεν ἡ καρδία μοῦ καὶ ἡ σάρξ μου; ψ lxxxi: 3 [פלט רדל ואביון] κρίνατε ὀρφανὸν καὶ πτωχόν; ψ xciii: 6 [אלמנה וגר יהרגו ויתומים ירצחו] χήραν καὶ ὀρφανὸν ἀπέκτειναν καὶ προσήλυτον ἐφόνευσαν; ψ xcv: 6 הוד והדר [לפניו עז ותפארת במקדשו] ἐξομολόγησις καὶ ὡραιότης ἐνώπιον αὐτοῦ ἁγιωσύνη καὶ μεγαλοπρέπεια ἐν τῷ ἁγιάσματι αὐτοῦ; ψ lxxxix: 10 [עמל ואון] κόπος καὶ πόνος; ψ lxviii: 23 ולשלומים [למוקש] καὶ εἰς ἀνταπόδοσιν καὶ σκάνδαλον; ψ xxxiv: 2 מגן [וצנה] ὅπλου καὶ θυρεοῦ; V. 3 [חנית וסגר] ῥομφαίαν καὶ σύνκλεισον.

The Septuagint's renderings of the tropes applied to God

---

¹ Driver, *Notes on the Hebrew Text of Samuel*, p. lxix.

are rather paraphrases than translations, with the single exception of צור which is regularly translated by ὁ θεός.[1]
ψ xvii: 31, 46; ψ xxvi: 5; ψ xxviii: 1; ψ xxx: 2; ψ lx: 2;
ψ lxi: 2, 7; ψ lxxxvii: 15; ψ lxxxvii: 20, 35; ψ lxxx: 16;
ψ lxxxviii: 26; ψ xci: 15, 22; ψ xciv: 1; ψ civ: 41; ψ cxiii: 8.

סלעי ומצודתי is rendered by στερέωμά μου καὶ καταφυγή μου
ψ xvii: 2; ψ xxx: 3; ψ lxx: 3; ψ xc: 2; ψ xliii: 2. When
occurring alone, סלע is translated πέτραν, ψ xxxix: 3; ψ lxxvii: 16;
ψ ciii: 18; ἀντιλήμπτωρ ψ xli: 10; מגני by ὑπερασπιστής μου,
ψ xxvii: 7; ψ xxxii: 20; ψ lviii: 11; ψ lxxxiii: 9; ψ cxiv: 9,
10, 11; ψ cxviii: 114; ψ cxliii: 2.

Such are the principle characteristics of the Septuagint Psalter. While there are places which are far from agreeing with our present Massoretic text, the version as a whole must be pronounced to be a fairly literal one; too idiomatic to be slavishly so, too faithful to its archetype to in any way resemble a paraphrase. Furthermore, the Pešiṭtâ and Septuagint have been found to have many characteristics in common.

---

[1] Wiegand (*Zeit. Alttest. Wissensch.* x: 1, cf. *Academy*, Aug. 23, 1890) points out that the name of the God Zur is met with in the O. T. The existence of this God is verified by a proper name which occurs in one of the Babylonian Contract Tablets, published by Dr. Strassmaier. There, one of the witnesses to a deed dated in the fourteenth year of Nabonidus, is called Zur-natanu, the son of Addu-Lagummu. The word Zur is preceded by the determinative for divinity (⊢⊣), showing that it is the name of a God. As the form "natanu" is Syrian or Hebrew, the Assyrian being nadanu, it is clear that Zur must be a deity of Syrian or Palestinian origin. (A. H. Sayce) cf. also *ZAW*, 1890, p. 85—92 where from the LXX φυλαξ (22: 3, 47; 23: 3 and Theod. in Dt. 32: 31, 37), צור is referred to √נצר.

§ 4. *Summary of Part I—The external evidence of a LXX influence upon the Pᵉšiṭṭâ Psalter*

Before proceeding to any investigation concerning the internal evidence of a Septuagint influence upon the Pᵉšiṭṭâ Psalter, let us first briefly summarize the external evidence already obtained.

I.

The origin of the Pᵉšiṭṭâ, as attested by the ablest scholars, was not later than the early part of the Second Century A. D. and may have been as early as the beginning of the first; a few facts point to an even earlier date.

II.

The authors of this version were probably Jewish-Christians, who finding Hebrew and Aramaic unintelligible to the masses, desired a translation in the Syriac vernacular: their motive being rather to secure a readable translation of the Scriptures than a critical version.

III.

While the general character of the Pᵉšiṭṭâ Psalter is in the main that of a slavishly literal translation, it yet bears many characteristics in common with the Septuagint. These characteristics further suggest that the translators were not perfectly familiar with the Hebrew. For this reason, it is possible that other translations, such as the Greek and the Aramaic, were at times called into requisition.

IV.

The principle version of the Scriptures at that period was the Septuagint, whose high literary and ecclesiastical standing is well attested by its universal use among sacred and profane Jewish and Christian writers, as well as in the synagogues and churches.

V.

Because of the authority it thus enjoyed, certain expressions and phrases of the Septuagint passed into current use.

VI.

The whole weight, therefore, of external evidence is on the side of a strong antecedent probability that the Septuagint was consulted by the Syriac translators.

Whether indisputable traces of this influence, as well as the method and extent of its exercise, can be discerned or not, can only be ascertained by a careful comparison of the Greek and Syriac variants from the Massoretic text. These must be compared not only with each other, but with the Aramaic Targum. This latter comparison will help us to decide whether or not both versions are simply following a common tradition.

PART II

THE INTERNAL EVIDENCE OF A SEPTUAGINT INFLUENCE UPON THE P^{E}ŠIṬṬÂ PSALTER

Chapter IV

TEXTS AND TEXT-CRITICISM

§ 1. *The superscription of the Psalms*

Before proceeding further, a word or two must be said by way of explanation of the fact that the Psalm Superscriptions have been wholly disregarded in the present investigation. As has before been intimated,[1] while there is no doubt concerning the antiquity of the titles of the Psalms, there is considerable dispute concerning their authenticity. A comparison with other literature offers no explanation as to the real significance of these superscriptions. True, Oriental poets usually prefix a title to their songs,[2] but even imagination can trace no resemblance between the instances found in Arabic poetry, for example, and the Hebrew inscriptions of the Psalms. There may be some slight analogy between these titles and the subscriptions of the Apostolic Epistles; but if so, the latter being undoubtedly spurious, so must be also the former.[3] Both

---

[1] Ch. ii, § 3, p. 28. [2] Tholuck, *Psalmen*, p. xxiv.
[3] Eichhorn, *Einleitung*, iii: 490—95.

Nestle[1] and Baethgen,[2] have convincingly shown that the Syriac superscriptions, which are partly historical and partly exegetical, were added by Theodore of Mopsuestia; who, accepting some from Eusebius and Origen, made many additions of his own. Prager,[3] judging simply by the similarity of certain Agadic passages with three superscriptions, has endeavored to prove them to be of Jewish origin. But Dr. Neubauer claims[4] that this is a mistake, observing, "As Dr. Nestle rightly says, the Agadic passages have no kind of superscription; to which it may be added that the Pirqe de R. Eliezer, the Midrasch Tilim, the Yalqoot and even the Thanḥuma, on which Dr. Prager bases his arguments, are of a later date than Theodore of Mopsuestia, and if there had been any borrowing on either side it will be the Midrash that has borrowed and not Theodore."

But long before the earliest times which can be assigned to the Pˢšittâ, the meaning of the Hebrew titles was lost. Even the Septuagint offers no explanation of them;[5] and probably as early as the time when the temple with its music was reorganized and the Psalter reëdited by Simon, the Jewish scribes themselves had forgotten their meaning.[6] Even the best Jewish commentators as Ibn Ezra and David Qamḥi are in the dark; the former treats them as the opening words of popular melodies, the latter as names of instruments; both confessing that the real meanings are unknown.[5] Staerk[7] has summarized the whole

[1] *Theologische Literaturzeitung*, 1876, col. 283.
[2] *Zeitschrift für Alttestament. Wissensch.* 1885, p. 66 seq.
[3] *De Veteris Test. Syr. Quaest. Crit.*, p. 52—56.
[4] *Studia Biblica* vol. ii, p. 9, *The Authorship and Titles of the Psalms according to Early Jewish Authorities.*
[5] Neubauer, *Studia Biblica*, vol. ii, p. 57.
[6] Cheyne, *Bampton Lectures*, p. 458.
[7] *Zur Kritik der Psalmen-Ueberschriften. Zeitschrift für Alttest. Wissenschaft* 1892, p. 91.

question thus: „Im Allgemeinen lässt sich für die Psalmenüberschriften der angegebenen Textzeugen ein dreifaches Charakteristicum ausstellen. Erstens liefern sie bei allen fast durchgehends den Beweis, dass schon die Uebersetzer den ursprünglichen Sinn der hebräischen Originale soweit sie musikalische Bemerkungen enthalten wenig oder gar nicht mehr verstanden haben; ferner, die Ueberschriften sind von den einzelnen Uebersetzern in gewissen stereotypen für jeden charakteristischen Formeln wiedergegeben worden; .... Endlich im grossen und ganzen haben die Uebersetzer unsern massorethischen Text (nach seinem Consonantenbestande) vor sich gehabt."

While the Septuagint evidently understood the meaning of the titles no better than did the P^ešittâ, yet it studiously avoided an untitled Psalm. David being the typical Psalmist, was probably credited by the Septuagint with more Psalms than belonged to him, e. g. ψ xliii;[1] and that titles are either omitted by the Hebrew or supplied by the Septuagint can be shown by numerous examples.[2]

It is evident in view of these facts that even if a resemblance could be shown to exist between the Greek and Syriac Psalm superscriptions, it would prove nothing as to the original relation of the Septuagint and P^ešittâ; and for this reason they have here received no consideration.

---

[1] Cheyne, *Bampton Lectures*, p. 458.

[2] Neubauer, *Studia Biblica*, vol. ii, p. 57, gives a list of such examples—among them: ψ xxiii (24), xxiv (25), xxvi (27), xxviii (29), xxx (31), xxxii (33), xxxvii (38), xlii (43), xlvii (48), lxv (66), lxix (70), lxx (71) et al.

§ 2. *Texts used in collecting the Greek and Syriac variants*

In compiling the Greek and Syriac variants from the Massoretic Text and comparing them with the Aramaic, the following texts have been consulted.

For the Hebrew, *Liber Psalmorum* (ספר תהלות), *Textum Massoreticum, accuratissime expressit e fontibus Masorae varie illustravit, notis criticis confirmavit S. Baer.* Praefatus est edendi operis adjutor Franciscus Delitzsch, Lipsiae 1880. The edition likewise contains "Appendices criticae et masoreticae".

For the Aramaic, *Hagiographa Chaldaice.* Edited by Paul de Lagarde, Lipsiae 1873. This text is based upon several codices, as stated by Lagarde in his preface as follows:—
"Quae in hoc volumine inde a 2, 1 usque ad 270, 5 habentur, ex editione Bombergii prima a Felice Pratensi curata desumpta sunt: quae post 270, 6 leguntur, e libro erfurtano fluxerunt ad cantabrigiensis et tertii codicis fidem hic illic reficto, de Paralipomenis quum mox uberius acturus sim, hoc loco non exponam, Bombergii scripturae a me mutatae hae sunt." Hereupon follows a list of the various readings.

For the *LXX,* I have used two editions; one, *The Psalms in Greek according to the Septuagint,* edited by Henry Barclay Swete D. D. Regius Professor of Divinity, Cambridge. Univ. Press. 1891. The text is that of the Vatican Ms. (B) where that Ms. is available; where it is defective, the lacuna is supplied from the Sinaitic Ms. (א); which, in those parts of the Psalter that are extant in B, seems to be more akin to B than the other uncial Mss. Four other Mss. supply the textual notes; the Psalter of the Codex Alexandrinus (A), the Verona and Zurich Psalters (R. T.), and the papyrus fragments at the British Museum (U). An Appendix records the unsubstantial variants; chiefly rejected spelling of no special interest. The other Septuagint text used is *Psalterii Graeci quinquagena prima* a

Paulo de Lagarde, Göttingen 1892. The work as far as ψ xlviii: 18 is that of Lagarde, from xlviii: 19 ad fin. of Alfred Rahlfs, who has followed strictly the method pursued by Lagarde. The work is chiefly valuable for its critical notes, based not only upon the original Greek codices, but upon many subsequent Greek and other translations.

For the Syriac, the main text is that of Dr. Samuel Lee[1] (1823). This edition is based mainly upon the text of the Paris Polyglot (g), from which it varies in only a few unimportant points—chiefly typographical errors, e. g. ψ xliii: 5 it reads ܒܐܠ ܟܝܐ for ܬܚܡܣܕ (LXX συνταράσσεις με), which reading is supported by the text of Ceriani and Urmia, which read ܟܝܐ ܠܒ; ψ l: 23 it stands alone in omitting ܟܠܗܘܢ, reading simply ܘܐܡܪ; ψ li: 1 it reads ܥܠ for ܠܒ; ψ lxiii: 7 ܐܫܬܟܚ] ܐܬܐܡܪ neither of which readings agree either with the Hebrew or LXX. The other variants are of too little importance to deserve special mention. More numerous, but

---

[1] The following mistakes have been noted by Baethgen (*J. P. T.* 1882, No. 3, p. 423) as occurring not only in the Text of Lee but in all the older Mss.:—ψ ii: 3 ܟܝܣܐ] ܟܣܝܐ; x: 6 ܟܐܢ] ܟܐܢ; v. 14 ܐܣܟ ܐܘܪܟܣ] ܐܘܪܟ ܐܢܐ ܟܠܗܘܢ ܟܠܗܘܢ ܐܘܪܟܣ; xxi: 4 ܐܒܗܬܗܘܢ; xxxv: 15 ܟܝܠܐܘ] ܟܝܠܐܘ or ܟܐܠܘ; xxxviii: 14 ܐܘܪܟܐ] ܐܠܗܢ—ܐܠܗܢ] ܟܬܝܘ (Bar 'Ebr.); xliv: 3 ܐܝܪܣܐ] ܐܝܪܣܐ; xliv: 20 ܟܠܘܕܐ] ܟܠܘܕܐ (as Z. D. M. G. 1849, p. 392); xlix: 16 ܡܣܒܥ] ܡܣܒܥ (Bar 'Ebr.); li: 3, 11 ܥܠ] ܠܒ (αβ CUP¹P³); li: 16 ܐܚܝܢܐ] ܐܝܣܐ; li: 16 ܣܝܒ] ܬܘܒ; lxiii: 9 ܐܣܢܝ] ܐܣܢܝ; lxv: 10 ܣܛܝܪܐ] ܣܛܝܪܐ; lxvi: 13 ܟܘܪܟܒ] ܟܬܝܒ; lxviii: 11 ܐܣܒܕ] ܐܘܒܕ; lxxv: 4 ܥܣܩܠܐ] ܥܣܩܠܐ; lxxv: 10 ܟܐܢ] ܟܐܢ; lxxvi: 5 ܢܣܬܒܩܘ] ܢܣܬܒܩܘ (Nestorian reading: cited by Bar 'Ebr.); xciv: 19 ܣܡܝܒܐ] ܣܡܝܒܐ; cii: 4 ܟܠܗܘ (Bar 'Ebr.); cx: 6 ܟܣܝܐ] ܟܣܝܐ; cxix: 131 ܢܐܣܝܠܐ] ܢܝܣܘܠܐ.

scarcely more important, are the variants in Walton's Polyglot from the Mss. of Usher (U) and Pocock (P). They consist chiefly of the omission and addition of a ܘ, the interchange of prepositions and conjunctions, and the omission of words and suffixes. A few variants may be mentioned:—ψ ix: 16 ܘܒܦܚܐ] ܘܒܡܨܝ̈ܕܬܐ CUPβ. LXX τοῖς ἔργοις τῶν χειρῶν; ψ x: 9 ܘܟܡܢ] ܘܟܡܢ ܒܡܛܫܝܬܐ ܐܝܟ ܐܪܝܐ ܒܡܫܟܢܗ U, supported by none of the other Mss.; ψ xix: 4 ܠܝܬ ܡܐܡܪܐ ܐܦܠܐ ܡ̈ܠܐ] ܠܝܬ ܒܡܐܡܪܐ ܐܦܠܐ ܡܬܡܠܠܐ P. Other Mss. as Lee. ψ xxxi: 4 ܡܢ ܦܚܐ] ܡܢ ܡܨܝ̈ܕܬܐ CUP, but LXX ἐκ παγίδος; ψ xxxviii: 19 ܘܚܝܘ] ܘܚܝܢ UP, LXX ζῶσιν; ψ li: 17 ܬܒܝܪܐ] + ܘܡܟܝܟܐ UP, LXX καρδίαν συντετριμμένην καὶ τεταπεινωμένην; ψ lxxiv: 11 ܕܦܩܘܕܬ ܡܢ ܥܘܒܟ ܥܠ ܦܘܪܩܢܗ ܕܥܡܟ] ܕܥܒܕ ܦܘܪܩܢܐ ܒܡܨܥܬܗ ܕܐܪܥܐ CU, LXX εἰργάσατο σωτηρίαν ἐν μέσῳ τῆς γῆς; ψ civ: 35 ܥܘ̈ܠܐ] ܚܛܝ̈ܐ, LXX ἁμαρτωλοί; ψ cxviii: 18 ܠܗ ܠܗ] > ܠܗ CβUP, LXX ἀποκάλυψον.

While the Ceriani (C) text presents many different readings from the text of Lee, they are of a kind similar to those in Walton's Polyglot, and very few are of any special significance; e. g. ψ ii: 11 ܫܡܫܘ ܡܪܝܐ] ܐܚܘܕܘ ܡܪܕܘܬܐ, but LXX δράξασθε παιδείας (ℵ παιδιαν); vii: 15 ܚܛܝܬܐ] ܥܘܠܐ, LXX ἀνομίαν; ψ xxix: 6 ܘܕܩܘܢ] ܪܩܕ, LXX λεπτυνεῖ; ψ xxxiii: 3 ܙܡܪܘ ܫܦܝܪ] ܘܐܙܡܪܘ ܕܫܦܝܪ, but LXX again ᾄσατε; ψ xxxv: 8 ܕܛܫܝܘ ܢܬܐܚܕܘܢ] . . . ܕܛܡܪܘ, in which reading C stands alone; ψ civ: 4 ܪܘܚܐ] ܢܘܪܐ, LXX πνεύματα (A, πυρος φλεγα); ψ cvi: 26 ܒܡܕܒܪܐ] ܒܥܡ̈ܡܐ, but LXX as Lee ἐν τῇ ἐρήμῳ; ψ cxi: 9 ܫܪܪ ܡܪܝܐ] > ܡܪܝܐ as LXX; ψ cxviii: 162 ܐܝܬ] ܐܝܟ, LXX ὡς; ψ cxxxix: 3 ܣܦܘܬ̈ܗܘܢ] ܠܫܢܗܘܢ, but LXX τὰ χειλη αὐτῶν as Lee.

In the Urmia (a) text, the following readings may be specially mentioned; together with a few from the Scholia of Bar 'Ebrayâ (β)[1]:—ψ vii: 10 ܐܪܥܐ] αβ (also g U. P. C.) in loc.

[1] The text used is *Praetermissorum libri duo* e recog. Pauli de Lagarde, Göttingen 1879. The following are the variants from the text of Lee, collected by Baethgen (see *Untersuchungen über d. Ps. nach d. Pesch.*, p. 20—23) from Ms. orient. Diez. A. octav. 160, (A. D. 1507), Ms. Diez quart. 118. (A. D. 1515), and Ms. orient. quart. 374 (beginning at ψ xxv: 9, of the xvii, or xviii centuries). ψ ii, 2 ܡܠܦܢܘܬܐ 118. 160; ψ iii: 2 ܠܢ ܠܒܝ; ψ iv: 5 ܚܠܦܬܢܝ 118. 160; ψ v: 3 ܨܗܝ 160; V. 12 ܘܢܨܝܕ 160; ψ vii: 10 ܐܪܥܐ] ܐܪܥܐ 118. 160. Erp.; V. 15 ܕܚܐ] ܕܠܐ 118. 160; ψ ix: 16 ܘܡܨܒ] ܘܡܨܒ̈ܐ 118. 160; x: 5 ܐܠܗܢ 118. 160; V. 18 ܘܠܐ] ܕܐ 118. 160; xii: 9 ܨܡܚܝ 118. 160; xiv: 5 ܙܕܝܩܐ ܕܚܠ ܪܒܐ ܗܘ] ܗܘ ܪܒܐ ܕܐܠܗܐ ܚܠܝ 118. (160. ܙܕܝܩܐ); xvii: 5 ܪܚܡܬ ibid. ܘܐܘܠܕ] ܘܐܘܠܕ 118. 160. Erp.; V. 6 ܘܚܠ ܐܢܫ 118. 160; V. 7 ܐܪܥܐ 118. 160; V. 10 ܢܣܠܩ 118. 160; V. 11 ܡܠܠ 118. 160; V. 12 ܕܗܘ 118. 160; xviii: 5 ܐܘܠܨܘ] ܐܘܠܨܘ A, V. 16 ܚܪܕܘܗܝ 118. 160; V. 24 ܫܠܡܝ 118. 160; V. 46 ܢܕܘܫ] ܢܕܘܫ 118. 160. Erp.; xix: 5 ܡܒܣܡ, V. 12 ܪ 118. 160; V. 15 ܘܢܗܘ 118. 160; xxi: 4 ܣܘܡܐܕ A, 118. 160. wrongly ܣܘܡܐܕ; xxii: 5 ܐܩܕܡ 160; V. 10 ܠܗ ܕܩܕܡ (Lee ܡܢ from LXX); xxvi: 1 instead of ܐܒܠܢ A has always ܐܠ ܢܒ, cf. xxxv: 24, liv: 1; xxvii: 9 ܘܗܘܐ ܠܝ ܣܘܥ] ܘܗܘܐ 374; xxix: 6 ܣܪܗܒ] Erp. ܢܘܗܪ; xxxi: 4 cf. ix: 16 ܒܗܘܢ ܗܘܘ] ܒܗܘܢ ܕܚܡܬܗܘܢ 118. 160; V. 19 ܕܬܩܒܠ ܚܘܒܝ 374; xxxiii: 3 ܝܫܘܥ ܙܕܝܩ] ܝܫܘܥ ܙܕܝܩܘܬܐ A. 118. 160; V. 8 ܠܘܚܕ] ܥܠܘܗܝ 118. 160. 374; xxxvi: 8 ܐܘܩܝ] ܐܘܩܝܕ 118. 160. (374 ܐܘܩܝ); xxxvii: 14 ܐܠܦܪ (Lee: printer's error ܐܠܦܪ); xxxviii: 13 ܪܠܐ ܗܘ] ܪܠܐ ܝܘ 118. 160.

ܒܝܫܬܐ LXX πονηρία ψ ix:16. As the other Mss. αβ read for ܥܒܕܐ] ܥܒܕܝܕܐ LXX τοῖς ἔργαις τῶν χειρῶν; ψ xvii:13 ܩܘܡ] ܩܘܡ α, but LXX as Lee ἀνάστηθι; ψ xix:4 ibid. ܐܪܥܐ] ܒܪܥܐ 118. 160; xxxix:3 ܘܚܕܝ ܘܬܕܚܠ 118. 160; xlii:8 ܠܬܘܝ] ܗܘ ܠܬܘܝ 118. 160; xliii:5 ܘܬܚܕܐ] ܠܒܝ 118. 160. 374; xliv:22 ܟܐܒܐ] ܟܐܒ; xlv:4 ܘܒܣܒܪܐ twice 118. 160. 374; xlviii:16 ܢܣܒܢܝ] ܢܣܒܢܝ 118. 160; li:1, 11 ܠܠܒܝ] ܠܒܝ 118. 160; V. 4 ܘܚܕܬ] ܘܚܕܬ 118. 160. 374; V. 14 ܢܘܕܘܢܟ] ܢܘܕܘܢܟ 118. 160; V. 15 ܘܠܒܝ] ܘܠܒ 118. 160. 374; lii:5 ܠܚܡܐ ܡܣܟܢܐ ܐܟܠ ܢܒܝܢ ܢܒܝܢܐ ܡܟܣܢ [ܡܢ ܘܡܣܟܢܘܬܝ ܐܟܠ ܘܡܝܢܝ ܘܡܢܝܢ ܡܣܟܢܐ ܥܡ ܠܚܡܐ 118. 160; liii:2 ܡܣܟܢܘܬܝ] ܡܣܟܢܘܬܝ 160. 374; lv:20 ܡܢܗܘܢ] ܡܢܗܝܢ 118. 160; lvii:8 ܐܪܬܝܪ; lxv:19 ܐܪܬܝܪ ܘܒܪܟܘܗܝ 118. 160; lxvi:3 ܢܘܕܘܢܟ] ܢܘܕܘܢܟ 118. 160; V. 5 ܠܚܕܐ] ܥܡ 118. 160. 374; lxvii:7 ܐܠܗܐ] ܐܠܗܐ 118. 160. 374; lxviii:9 ܘܣܘܚܘܗܝ] ܘܣܘܚܘܗܝ 118. 160; V. 20 ܩܕܡܝܢ 118. 160; lxxi:15 ܐܟܣܐ 118. 160; V. 19 ܘܣܒܬܐ 118. 160; lxxiii:13 ܕܓܒܝ 118. 160. 374; lxxiv:2 ܚܠܡ ܕܒܒܪܝܐ] ܚܒܪܝܐ (118. 160. ܚܠܡ 378 ܚܒܪܝܐ); V. 11 ܬܚܣܡ ܥܡ ܒܕܡܣ. ܒܕܡܣ ܘܦܘܩܝܐ ܥܡܝ ܡܘܚܬ ܕܐܝܟ] ܠܚܕ ܦܘܩܝܐ ܕܣܘܣ. 118. 160; V. 12 ܡܠܟܢ] ܡܠܟܐ 118. 160; lxxvi:4 ܘܚܕܣܡ] ܘܚܕܣܡ (read acc. to 118. 160. Erp. ܘܚܕܣܐ); V. 6 ܐܪܥܣܬ 118. 160. 374; lxxx:16 ܐܟܠܘ] A ܐܟܠܘܗܝ, 118. 160. ܐܟܠܘܗܝ; lxxxi:5 ܡܢ ܐܪܝܐ] ܐܪܝܐܠ 118. 160; lxxxv:2 ܠܒܝ]*; xc:15 ܘܐܬܚ] ܘܐܬܘܝ; xcii:6 ܚܒܕܠ 118. 160; xcviii:7 ܘܒܣܐܘܗܝ ܘܝܬܒܝܗ] ܘܝܬܒܝܗ 118. 160; V. 9 ܒܣܐܬܐ] ܕܘܣܬܐ; cii:23 ܣܠܩ] A. 374 ܣܠܩ; civ:4 ܘܝܬ] ܘܝܬ A, ܝܬ 118. 160. 374; V. 10 ܓܙܬ; cv:45 ܒܓܣܡܘܣ 118. 160. 374; cvi:4 ܒܣܦܪܐ] ܒܣܦܝܪܐ (118. 160. ܒܣܦܝܪܘܢ);

ܘܠܥܡܗ ܬܫܒܘܚܬܐ] ܘܠܥܡܗ ܬܫܒܘܚܬܐ α; .. ܬܫܒܘܚܬܐ β
LXX ἀκούονται; ψ xxi : 13 ܬܘܕܐ] ܬܚܕܐ β LXX θήσεις;
ψ xxxi : 4 ܡܢ ܩܫܐ ܩܝܛܐ] ܡܢ ܩܘܛܪܓܐ ܩܝܛܐ α β, LXX
as Lee, ἐκ πάγιδος; V. 16 ܦܨܢܝܗܝ] ܚܠܨ ܢܦܫܝ ܦܨܢܝܗ β,
LXX simply ῥυσαί με; ψ xxxv : 8 ܢܣܬܬܪܘܢ] ܢܣܬܬܪ ܒܛܠܠܟ α, LXX ἐκρύψαν; ψ xxxviii 13 ܐܘܠܨܢܝ]
ܚܪܫܐ αβ, but LXX κωφός; ψ xxxix : 3 ܐܬܡܠܠܬ] αβ ܚܘܝܬ LXX ἐλάλησα, as Targ. אתאלמית; ψ xl : 14 ܕܒܥܝܢ] ܕܒܥܝܢ β,
LXX οἱ ζητοῦντες, which corresponds to the reading of Lee;
ψ xliii : 5 ܕܡܚܫܘܠܐ] ܠܒܝ ܢܒܝܥ α, LXX συνταράσσεις με,

V. 16 ܕܟܬܝܒܐ 118. 160; V. 42 ܬܫܘܐ; cviii : 2 ܐܬܚܪܟܬ
374; V. 12 ܕܢܣܒܝܢ] ܣܒܠ (118. 160. 374 ܢܣܒܠ); cix : 16
ܠܒܝܫܐ 118. 160. 374; V. 26 ܐܝܬܝܟܐ] ܐܝܟܐ 160; cxi : 9
ܩܝܛܐ]* 118. 160. 374; cxii : 10 ܘܢܫܕܘܢ] ܘܢܫܕܘܢ 118.
160; cxvii : 16 ܕܐ] ܘܕܐ 118. 160. 374; V. 19 ܐܘܬܚ; cxviii : 8
ܪܚܒܬܐ 118. 160. 374; V. 18 ܕܠ 118. 160. 374; V. 24 ܝܬܚܙܝܘܢ
118. 160. 374; V. 57 ܕܡܠܬܟ ܚܘܕܘܝܢ] ܩܝܛܐ܆ ܚܘܕܘܝܢ;
v. 74 ܘܢܣܟܐ] ܘܢܣܟܐ Erp.; V. 162 ܐܝܟ] ܐܝܟ 118.
160. 374. Erp.; cxxxi : 17 ܠܒܫܘ; cxxxvi : 8 ܕܨܒܝܘܢ]
ܠܨܒܝܢܝܘܢ A, ܠܨܒܝܢܝܘܢ 118; cxxxvii : 1 ܕܒܠܟ] ܠܝ
ܩܝܛܐ 118. 160. 374; cxxxix : 11 ܕܚܫܟܐ 374; cxli : 7 ܠܕ 118.
160. 374; cxlii : 8 ܩܝܛܐ 118. 160. 374; V. 10 ܢܝܘܒܪܕ 118.
160; cxliii : 10 ܒܚܝܘܗܝ] ܒܚܘܗܝ; ibid. ܝܚܕܕܗ] ܝܚܕܕܗ; V. 12
ܚܢܘܬܢ] ܚܢܝܢ; ibid. ܘܢܬܚܣܕܘܢ] ܘܚܣܕܘ and so forth
throughout the ψ, the first person in place of the third; cxlvii
ܘܡܠܓܠܐ ܘܩܪܝܫܐ; V. 19 ܘܢܡܣܘܢ] ܘܢܡܣܘܢ; cxlix : 7
ܠܚܒܫܬܐ ܠܚܕܕܗ 118. 160. 374; cl : 4 ܕܢܨܚ] ܫܒܚܘܗܝ
118. 160. 374.

As these variants are similar to those of α and β, they require no especial comment.

Hebrew עלי ומהרתם; ψ xlviii: 1 ܒܩܪܝܬܐ] ܩܪܝܬܐ β LXX
πόλει; ψ xlix: 7 ܐܚܘܗܝ .. ܠܗ ܠܐ] ܠܗ ܢܬܠ ܡܟܐ β,
LXX οὐ δώσει ... ἐξίλασμα αὐτοῦ; ψ lxvi: 5 ܢܚܠ] ܢܚܠܝ
αβ, LXX ποδί; ψ lxviii: 22 ܐܦܢܐ] ܐܦܢܐ αβ as LXX ἐπισ-
τρέψω; ψ xc: 13 ܣܒܥܬܢ] ܣܒܥܬܢܝ αβ, LXX ἐνεπλήσθημεν
Hebrew שבענו. The last two books of the Psalter (iv, v)
contain no important variants. A large proportion of the
variants of these two Mss. consist in a different spelling of
several words, ܐܘܪܚܬܐ, α ܐܘܪܚܐ and β ܐܘܪܚܬܐ, ܐܪܥܬܐ,
α and β ܐܪܥܬܐ; also ܗܘܬ usually ܗܘܐܬ. C often writes
ܥܠ in full ܥܠܘ; as do also α and β occasionally. The following
is a complete list of all the variants of the several Mss. from
the text of Lee.

I: 3 ܕܠܐ ܡܥܒܕ] ܕܠܐ ܡܥܒܕ C; 4 ܐܙܪܥܐ] + ܗܘܐ ܠܐ U;
5 ܘܐܠܗܐ]ܘܐ C; 6 ܒܪܗ C. II: 1 ܘܐܬܪܓܙܝ C | ܐܬܒܘܣܘܐܐ P |
ܘܐܠܝܠܐ CU; 3 ܪܡܣܝ]ܣ U; 8 ܐܝܕܥ C | ܐܒܕܒܘ UP; 9
ܐܘܕܝܕܪܐ C | ܐܝܓܝ CU; 10 ܐܘܕܘܒܪܐ UP; 11 ܐܢܐ
ܒܝܐ] ܐܗܘܪܒܝ ܪܐܘܪ C | ܠܒܝ]+ܐܒܝܢ C | ܐܘܒܕܐܪܐ]
ܘܐ C | ܐܘܣܒܝ] + ܐ C. III: 3 ܡܒܪܪܐܣ C; 4 ܘܪܐܘ]ܘܐ C;
5 ܐܟܝܢ] + ܐܠܡܝܢܣ P. IV: 3 ܠܠܠܐ C; 4 ܐܗܝܐܘܣܒܝ]
ܐܗܝܒܒܕܝ P | ,ܡܘܒܝܘܐ] + ܐܠܡܝܢܣ P; 5 ܐܕܗܒܬܠ]
ܐܕܚܝܒܬ C; 7 ܣܒܘ C | ܠܠܝ C; 9 ܢܐܘܣܠܢܐ U (fortasse
conject. ex Hebr.). V: 2 ܒܝܠܣ] ܒܠܝܣܒ P¹ | ܣܟܠܝܢ P²;
3 ܗܘܘܐ]ܘܐ C; 4 ܣܒܝܣܐ] ܣܒܝܣ P² C | ܬܩܢܒܝ ܐܒܝܣ
P¹; 5 ܘܐܠܗܐ]ܘܐ C; 6 ܕܠܐ P; 9 ܘܒܘܣܝܣܕܘ] ܘܣܒܘܐ P¹;
11 ܚܣܝܕ C P; 12 ܐܚܕܣܐܕܘܐ C. VI: 2 ܟܐܠܐܐ C; 3 ܐܪܒܘܣ
C; 7 ܐܠܟܝ ,ܘܪܝܐ C | ܠܠܠܐ] ܠܠܠܝ C ܠܠܠܝ P | ,ܕܡܕܒܝܐ
ܐܘܪܚܕ C; 9 ܐܘܣܝܣܐ ܡܣ C. VII: 5 ܐܝܕ ܐܚܘ C | ܐܚܕܠܚܠ C;
7 ܘܕܒܠܒܣܘܟܝ P²; 10 ܕܟܣܝ C | ܐܪܥܝܝ] ܐܪܥܝܝ α C,

 U (> in marg.); 13 C; 15
C. VIII:4 C; 6 , CU (U > in marg.);
7 C; 8 C;
9 C | C. IX:3 P²;
4 C; 16 CU
 P². X:5 CU; 9 C |]
 U (et
 ad marg.); 13 U and in marg. I
 P²; 15 C. XI:4
 U; 6 U P² I
 C. XII:3 U; 9 U. XIII:3
 C. XIV:4 C. XIV:5]
 C. XV:4 P² |, C.
XVI:4 P² C; 5 C; 6
P²; 9 C; 10 . XVII:1 C;
7 P² | U |])>C; 10
 C; 11 C; 12 C. XVIII:5
 C; 6 C; 7 U | C;
9 C; 10 C; 24 P² C;
26 C; 31 P²; 34 C; 41] +
 P²; 46 U; 47 C. XIX:3]
 C; 4
 P² |
C | U; 5 gC; 7 U |
P²; 10 C; 12 CU | C; 13 U I
 C. XX:4 P²; 6 P²;
7 P²C. XXI:4 U; 5 C;
7 C; 8 C; 10 C; 12.
 C; 11 C. XXII:2 C; 3 C;

 C; 6 U (in marg.); 8 C; 14 UP²; 20 C; 27 C. XXIII:4 U P² C; 5 P². XXIV:6 P¹P² (semper). XXV:3 C; 10 P¹; 18 C; 19 C. XXVI:1 C; 3 C; 4 C. XXVII:4 P²; 6 C I C; 9 C. XXVIII:9 C. XXIX:6 U C I C. XXX:5 CU; 7 C; 11 U (ad marg.). In CP¹P²U, XXX and XXXI form one Psalm. XXXI:4 UP², C; 7 C; 8 C; 18 U; 19 P¹C; 23 C. XXXII:6 C I C. XXXIII:3 C; 4 UP¹P²; 7 C; 8 CU; 9 C; 11 C. XXXIV:8 UP² I C; 20 UP¹. XXXV:3 U; 8 C; 19 U in marg. I UP¹, P², C; 22 g; 24 C. XXXVI:1 U (in marg.) CU; 7 UP¹P²; 8 C; 12 U (in marg.)). XXXVII:3, 4 C; 7 U; 9 C; 11 UP¹; 19 C; 25 C; 30 UP¹P², + UP²; 33 UP¹P²; 39 CU. XXXVIII:1 C; 4]

 C | C; 6 CU; 9]> U; 13
 CU | C; 19
P¹UP². XXXIX:3 CU; 8]> CU |
]> U; 10 C; 13 U.
XL:1 U; 2 C;
3 U; 4]> C; 5 U | C |
 U; 11]> CU. XLI:9 U; 10]
> U |]> gUP¹ | + P¹.
XLII:8 C. XLIII:1]
> UP² (.... in marg.); 5
 g C. XLIV:1]> CUP²; 3 C;
13]> C; 21 U, P¹ |
 C. XLV:2 C; 4
 P¹UP² |
]> C; 6 C; 13
 C; 14 C; 17 C | C.
XLVI:5 C; 9]> CP². XLVII:3 C;
9 U. XLVIII:6 C; 10 C;
14 U | C | U, C.
XLIX:17 > C. L:1 CU; 3]
> U | CU; 4 C; 6 C; 7
 Cg; 8 U,
 C |]> C; 23 > CP² |
]> g. LI:1 CUP¹P²g;
9 C; 14 C; 15]
 C; 16]> C; 17 UP¹;
18 U. LII:5
 C | C; 8 C | C. LIII:3
]> CU; 4]> U. LIV:3 U;

4 U. LV:6 UP¹ | ;
C | C; 12 CUP²; 20 CUP².
LVI:1 P²; 2 C; 8
U; 13 U, C. LVII:3
UP; 4 U; 7 C; 8 U.
LVIII:1 C; 4 C; 6 U; 8]
 U, PC; 11 C |
 C | CUP². LIX:4 U; 8]
) U; 13 U. LX:1 C; 4 U;
7 P¹U^m; 8 CUP¹P² (U ad
marg. C. LXI:2 UP²;
4 C; 7 U^m; 8 C. LXII:11
 P², U. LXIII:3
 P², U^m; 7]
 gU^mP¹, U; 9 C; 11]
) U. LXIV:3 U; 5 UP².
LXV:1 P¹UP²; 12
 U^m; 13 C. LXVI:1 ; 2
 U^m; 4 U; 5 CU; 7
 C. LXVIII:2 C; 4]
) CU^mP²; 8 C; 12 P²; 16
C; 18 U | C; 21 U,
P¹P²; 24 U; 25 C; 26
 gCUP¹P²; 27
P¹U^m; 34 GU, P¹
(vel). LXIX:2 UP¹P²; 3
 C | CP²; 17 C; 24 C; 27]
 C; 28 C | U. LXX:6
U— P². LXXI:6

CUP¹P²; 9]+ o U; 12]+ o U; 15
U; 18]+ o C |]> o UP²; 19 C |
 C. LXXII:6 C; 10]>C;
11] + o C; 14 U; 15 ; 18
]> o CU^m P¹P² | C. LXXIII:9
U; 10 UP²; 13 C; 15
 UP¹P²; 24]>C | C. LXXIV:2
]>C; 6 C; 8]> o C; 11
 CU; 12 C. LXXV:3]
in sing. P; 4, 5 UP²; 6]> o C. LXXVI:1
 U^m; 8 C; 12 . LXXVII:1
 C; 5 C; 16
 UP¹P²g, C. LXXVIII:5 C |]
 C |]> U^m; 14]> o CUP²; 18
, U U^m; 19
CUP²; 20 C; 21]> o C; 25]+ o C;
26]> o U; 27 C; 33 C; 34]
> o U; 42
P¹UP² C; 45 U, C;
56 U; 59]> o U; 64
U; 70]+ o UP² | U. LXXIX:3 o. U, C;
8 o U; 10 UP²| C. LXXX:4 C;
8 U; 12 C; 18 C. LXXXI:5]
 U^m CP²;9 U, CP²; 11
C; 12 U; 16 U^m. LXXXII:5
 U | U. LXXXIII:15 C;
16 U, U^mP¹P²; 17 C.

LXXXIV : 2 P², U; 3, 6
C; 7 . LXXXV : 3 C; 6
 C; 7 C; 10
CU^m, UP²; 12 C. LXXXVI : 2 C; 5 C ;
6 g; 8 CUP²; 11 U;
13 U; 14 Us.; 16 U; 17]
 C. LXXXVII : 5 CUP². LXXXVIII : 3
 U; 8 C; 12 C; 13
 UP¹P²; 18 C. LXXXIX : 2
C; 4 U; 5 C; 8 CUP²;
11 C C; 20 U
CU; 21 C; 27 C; 45 C; 52
 C. XC : 1 C; 5 C; 10
P¹U C; 15 C; 17 UP².
XCI : 2 U^mP¹P²; 5 U; 8]
 U^mC; 9 UP¹; 15
 C. XCII : 7 C; 15 C.
XCIII : 1 C; 4 UP¹P²; 5]
 UP² U^mP²C. XCIV : 2 C
 C; 10 U^m; 13 U^m; 23
 C. XCV : 1 U; 3 U^m;
5 C; 9 U^m; 10 U. XCVI : 5
 UP²; 11 C C. XCVII : 3
 C C. XCVIII : 7 U^mP²C.
XCIX : 7 U. C : 3 U,
 P², C; 5
C. CI : 7 CUP². CII : 3 U^mP¹; 5 C;
8 U, P²; 16 CU^mP²; 18

6

 CUP²; 22 C | g; 23]
 P¹U; 24 C. CIII:5 C; 10
 C; 24 CUP²; 26 U |
 C. CIV:1 U; 4 C | C; 5 C;
8 UP¹; 10 C | C; 11 C;
12 C; 14 C; 15 U |
 C; 17 U C; 20]
 U; 24 C; 25 C | C |
 C; 30 U P¹; 34]
+ CUP¹; 35 U. CV:3 g; 15
 UP¹P²; 16 UP²; 17 CU;
18 C; 20 CU; 21
 U, P¹P²; 22
CUP¹P²; 23 CUP¹; 31, 34 C;
41 U; 42 U; 44 C. CVI:4
 C | C; 5 U; 9
 CU | CUP²; 11 C; 16
 C; 17 C; 21
.. U; 26 C; 31 C |
 UP²; 37 Cg; 42 C;
43 CU; 45 UP²; 46 U|
 C; 47 C; 48 C | C. CVII:1
 C; 12 CUᵐP² |]
 U; 14 C; 18 C; 29
 U; 39 UP²; 40]
 CU; 41 C. CVIII:1 C; 4...
 C; 9
CU; 12 C. CIX:3 U; 16

UPON THE PĔSHITTÂ PSALTER

 Cg | UP¹P²; 22 C; 23
 C; 25 C; 26 C | U
CX:2 C> C. CXI:5 U
 UᵐP¹; 8 C | CUP¹P²; 9
]> C | U. CXII:3 C; 9
 C | U. CXIV:7 UP¹P²; 11
 C; 13 g; 16 C; 17
 UP¹. CXV:4 U Uᵐ; 6]
 U; 8 UP² P¹ Uᵐ;
9 CU; 19 CUᵐP². CXVII:17
 C; 23 C; 25 U |]
 UP¹P². CXVIII:18 CUᵐP¹P²> UP²;
42 UP¹; 43 U; 44 C; 46
UP¹P²; 57 CUP¹P²; 82 C; 90 C;
96 UP¹P²; 97 g; 104 C; 106
 C; 109 Cg; 120 U; 123]
 g C; 133 C | C; 141 CUᵐ>;
145 C; 146 C; 151 C; 159
 C; 162 Cg; 170]
 C. CXX:5 U; 6 U. CXXI:1
 UP¹P². CXXII:2 P² | U.
CXXIV:2 UP²; 5 CUP¹P² Uᵐ.
CXXVII:2 C. CXXVIII:3 C;
6 C; 7 C. CXXXI:12]
> C | C; 14 C. CXXXIV:3 C;
6 C; 12 UᵐC; 13
 C; 21 C. CXXXV:15 C;
18 C. CXXXVI:1 C; 6 C.

6*

CXXXVII:1 C. CXXXVIII:2]
 C; 3 C; 10 C. CXXXIX:3
 C; 5]> U; 10]
+ C | C. CXL:6]> U | C.
CXLI:4 C; 7]> C. CXLII:2 Uᵐ;
10 Uᵐ | CUPᵃ. CXLIII:2
]> UP¹; 14 C; 13 C. CXLIV:1
 C; 8 Uᵐ; 10 U; 13 C;
14 UP¹P²; 21 C. CXLV:7 C;
10 C | C. CXLVI:10]> C.
CXLVII:13 C; 18 Uᵐ; 20 U.
CXLVIII:4 C; 6 C; 13]> C.
CXLIX:6 C; 9]> UCgP¹P².

The variants of the texts of the Urmia Edition and the
Scholia of Bar ʿEbràyà from the text of Lee are as follows.[1]

I:6 α. II:2 α;
4]> β; 10 α |]
 α; 11 β. III:3 α |
 α |]> α; 5 α. IV:2]
+ α; 5 α β. V:2]
 α β; 4 β; 5]> β; 6 α;
9 α; 12 α > . VI:7]
 α | β. VII:6]
 α; 9 α; 10
α | α β; 11]> β; 12 α;
13 α β; 16 β; 17 α |
 α β. VIII:3 β; 4]> α |

---

[1] α = Urmia Edition; β = Scholia of Bar ʿEbràyà.

5 αβ; 7
α | β α; 9 α | α.
IX : 2 α; 4 α;
6 α; 9 αβ; 16 α
X : 5]> α | αβ; 6]
 α; 7 α |]> α; 11]
 α; 14 α | α; 17]
 β | αβ | β. XI : 1
 β. XII : 6 β;
7 α > . XIII : 6 α. XIV : 5
 α; 7 β. XVI : 2]
+ β; 3 αβ; 4 αβ; 5 α; 6]
+ α; 7 αβ. XVII : 1 α; 5]> α;
7]> α | α>]>,β α; 13 α.
XVIII : 3]> α; 6 α; 7]
 α; 9 α; 10]> α | αβ;
16]> β; 17 α; 19 β; 21]
> α; 25 α |]> α; 26]
 α; 33]> α; 37 α; 39 α;
44 α; 48 α. XIX : 4
 β | α | β;
5] β | β | β; 7]
> α; 11 α; 12 α |]> αβ.
XX : 2 α; 7 α. XXI : 4
 αβ; 5 α; 7 α; 8]> α;
9a α; 9b α; 10 β |
 α; 13 αβ |]
 β. XXII : 3 α; 4 αβ;
7 β | α; 8]

 α; 11 α; 14 α;
15 α; 20 α β; 24 α β;
25 α; 27 α | α. XXIII: 5
 α. XXIV: 2 α β; 7, 9 α β. XXV: 5
 α; 10 α |]
 α; 12 α; 13 α;
17 α; 18 β; 19 α;
21 α, β. XXVI: 3 β. XXVII: 6
 α; 9 α; 10 α;
12 β. XXVIII: 6 α;
8 α. XXIX: 4 α; 6]
) β | α | α; 9 β |
 α β. XXX: 5 α; 7 α.
XXXI: 4 α β; 8]
 α β | α β; 9 α β;
10 α; 14 α; 15
 β; 19
 α; 20 β; 21 α. XXXII: 2
 α; 4 α; 8 α; XXXIII: 3
 α; 7 α | α β;
8 α β; 9 α; 13 α; 16]
+ α; 18 α; 21 α. XXXIV: 2
 α; 3 α; 6]
 α β; 9 α. XXXV: 3]
 β; 6 α; 8]
 α; 9 α |]
 α; 12 β | β;
16 β; 19 α β; 24
 α; 27 α; 28 α. XXXVI: 5]

ܐܢܬ] α; 6 ܬܫܒܘܚܬܝ]+ο αβ | ܐܠܗܐ]+ܘ α | ܚܢܢܬ]
ܚܣܕܐ α | ܘܪܚܡܐ] ܪܚܡܐ α; 8 ܐܢܬ]+ο α | ܐܢܬ β;
12 ܬܚܣܡܘ]+ο α. XXXVII:11 ܘܡܚܣܕܐ]>ο α;
19 ܠܐ]+ο α; 25 ܘܠܐ]>ο β; 35 ܙܪܥܗ] ܙܪܥܗ α.
XXXVIII:2 ܘܐܡܪܬ]>ο β; 4 ܚܕܬ] ܚܕ α | ܐܢܐ αβ |
ܝܡܝ] ܝܡܐ α; 5 ܝܡܝ] ܝܘܡܝ α; 6 ܘܟܠ]+ο α; 13 ܐܢܬ]
ܚܝܝ β α | ܘܨܠܘ] > ο α | ܐܘܪܚܐ] ܐܢܬ αβ; 18 α >
om. XXXIX:3 ܐܬܚܒܠ] ܢܦܫܝ αβ; 4 ܣܡܟܢܝ]+ο α | ܣܡܘ αβ;
7 ܐܩܝܡܝܢ] ܐܩܝܡ α; 8 ܐܡܪ]>ο α | ܘܐܡܪܬ]>ο α; 10 ܐܡܪܬ]
ܐܡ α. XL:1 ܡܣܟܢܐ] ܡܣܟܢܐ α; 6 ܘܡܚܣܒܝܢ]
ܘܡܚܣܒܝܢ α; 8 ܕܒܝܫ αβ; 11 ܐܪܚܡ]>ο α; 12 ܕܐܝܢ αβ|
ܚܠܦ]>ο β; 14 ܕܐܡܪ] ܕܪܚܡ β; 16 ܚܝܝܢ α; 17 ܐܣܕܪ]
ܐܬܣܕܪ β. XLI:1 ܟܚܝܠܐ]>ܕ α; 6 ܫܒܚܗ]+ο α;
10 ܐܘܒܕܘ]+ο α | ܕܥܘܪܝܝܢ] ܥܘܪܝܐ β; 13 ܫܡܝܢܝ α|
ܫܒܚ]>οβ. XLII:2 ܗܢܐ α; 7 ܘܐܠܗܝ]>ο αβ|ܚܢܢܬ]ܚܣܕܐ α;
8 ܠܝܠܝܐ] om ܠܝܠܝܐ α; 9 ܠܐܠܗܐ]>ܕ β; 10 α > ܡܐ
XLIII:1 ܒܚܣܝܘܗܝ]>οβ; 2 ܐܬܘܪܝܐ α; 5 ܫܒܚܬܗ]
ܠܐܠܗܐ α. XLIV:2 ܐܡܪܢܐ]+ο αβ; 4 ܐܬܘܪ α;
6 ܘܚܠܦ] ܚܣܝܢܝܢ ܣܡ α | ܘܟܠܐ]+ο α; 7 ܐܬܘܪ α;
12 ܕܐܢܬ] ܐܢܬ α; 14 ܟܪܝܢ αβ; 16 ܗܘܘ] ܕܗܘܘ α;
23 ܐܚܖܢܐ] ܟܠܗ α | ܚܠܦ β; 24 ܩܘܝܐ] ܣܝܡ ܣܘܪܝܝܐ α.
XLV:4 ܡܝܒܒܘ ܣܕܪܝ] ܣܘܒܒܘ ܣܘܒܒܘ ܣܕܪܝ
ܐܪܐ α; 6 ܟܠܗ α; 8 ܟܪܝܢ αβ | ܗܘܘ]>ο α; 12 ܐܩܦܝ]
ܐܦܩܝ α; 13 ܢܫܒܚ] ܘܢܫܒܚ β; 14 ܘܨܠܘ]>οβ;
15 ܕܐܝܪܘ]>οα; 16 ܐܬܢܣܒܬ] ܐܣܬܒܪ α | ܕܢܫܕܐ] ܚܢܢܬ α;
17 ܚܠܡ α. XLVI:4 ܐܪܥܐ α; 5 ܣܠܩܝܗܝ] ܣܠܩܝܗ α; 6 ܙܘܝܐ]
ܙܘܐ α. XLVII:3 ܚܘܫܒ α; 5 ܘܐܪܙܐ]>ο αβ. XLVIII:1
ܐܢܬ α | ܘܚܝܒܘ] ܚܣܕܐ β; 7 ܐܠܗܐ]+ο α; 8 ܗܢܐ]
ܐܡܐ αβ | α > ܠܗܠܟܝܢ ܟܪܝܢܐ ܘܚܝܒܘ; 10 ܗܢܐ]

] α ا | 14 ;β α
XLIX:2 β; 7 [β |
 β; 9 [αβ | α | α;
12 β; 18 [β; 19 [αβ.
L:2 [α; 3 []> β | α;
6 α; 7 α, β |]
 αβ; 8 > αβ; 9 []> β; 12 β;
16 []> α; 23 [α. LI:2]
 β, α; 4 [αβ; 7 []> β;
9 [α; 10 [αβ; 14 []
 αβ; 15 [αβ; 16 [] > αβ.
LII: 5 [α, > β;
8 [β; 9 []> α | α. LIII:1
[β; 2 [β; 3 []
> α; 4 []> α; 6 α. LIV:1 [
 α; 3 [α; 4 []
 α. LV:10 [α; 13 [β;
20 [β α. LVI:2 [α;
4 [β; 5 []> β | β >]> β.
LVII:4 [β | [β; 6 α;
7 α. LVIII:1 [β |
[β; 4 [αβ; 5 []
 α; 7 [α; 8 [β α; 11 [β
[α. LIX:5 α; 7 [αβ;
9 [α; 10 β > α; 16 []
> α. LX:1 [β | [β;
7 [β; 8 [α, [β | []
[α; 9 []> β. LXI:4 []>
 α; 8 [α. LXII:6 [α; 8 []

 α β. LXIII : 5 α. LXIV : 5 α.
LXV : 5 α ; 11 α.
LXVI : 1 α β ; 4 α ; 5]
 β α ; 6 α ‖ α ; 11 α β ;
13 α ‖ α. LXVII : 1]
 β ; 4 β > β. LXVIII : 5 α > ;
7 α β ; 8 α β ‖
 α ; 12 α ; 14 β >]
 β ; 18 α ; 21 α ‖]
 α, β ; 22 α β ; 23]
 α ; 26 α β ‖
 α, β ; 27 β ‖]
 α ; 31 α ; 34 α,
 β ; 35 α ‖ α. LXIX : 3]
 α ‖]> β, α ; 6]> α ‖ α ;
8]> β ; 13 β>]> α ‖]
 α ‖ α ; 21]> α ;
25 α ; 26 α ; 33 α ;
35 β. LXX : 2 α ‖]
+ α ; 4 α ; 6 α. LXXI : 4]
 β ; 5 α β ‖]> α ; 9]> α ;
13]> α ; 14 α ; 21]
+ α ‖ α ; 22]> α. LXXII : 9]
 β ; 10 α β ‖ α > α ;
14 α ; 15 α ; 17 α ‖ α ;
18]> α β. LXXIII : 1 α, β ;
8 α ; 10]> α β ; 20 α ; 23 α ;
24 β. LXXIV : 1 β ; 2 α >
 α β ‖ i α β ; 13 i α β ;

16 α; 18 α; 22] >ο β. LXXV:3 α | β; 5])ο α; 6])ο β; 10] >ο. LXXVI:1 α, β; 5 α; 8 α; 10 β; 10 α. LXXVII:6 α; 8 α; 10] +ο β; 16 α; 17 |] +ο α; 18]>ο β; 20 α. LXXVIII:1 , β; 5 α | α; 6 α; 14])ο αβ; 18] >ο α; 19 α; 21 α; 24 β; 25] +ο α; 28 α | α; 31 . α; 34])ο β; 39 β; 41 . α, . β; 42 . α | α; 44 . α; 46 α; 51] +ο α | αβ; 56 . α; 60 . α; 64 α |] >ο β; 70] +ο α; 72 α. LXXIX:1])ο β; 4])ο β; 10 αβ | β; 11 α. LXXX:1 . α, . β; 18 αβ. LXXXI:3 β | αβ; 4 α, β; 5 αβ; 6 β; 8 α | α; 11] +ο α | α, β | α; 12 α; 13 α; 16 β. LXXXII:5 αβ | α; 7 β. LXXXIII:2 α; 3 β; 5 . α; 15 α; 18 α | .] +ο α. LXXXIV:3])ο αβ; 5]

 a | a.   LXXXV : 2 a a;
10 a;   12 β | a.   LXXXVI : 8
 a, β; 11 a; 14]
 a.   LXXXVII : 3 a; 5 αβ;
6 a. LXXXVIII : 2 a; 8]
 a; 9 a;   12 a; 13 a;
14 a; 15 β.   LXXXIX : 2
 a; 3 a; 5 a; 11 a;
 αβ | αβ; 13 a |
 a; 17 a | a; 20 a |
 a; 33 a; 43 αβ; 44
 a αβ; 49]
+ a.   XC : 2 a | a | αβ; 3 β;
4 a] αβ; 5 αβ;
8 β;   13 a | αβ; 16 a;
17 β.   XCI : 8
 αβ | a | a; 10]
+ β; 14 β; 15 a.   XCII : 2
 αβ; 4 a; 7 a; 10]
+ a; 12 a; 15 a.   XCIII : 1 αβ;
3 a.   XCIV : 1 a; 12
 β; 18 a; 20 a; 23]
 | a.   XCV : 5 a;
6 β; 9 a β.   XCVI : 4]
 a; 5 αβ | β; 10
 αβ | β | a | a;
12 a; 13 a.   XCVII : 1 a;
3 a; 4 αβ; 6 a; 8 a; 10
 a | a.   XCVIII : 3 a; 7

92   THE INFLUENCE OF THE SEPTUAGINT

 α ǀ α) ǀ α; 9 α.
XCIX: 1 α. C: 3 α. CI: 2
 α; 3 α; 7]
+ α. CII: 2 α; 3 α; 8]
 β; 10 β; 11 αβ; 16
 α; 18 α; 19]
 α; 23 α; 25 α. CIII: 3
 α; 7 α; 11 α ǀ] +
 α. CIV: 1 α ǀ α; 2
 α ǀ α; 4 αβ;
5 α ǀ α; 7 α; 8 α;
12 α; 14 α ǀ α; 16]
) α; 17 α ǀ α; 21 α;
25 α; 33 β; 34 α. CV: 4
 α; 5 α; 10 α; 12
 α; 15 β; 17 α; 18
 α; 23 α,
 β; 24 α; 31 α;
36 αβ; 44 α. CVI: 3 α;
4 α; 5 α; 9 α ǀ
 α; 16 α ǀ α; 17
 αβ; 26 α ǀ]
 α; 31 β; 32 β; 34
 α; 37 α; 42 α; 47
 β; 48 α;
48 α. CVII: 1 α; 13 α; 14
 α; 14 β; 17 α; 18]
) α; 23 α; 30 α; 31]
 α; 38 α; 40 α; 41 α.

CVIII: 4 α;
8 α | α β; 9 α β; 11]
 β; 12 α; 13] > α. CIX: 12
 α; 16 β |] > β;
18 α; 23 α; 25 α; 26]
 α. CX: 2 α > α β; 7 α . CXI: 8
α <[ܘܕܚܣܡܐ] > α | | + α | | α |]
9 α β > α β. CXII: 3 α; 9
 α | α; 10] > α β |]
 α | α. CXIII: 4 α; 8]
 α β. CXIV: 1, 12 α, β α;
6 α; 7 α; 5 α; 7]
> α | α; 9 α |] > α; 10
] > α; 16 α; 17 α β. CXV: 4
 α; 8 α; 9 α β;
11 α; 14] > α; 15 α; 18]
> α; 19 α. CXVII: 2 α; 9 α, 17
 α; 20] > β; 22 α β; 23
 α; 26 α; 27
 β. CXVIII: 4 α;
8 α; 18 α >] > α; 43 α; 44
 α; 57 α β; 72 α; 82 [
 α; 98 α; 109 α β; 120 β;
121 α; 122 α β; 123
 α; 125 α; 133 β;
137 α; 141 α α; 148
 α; 149 α; 159] > α; 160 α β;
162 α; 169 α; 170 α; 175
 α β; 176 α.

CXX:3 αβ; 4 α; 5 α;
7 α. CXXI:2 α; 4 α | α,
 β; 6 α. CXXIII:1 α;
3 α; 6 α. CXXIV:5 α. CXXVI:1
 β; 5 β. CXXVII:2
 β; 3 α; 6
 α. CXXVIII:1 α, β; 3]
 α; 6 α | β; 7 β.
CXXIX:6 β; 7 α; 8 α |
 α. CXXX:2 α; 3 α.
CXXXI:4 α | α; 8]
 β; 11 α; 12 α |
 α; 14 α. CXXXII:2 αβ; 3]
 αβ. CXXXIV:3 α; 4 α,
 β; 7 β; 12 α; 14]
 αβ; 16 α; 19 α; 21 α.
CXXXV:1 α; 11 α; 14 α; 22
 α. CXXXVI:1 α; 4 α;
6 αβ | α; 4 α.
CXXXVII:1 β | β.
CXXXVIII:1 β; 2 α;
3 α; 14 α; 16 αβ | α;
17 β. CXXXIX:3 α | β
6 α; 7 αβ; 8]
 α; 10 α | α; 11
 β; | α | α; CXL:5
 α; 6 α. CXLI:5] +
 α; 7 αβ. CXLII:3 α; 5
 αβ; 8 α >]

] α; 11 α; 11 α; 12
 α. CXLIII:2 α;
8, 11 α; 13 α;
15 α ! α. CXLIV:2 α;
11 α; 13, 21 α; 18 α. CXLV:1
 α; 3 β; 7 α.
CXLVI:1 α; 3 α; 5 α;
9 α; 10 α. CXLVII:13]
 α; 19 α ! α.
CXLVIII:4 α ! α β; 6 α;
10 α; 11 α; 12]
 α; 13 β !]
 α. CXLIX:2 β; 8]
 α. CL:4 α; 5 α !
 α.

§ 3. *The Greek and Syriac variants compared*

Psalm ii.

3. שלשלותימו τὸν ζυγὸν αὐτῶν עבתימו
9. תרעם ποιμανεῖς αὐτοὺς תרעם
12. כמעט ἐν τάχει בועיר

Psalm iv.

2. עננ εἰσήκουσεν קבל מני
8. ~ καὶ ἐλαίου αὐτῶν ~

ii:9 LXX and read תְרָעֵם from רעה. 12 may agree with LXX or N. T.
iv:2 εἰσήκουσεν ABDMRSW. εἰσηκουκας, a — עניתי.

Psalm v.

11. ארום מרדו במימרך ܕܐܡܪܡܪܘܟ ὅτι παρεπίκρανάν σε מרו בך
12. ותסך עלימו ܘܬܛܠ ܥܠܝܗܘܢ καὶ κατασκηνώσεις ἐν αὐτοῖς ותמיל עילויהון

Psalm vii.

3. ܡܐ ܕܠܝܬ ܕܦܪܩ ܘܡܚܐ μὴ ὄντος λυτρουμένου μηδὲ σώζοντος יפשח ולית דיפצי
5. ܐܢ ܦܪܥܬ ܠܡܢ ܕܓܡܠ ܠܝ ܒܝܫܐ εἰ ἀνταπέδωκα τοῖς ἀνταποδιδοῦσίν μοι κακά אין פרעית לבעיל שלמי ביש
12. ܘܠܐ ܢܓܕ ܥܠ ܢܦܫ ܐܠܗܐ ܪܘܓܙܐ ܒܟܠܝܘܡ ὀργὴν ἐπάγων καθ' ἑκάστην ἡμέραν ובתקוף רגיז על רשיע כל יומא

Psalm viii.

3. עז ܕܬܫܒܘܚܬܐ αἶνον עושנא
6. מלאכיא ܡܠܐܟܐ ἀγγέλους אלהים

Psalm ix.

7. ܕܒܒܐ ܢܦܠ ܒܥܝܠ ܚܪܒܗ ܠܚܠܛܝܢ τοῦ ἐχθροῦ ἐξέλιπον αἱ ῥομφαῖαι εἰς τέλος וכד נפל בעיל דבבא אישתציו חילוותיה וכרכיהון אצתריו לעלמא
21. ܐܩܝܡ ܠܗܘܢ ܡܪܝܐ ܡܫܘܕܥܢܐ שיתה יהוה מורה להם κατάστησον Κύριε νομοθέτην ἐπ' αὐτούς שוי יהוה דחלתא להון

v: 11 LXX, ܣ read מרו for מרה.
v: 12 LXX, ܣ, ܬ read סכך for גסך.
vii: 3 LXX, ܣ take פרק in the sense of "to deliver"; T. "to rend in pieces".
vii: 5 The rendering of the ܣ and LXX is possible.
vii: 12 ܣ and LXX read וְאֵל.
ix: 7 LXX, ܣ read אוֹיְבִי תַּמּוּ בָחֳרָבוֹת לָנֶצַח.
ix: 21 LXX, ܣ read מוֹרָה from ירה.

Psalm x.

2. ܒܫܘܒܗܪܗ ܕܪܫܝܥܐ ܝܩܕ ܡܣܟܢܐ בגאות רשע ידלק עני
ἐν τῷ ὑπερηφανεύεσθαι τὸν ἀσεβῆ ἐνπυρίζεται ὁ πτωχός
בגסות רשיעא ידלק ענייא

3. ܥܘܠܐ ܡܬܒܪܟ ܘܪܓܙ ܡܪܝܐ ובצע ברך נאץ יהוה
ὁ ἀδικῶν ἐνευλογεῖται παρώξυνεν τὸν Κύριον דמברך גברא
טלומא מרחק מימרא דיהוה

5. ܘܠܟܠܗܘܢ ܒܥܠܕܒܒܘܗܝ ܢܫܠܛ כל צורריו יפיח בהם
πάντων τῶν ἐχθρῶν αὐτοῦ κατακυριεύσει בכל מעיקני יזעוף בהון

12. ܐܠܗܝ אל ὁ θεός μου יהוה

17. ܘܠܛܘܝܒܐ ܕܠܒܗܘܢ ܬܨܘܬ ܐܕܢܟ תכין לבם תקשיב אזנך
τὴν ἑτοιμασίαν τῆς καρδίας αὐτῶν προσέσχεν τὸ οὖς σου
תתקין לבהון תצלי אדנך

Psalm xi.

3. ܡܛܠ ܕܡܕܡ ܕܬܩܢܬ ܣܚܦܘ כי השתות יהרסון ὅτι ἃ
κατηρτίσω καθεῖλον מטול דאין אשייתא יתרעון

7. ܘܬܪܝܨܘܬܐ יָשָׁר εὐθύτητα תקניא

Psalm xii.

5. ܠܫܢܢ ܢܪܘܪܒ ללשננו נגביר τὴν γλῶσσαν ἡμῶν μεγαλυνοῦμεν בלישננא נתגבר

7. ܕܒܚܝܪ ܒܐܪܥܐ בעליל לארץ δοκίμιον τῇ γῇ על ארעא

Psalm xv.

3. ܘܠܐ ܢܟܠܬ לא רגל οὐκ ἐδόλωσεν לא אכל

4. ܠܚܒܪܗ לרעהו τῷ πλησίον αὐτοῦ לגרמיה

x : 2 The rendering of the ס and LXX is possible.
x : 3 ס and LXX read בֹּרַךְ as passive בֹּרַךְ.
x : 5 ס and LXX have expressed the sense of the M. T. in a different way. x : 12 ϑεος] + μου $\aleph^{ca}$ AR.
xi : 3 ס and LXX read הַשַּׁתּוֹת. xi : 7 ס and LXX read יֹשֶׁר.
xv : 4 ס and LXX read לְרֵעֵהוּ for לְרֵעֵהוּ.

Psalm xvi.

2. אָמַרְתְּ ܐܡܪܬ εἶπα אנת מלילת

5. תומך גורלי אתה ܐܢܬ ܗܘ ܡܦܢܐ ܠܝ ܝܪܬܘܬܝ. σὺ εἶ ὁ ἀποκαθιστῶν τὴν κληρονομίαν μου ἐμοί אנת תסובר עדבי

Psalm xvii.

3. זמתי בל־יעבר־פי צרפתני בל־תמצא ܟܕ ܘܒܚܢܬܢܝ ܘܠܐ ܐܫܟܚܬ ܒܝ ܥܘܠܐ ܘܠܐ ܢܥܒܪ ܥܠ ܦܘܡܝ ܥܒ̈ܕܐ ܕܒܢܝܢܫܐ καὶ οὐχ εὑρέθη ἐν ἐμοὶ ἀδικία ὅπως ἂν μὴ λαλήσῃ τὸ στόμα μου τὰ ἔργα τῶν ἀνθρώπων סנגתא לי לא אשכחתא שחיתא חשבית בישותא לא עברת פומי

8. כאישון בת־עין ܐܝܟ ܒܒܬܐ ܕܥܝܢܐ ὡς κόραν ὀφθαλμοῦ כגילגול די במציעות עינא

Psalm xviii.

8. כי חרה לו ܡܛܠ ܕܐܬܚܡܬ ܥܠܝܗܘܢ ὅτι ὠργίσθη αὐτοῖς מטול דתקיף ליה

9. ואש מפיו תאכל ܘܢܘܪܐ ܡܢ ܦܘܡܗ ܐܬܓܠܚܬ καὶ πῦρ ἐναντίον αὐτοῦ κατεφλόγισεν כאישא בערא דמן קדמוי

15. וברקים רב ܒܪ̈ܩܘܗܝ ܐܣܓܝ. ἀστραπὰς ἐπλήθυνεν וברקין סגיאין

27. עם־נבר תתברר ܘܥܡ ܓܒܝܐ ܬܗܘܐ ܓܒܝܐ καὶ μετὰ ἐκλεκτοῦ ἐκλεκτὸς ἔσῃ עם יעקב דהוה בריר קדמך בחרתא בנוי מן כל עממיא ואפרשתא זרעיה מן כל פסילא

xvii : 3 ܦ and LXX read בל־תמצא וְמָתִי בל־יַעֲבְרוּ פי פעלות אדם בדבר.

xvii : 8 ܦ and LXX give the correct meaning of the M. T., but we would expect ܦ to use an expression similar to אישון. cf. Arab. إِنْسَانُ ٱلْعَيْنِ. xviii : 9 καταφλεγησεται $\aleph^{ca}$ R^{a}.

xviii : 15 רבב means either "to multiply" or "to shoot". ܦ, LXX, T have interpreted according to the latter meaning.

35. ונחתה קשת־נחושת זרועתי ܘܫܘ̈ܝ ܐܝܟ ܩܫܬܐ ܕܢܚܫܐ ܕܪ̈ܥܝ καὶ ἔθου τόξον χαλκοῦν τοὺς βραχίονάς μου ומתקיף היך קשת כרכומיא דרעי

36. ועגותך תרבני ܘܡܪܕܘܬܟ ܗܝ ܬܪܒܝܢܝ καὶ ἡ παιδία σου αὐτή με διδάξει ובמימרך אסגעתני

46. ויחרגו ממסגרותיהם ܢܬܚܓܪܘܢ ܡܢ ܫܒ̈ܝܠܝܗܘܢ καὶ ἐχώλαναν ἀπὸ τῶν τρίβων αὐτῶν ויטלטלון מבירנתהון

Psalm xix.

5. קום ܡܫܘ̈ܚܬܗܘܢ ὁ φθόγγος αὐτῶν מתח עיניניהון

Ibid. לשמש ܒܫܡܫܐ ܥܠ ἐν τῷ ἡλίῳ לשמשא

8. פתי ܛܠܝ̈ܐ νήπια שיברא

11. פז רב ܟ̈ܐܦܐ ܝܩܝܪ̈ܬܐ λίθον τίμιον πολὺν ומן אובריזין סגי

12. עבדך נזהר בהם ܥܒܕܟ ܢܙܕܗܪ ܒܗܘܢ ὁ δοῦλός σου φυλάσσει αὐτά ברם עבדך איזדהר בהון

Psalm xx.

6. נדגל ܢܬܬܪܝܡ μεγαλυνθησόμεθα ניסקם

8. נזכיר ܢܬܥܫܢ μεγαλυνθησόμεθα נדכר

Psalm xxii.

2. דברי שאגתי ܡ̈ܠܝ ܕܣܟ̈ܠܘܬܝ οἱ λόγοι τῶν παραπτωμάτων μου מילי אכליותי

xviii : 35 LXX, ܦ, T read נחתה.

xviii : 46 the M. T. is doubtful. cf. ii Sam. xxii : 46.

xix : 5 ܦ and LXX read קולם. xix : 12; this is an instance where the ܦ translators have slavishly rendered the Hebrew by a kindred root, regardless of idiomatic meaning; ܙܗܪ in the Ethpeʿel means "to observe carefully."

xx : 6, 8 ܦ and LXX read נגדל.

xxii : 2 ܦ and LXX read שגיאתי; 18 ܦ and LXX read יספרו.

3. אקרא ܐܩܥܐ ܠܘܬܟ κεκράξομαι . . . . πρός σέ קרי

10. מבטיחי ܣܒܪܝ ܗܘܝܬ ἡ ἐλπίς μου אסברתני

14. אריה ܐܝܟ ܐܪܝܐ ὡς λέων היך כאריא

17. כארי ידי ܒܙܥܘ ܐܝܕܝ ὤρυξαν χεῖράς μου היך כאריא אידי

18. אספר כל־עצמותי ܘܐܬܡܠܠܘ ܟܠܗܘܢ ܓܪ̈ܡܝ ἐξηρίθμησαν πάντα τὰ ὀστᾶ μου אחוי כל הלבשוש גרמיי

22. ומקרני רמים עניתני ܘܡܢ ܩܪ̈ܢܐ ܕܪ̈ܝܡܐ ܡܘܟܟܝ καὶ ἀπὸ κεράτων μονοκερώτων τὴν ταπείνωσίν μου ומלכין דתקיפין ורמין כרימנא קבילתא צלותי

27. לבבכם ܠܒܗܘܢ αἱ καρδίαι αὐτῶν לבכון

30. ונפשו לא חיה ܘܢܦܫܝ ܠܗ ܗܘ ܚܝܐ καὶ ἡ ψυχή μου αὐτῷ ζῇ ונפש רשיעא לא ייחי

31. זרע יעבדנו יספר לאדני לדור ܘܙܪܥܐ ܕܢܦܠܚܘܢܝܗܝ ܢܫܬܥܐ ܠܡܪܝܐ ܕܪܗ καὶ τὸ σπέρμα μου δουλεύσει αὐτῷ ἀναγγελήσεται τῷ κυρίῳ γενεὰ זרעיה דאברהם יפלחון קדמוי ויחוון כח גבורתא דיהוה לדרא בתראה

32. לעם נולד כי עשה ܠܥܡܐ ܕܡܬܝܠܕ ܕܥܒܕ ܡܪܝܐ λαῷ τῷ τεχθησομένῳ ὃν ἐποίησεν ὁ κύριος לעמיה דעתיד למילד פרישן דעבד

Psalm xxiii.

1. יהוה רעי לא אחסר ܡܪܝܐ ܢܪܥܝܢܝ ܘܡܕܡ ܠܐ ܢܚܣܪ ܠܝ Κύριος ποιμαίνει με καὶ οὐδέν με ὑστερήσει יהוה רחן ית עמיה במדברא לא חסרו כולא

xxii: 22 ܦ and LXX read עני or ענותי; 30 ܦ and LXX read לו, and changed the rest of the sentence in consequence; 31 the first clause of ܦ agrees rather with T., the second clause with LXX.

xxiii: 1 only LXX influence can explain the unnecessary circumlocution of ܦ; 5 On the LXX reading, cf. *Psalterii Graeci quinquagena prima* a Paulo de Lagarde, p. 31 in loc. The ܦ verb is the same as the Hebrew; but in the Aphel it signifies "to inebriate".

5. כוסי רויה ܟܣܟ ܡܪܘܝܐ ܐܝܟ ܫܦܐ καὶ τὸ ποτήριόν σου μεθύσκον ὡς κράτιστον כלידי רוותא

6. אך טוב ܛܝܒܘܬܟ τὸ ἔλεός σου ברם טבתא

Psalm xxiv.

1. וישבי בה ܘܟܠܗܘܢ ܥܡܘܪ̈ܝܗ καὶ πάντες οἱ κατοικοῦντες ἐν αὐτῇ ודיתבין בה

6. פניך יעקב ܕܐܦ̈ܝܟ ܐܠܗܗ ܕܝܥܩܘܒ τὸ πρόσωπον τοῦ θεοῦ Ἰακώβ אפוי יעקב

Psalm xxv.

5. אלהי ישעי ܡܛܠ ܕܐܢܬ ܗܘ ܐܠܗܝ ܘܦܪܘܩܝ כיאתה אלהי ישעי ὅτι σὺ εἶ ὁ θεὸς ὁ σωτήρ μου ארום את הוא אלהא פורקני

21. תם־וישר יצרוני ܬܡܝܡ̈ܘܬܐ ܘܬܪ̈ܝܨܘܬܐ ܢܩܦܘ ܠܝ ἄκακοι καὶ εὐθεῖς ἐκολλῶντό μοι שלמתא ותריצותא ומרוגני

Psalm xxvii.

9. אלהי ישעי ܐܠܗܝ ܘܦܪܘܩܝ ὁ θεὸς ὁ σωτήρ μου אלהא פורקני

10. כיאבי ואמי עזבוני ויהוה יאספני ܡܛܠ ܕܐܒܝ ܘܐܡܝ ܫܒܩܘܢܝ ܘܡܪܝܐ ܩܒܠܢܝ ὅτι ὁ πατήρ μου καὶ ἡ μήτηρ μου ἐγκατέλιπόν με ὁ δὲ κύριος προσελάβετό με מטול דאבא ואימא ישבקו יתי יהוה יכנוש לי

13. לולא האמנתי לראות ܐܢܐ ܕܝܢ ܗܝܡܢܬ ܕܐܚܙܐ πιστεύσω τοῦ ἰδεῖν אילולי די הימנית למחמי

Psalm xxviii.

1. צורי ܐܠܗܝ ὁ θεός μου תקיפי

xxv : 21 ܦ and LXX have used the concrete for the abstract.

xxvii : 10 By the use of the perf. for the imperf. ܦ and LXX have changed a prediction into a fact.

xxviii : 1 LXX invariably translates צור by θεός; 8 ܦ and LXX read עז לעמו.

7. ܥܕܘܪܝ ܘܡܣܝܥܢܝ ܒܘܗθός μου καὶ ὑπερασ-
πιστής μου; ibid. עוֹשֵׂנִי וּתְרִים; ונעזרתי ויעלו לבי ומשרי אהדונו
ܘܣܠܩ ܒܣܪܝ ܘܡܢ ܨܒܝܢܐ ܐܘܕܐ ܠܗ καὶ ἀνέθαλεν
ἡ σάρξ μου καὶ ἐκ θελήματός μου ἐξομολογήσομαι αὐτῷ
וסעדתני ודאיץ לבי ומתושבחתי אודה קדמוי
8. ܡܪܝܐ ܥܫܝܢܐ ܗܘ ܕܥܡܗ Κύριος κραταίωμα יהוה עזלמו
τοῦ λαοῦ αὐτοῦ יהוה תקוף להון

Psalm xxix.

1. ܐܘܒܠܘ ܠܡܪܝܐ ܒܢܝ ܕܟܪܐ ἐνέγκατε הבו ליהוה בני אלים
τῷ κυρίῳ υἱοὺς κριῶν בני מלאכיא כתי תושבחתא יהוה קדם הבו
ibid. כבוד ועז; ܫܘܒܚܐ ܘܐܝܩܪܐ δόξαν καὶ τιμὴν
איקר ועישונא

2. ܒܕܪܬܐ ܡܩܕܫܬܐ ἐν αὐλῇ ἁγίᾳ αὐτοῦ בהדרת קדש
בשיבהורת קודשא

6. ܘܕܩܩ ܐܢܘܢ καὶ λεπτυνεῖ αὐτάς וַיְרַקְּדֵם ישוורינון

Psalm xxx.

4. ܡܢ ܢܚܬܝ τῶν καταβαινόντων (מִיֹּרְדִי קרי) מִיָּרְדִי מן למיתת
6. ܒܪܘܓܙܐ ܪܢܐ ܒܐܦܘ ὀργὴ ἐν τῷ θυμῷ αὐτοῦ רגע באפו
ממול דשעתא רוגזיה

8. ܘܡܣܩܬܐ ܚܝܠܐ ܠܛܘܪܝ ܥܘܫܢܐ παράσχου העמדתה להררי עז
τῷ κάλλει μου δύναμιν איתעתדתא לטוריא עושנא

Psalm xxxi.

3. ܗܘܝ ܠܝ ܐܠܗܐ ܡܣܬܪܢܐ γενοῦ μοι היה לי לצור־מעוז
εἰς θεὸν ὑπερασπιστήν הוי לי לכרך עשין לחוסנא

xxix: 1 ܦ and LXX read בני אילים; 2 ܦ and LXX undoubtedly
read בחדרת־קדש i. e. the Holy of Holies; 6 ܦ and LXX
read וירקדם for וירקדם.

xxx: 4 The unpointed M. T. will bear the interpretation of ܦ,
and LXX; 6 ܦ and LXX read רנו באפו; 8 ܦ and LXX read להררי.

4. כי־סלעי ומצודתי אתה ܡܛܠ ܕܬܘܩܦܝ ܘܡܥܘܕܪܢܝ ܐܢܬ ܗܘ ὅτι κραταίωμά μου καὶ καταφυγή μου εἶ σύ מטול דתוקפי ורוחצני את

7. שנאתי ܣܢܝܬ ἐμίσησας שנאתי

18. ידמו ܢܫܬܘܩܘܢ καταχθείησαν ויתתון.

25. ויאמץ לבבכם ܘܢܬܚܝܠ ܠܒܟܘܢ κραταιούσθω ἡ καρδία ὑμῶν ויתעלים רעיונכון

Psalm xxxiii.

7. כַּנֵּד ܐܝܟ ܕܒܙܩܐ ὡσεὶ ἀσκόν היך זיקא

9. ויהי ܘܗܘܘ καὶ ἐγενήθησαν והוי

Psalm xxxiv.

6. הביטו אליו ונהרו ופניהם אל־יחפרו ܩܪܘܒܘ ܠܘܬܗ ܘܐܬܢܗܪܘ ܘܐܦܝ̈ܟܘܢ ܠܐ ܢܒܗܬܘܢ προσέλθατε πρὸς αὐτὸν καὶ φωτίσθητε καὶ τὰ πρόσωπα ὑμῶν οὐ μὴ καταισχυνθῇ אסתכלו לותיה ואתנהרו ואפיהון לא עצבו

11. כפירים ܥܬܝܪ̈ܐ πλούσιοι בני אריוא

13. אהב ימים לראות טוב ܘܪܚܡ ܝܘ̈ܡܬܐ ܛܒ̈ܐ ܠܡܚܙܐ ἀγαπῶν ἰδεῖν ἡμέρας ἀγαθάς רחים יומיא למחמי טבא

18. ~ ܘܙܕܝ̈ܩܐ δικαίοι ~

Psalm xxxv.

1. ריבה ܕܘܢ δίκασον איתגר

2. מגן ܙܝܢܐ ὅπλου תרים

3. חנית ܪܘܡܚܐ ῥομφαίαν מורניתא

Psalm xxxvi.

2. לבי ܒܠܒܗ ἐν αὐτῷ לבבי

xxxiii : 7 ס, LXX, T. read נֹד or נאד.

xxxiv : 6 In the M. T. the verbs are not in the imperative, and the noun has the suffix of the third person.

4. חדל להשכיל להיטיב ܘܠܐ ܨܒܐ ܠܡܣܬܟܠܘ. ܠܛܒܬܐ οὐκ ἐβουλήθη συνιέναι τοῦ ἀγαθῦναι פסק למשכל לאוטבא

8. מה־יקר ܡܢܐ ܣܓܝܐܝܢ ὡς ἐπλήθυνας כמה יקר

13. פעלי ܟܠ ܥܒ̈ܕܝ. πάντες οἱ ἐργαζόμενοι עבדי

Psalm xxxvii.

2. כי כחציר מהרה ימלו ܡܛܠ ܕܐܝܟ ܥ̈ܡܝܪܐ ܒܥܓܠ ܢܒܫܘܢ ὅτι ὡσεὶ χόρτος ταχὺ ἀποξηρανθήσονται מטול דסופיהון היך עסבא בסרהוביא יתמוללון

7. והתחולל ܘܨܠܐ καὶ ἱκέτευσον ואוריך

16. מהמון רשעים רבים ܡܢ ܩܢܝܢܐ ܣܓܝܐܐ ܕܪ̈ܫܝܥܐ ὑπὲρ πλοῦτον ἁμαρτωλῶν πολύν מריכפת רשיעין סניעין

20. כיקר כרים ܘܐܝܟ ܬܢܢܐ ὡσεὶ καπνός היך יקר פלניסין

35. כאזרח רענן ܐܝܟ ܐܪ̈ܙܐ ܕܠܒܢܢ ὡς τὰς κέδρους τοῦ Λιβάνου היך אילן יציב ועבוף

36. ויעבר ܟܕ. ܥܒܪܬ καὶ παρῆλθον ופסק

37. אחרית לאיש שלום ܡܛܠ ܕܐܝܬ ܫܪܬܐ ܠܛܒܬܐ ܠܓܒܪܐ ܕܫܠܡܐ ὅτι ἐστὶν ἐνκατάλιμμα ἀνθρώπῳ εἰρηνικῷ ארום דסוף בר נשא שלמא

Psalm xxxviii.

4. חטאתי ܚܛܗ̈ܝ τῶν ἁμαρτιῶν μου חובי

11. סחרחר ܐܬܕܠܚܬ ἐταράχθη צמרמר

18. לצלע ܠܢܓܕܐ μάστιγας לתברא

Psalm xxxix.

3. נאלמתי דומיה ܫܬܩܬ ܘܐܬܡܟܟܬ ἐκωφώθην καὶ ἐταπεινώθην אתאלמית שתקית

xxxvii : 35 The ܦ reading is that of Aphraates (vid Baethgen, *Der text-krit. Werth d. alten Uebersetzungen zu den Ps. J. P. T.* 1882, No. iv, p. 626). The other Mss. read ܐܝܟ ܐܝ̈ܠܢܐ ܕܥܒܐ.

xxxvii : 37 ܦ and LXX seem to have taken ישר and תם as abstract nouns instead of concrete; and איש as construct before שלום.

7. מי־אספם ܠܡܢܘ ܟܢܫ ܠܗܘܢ τίνι συνάξει αὐτά מטול מנא
מן כנשינן

8. ועתה מה־קויתי אדני תוחלתי לך היא ܡܟܝܠ ܡܢܘ ܣܒܪܝ. ܐܠܐ
ܐܢ ܐܢܬ ܡܪܝܐ καὶ νῦν τίς ἡ ὑπομονή μου οὐχὶ ὁ κύριος
וכדון מנא סברית יהוה אוריכותי לותך היא

13. שמעה תפלתי יהוה ושועתי האזינה ܫܡܥ ܡܪܝܐ ܨܠܘܬܝ.
ܘܒܥܘܬܝ. ܘܨܘܬ ܠܬܟܫܦܬܝ. εἰσάκουσον τῆς προσευχῆς μου
καὶ τῆς δεήσεώς μου קביל צלותי יהוה ובעותי אצית

Psalm xl.

5. אשר־שם יהוה ܕܥܠ ܫܡܗ ܕܡܪܝܐ ܬܘܟܠܗ οὗ ἐστιν τὸ
ὄνομα Κυρίου ἐλπὶς αὐτοῦ דשוי יהוה רוחצניה; ibid. אל־רהבים
ושטי כזב ܠܣܪܝܩܘܬܐ ܘܐܦܠܐ ܠܡܡܠܠܐ ܕܓܠܐ εἰς
ματαιότητας καὶ μανίας ψευδεῖς לות סורבניא וממללי כדיבותא

8. במגלת־ספר ܕܪܝܫ ܒܟܬܒܐ ἐν κεφαλίδι βιβλίου במגילת סיפרא

Psalm xli.

3. יְאֻשַּׁר ܘܢܛܘܒ ܠܗ καὶ μακαρίσαι αὐτὸν ויוטיביניה

9. דבר־בליעל יצוק בו ܡܠܬܐ ܕܥܘܠܐ ܪܫܡ ܗܘܘ λόγον
παράνομον κατέθεντο ממלל טלומא יתיך ביה

Psalm xlii.

5. כי אעבר בסך ܡܛܠ ܕܐܥܒܪ ܒܡܛܠܬܢ ܒܥܫܝܢܐ ὅτι
διελεύσομαι ἐν τόπῳ σκηνῆς θαυμαστῆς כד אעבר טללא בלחודי
אתחייל במשריין דצדיקי

6. כי עוד אודנו ישועות פניו ܡܛܠ ܕܬܘܒ ܐܘܕܐ ܠܗ ܠܦܪܘܩܐ

xl : 5 The reading of ܦ and LXX was doubtless שֵׁם יהוה.

xli : 3 ܦ and LXX agree more nearly with the Kerē וְאֻשַּׁר.

xli : 9 Possibly ܦ and LXX read יצקו, the T. יָצוּק; but more probably they mistook the word and read יצורו, from the root צור "to conceive, to imagine".

xlii : 6 In M. T. אלהי is construed with the following verse.

ܕܐܦ̈ܝ ܘܐܠܗܝ ὅτι ἐξομολογήσομαι αὐτῷ σωτήριον τοῦ προσώπου μου ὁ θεός μου ארים תוב אשבחיניה בפורקנא דמן קדמוי

Psalm xliii.

1. מרמה ועולה ܢ̈ܟܠܐ ܘܥܘܠܬܢܐ ἀδίκου καὶ δολίου נכיל ושלומא

4. אֶל־אֵל שמחת גילי ܘܠܘܬ ܐܠܗܐ ܕܡܚܕܐ ܠܛܠܝܘܬܝ τὸν εὐφραίνοντα τὴν νεότητά μου לות אלהי די מיניה חדות בעותי

Psalm xliv.

5. צוה ܕܦܩܕܬ ὁ ἐντελλόμενος פקיד

Psalm xlv.

3. יפיפית ܫܦܝܪ ܒܫܘܦܪܗ ὡραῖος κάλλει שופרך מלכא משיחא עדיף

10. שגל ܡܠܟܬܐ ἡ βασίλισσα אורייתא.

ibid. בכתם ܒܠܒܘܫܐ ܕܕܗܒܐ ἐν ἱματισμῷ διαχρύσῳ באובריזן דמן

13. ובת־צר במנחה ܘܒܪ̈ܬ ܨܘܪ ܬܣܓܘܕܝܢ ܠܗ καὶ προσκυνήσουσιν αὐτῷ θυγατέρες Τύρου ἐν δώροις ויתבי כרכא דצור בתקרובתא

14. כל־כבודה בת־ ܟܠܗ ܫܘܒܚܐ ܕܒܪ̈ܬ πᾶσα ἡ δόξα αὐτῆς θυγατρός כל שפר ארג נכסי

Psalm xlvi.

4. בגאותו ܒܥܘܫܢܗ ἐν τῇ κραταιότητι αὐτοῦ בגיוותנותך

7. תמוג ܘܙܥܬ ἐσαλεύθη איתמטנו

9. שמות ܬܕܡܪ̈ܬܐ τέρατα ברישעי.

xliii : 4 Possibly this mistake may be accounted for by comparing the Arab. غيل, (vid. Oliver, *Translat. of the Syriac Ps.* p. 81, note), or the use of גיל Dan. i : 10 (vid. Baethgen, *Der textkrit. Werth d. alt. Uebersetz. zu d. Ps. J. P. T.* 1882, No. 4, p. 631).

xlv : 14 פ and LXX read כבוד as construct before בת

Psalm xlvii.

10. עַם נֶאֶסְפוּ ܠܥܰܠ ܐܶܬܟ݁ܰܢܰܫܘ݂ συνήχθησαν μετά רבני עממיא

ibid. מִגִּנֵּי־אֶרֶץ ܢܣܰܒܘ݂ܡܣܳܐ݂ ܘܐܺܝܪܳܟܶܐ݂ οἱ κραταιοὶ τῆς γῆς תרימי ארעא

Psalm xlviii.

3. שַׁפִּיר ~ ~ יפה נוף
6. עַרְקוּ ~ ~ נחפזו
8. בְּקָדִים βιαίῳ ܩܰܕܺܝܡ ܒܶܐܣܢܳܐ
12. דִּינָךְ κριμάτων σου Κύριε ܕܺܝ̈ܢܰܝܟ ܡܳܪܝܳܐ ܬܶܠܬܳܗ̇ מִשְׁפָּטֶיךָ
14. רָם καταδιέλεσθε ܦܰܣܶܩܘ ܣܰܘ̈ܦܶܝܗ̇

Psalm xlix.

9. וּמוּרְעָנוּתָא לְעָלַם καὶ ἐκοπίασεν εἰς τὸν αἰῶνα ܘܠܳܐ ܠܥܳܠܰܡ ܚܳܕܶܠ לְעוֹלָם וְחָדַל
11. וּשְׁטַיָּא ܫܰܛܝܳܐ ܘܰܣܟ݂ܳܐ ἄνους וָבָעַר
12. קִבְרָם ܩܰܒ݂ܪܰܝ̈ܗܘܢ οἱ τάφοι αὐτῶν בבית קבורתהן
13. לָא בַּיְתִי בְּלִילִין ܠܳܐ ܐܶܬ݂ܚܰܟܰܡܘ οὐ συνῆκεν
13, 21. אִשְׁתַּוִּיו לִלְמָא ܐܶܬܕܰܡܺܝ ܠܗܘܢ καὶ ὡμοιώθη αὐτοῖς נִדְמוּ
14. שְׁטוּתָא לְהוֹן ܡܰܩܠܳܬ݂ܳܐ ܠܢܰܦ݂ܫܗܘܢ σκάνδαλον αὐτοῖς כְּסֵל לָמוֹ
15. מִן יְקָרָם ܡܶܢ ܐܺܝܩܳܪܬ݂ܗܘܢ ἐκ τῆς δόξης αὐτῶν מִזְּבֻל
19. אֲרוּם תִּיטִיב לְפוּלְחָן קֳדָמָךְ ܟܰܕ ܬܰܛܐܶܒ ܠܗ ὅταν ἀγαθύνῃς αὐτῷ כִּי־תֵיטִיב לָךְ
20. יַחְמוֹן ܢܶܚܙܘܢ ὄψεται יִרְאוּ

xlvii: 10 For עַם, ܐ and LXX read עִם.
xlix: 12 ܐ and LXX read קִבְרָם.
xlix: 12 ܐ and LXX read יָבִין.
xlix: 13, 21 דָּמָה — either "to be like", or "to destroy". ܐ and LXX interpreted it in the latter meaning; T and the other versions in the former. xlix: 14 ܐ and LXX read כְּשֶׁל.

Psalm l.

5. אספרלי חסידי כרתי בריתי ܐܬܟܢܫܘ ܠܗܘܢ ܟܠܗܘܢ ܚܣܝ̈ܕܘܗܝ.
ܕܡܩܝܡܝܢ ܩܝܡܗ συναγάγετε αὐτῷ τοὺς ὁσίους αὐτοῦ τοὺς
διατιθεμένους τὴν διαθήκην αὐτοῦ כנושו לותי חסידי די גזרו קיימי
7. ואדברה ܘܐܡܠܠ ܠܟ καὶ λαλήσω σοι ואמליל
10. בהררי־אָלֶף ܒܛܘܪ̈ܐ ܘܬܘܪ̈ܐ ἐν τοῖς ὄρεσιν καὶ βόες
טורין אלפא
11. עוף הרים ܦܪܚܬܐ ܕܫܡܝܐ τὰ πετεινὰ τοῦ οὐρανοῦ
עופא דפרחין באויר שמיא
21. דמית ܣܒܪܬ ܥܘܠܐ ὑπέλαβες ἀνομίαν דתיתיב חשבתא
22. פן־אטרף ܕܠܡܐ ܢܚܛܘܦ μή ποτε ἁρπάσῃ דילמא איתבר
23. ושם דרך אראנו בישע אלהים ܘܬܡܢ ܐܚܘܝܘܗܝ ܐܘܪܚܐ
ܕܦܘܪܩܢܗ ܕܐܠܗܐ καὶ ἐκεῖ ὁδὸς ᾗ δείξω αὐτῷ τὸ σωτήριον
τοῦ θεοῦ ודי יעדי אורחא בישא אחמי ליה בפורקנא דיהוה

Psalm li.

8. ובסתם חכמה תודיעני ܘܟܣܝ̈ܬܐ ܕܚܟܡܬܟ ܐܘܕܥܬܢܝ τὰ
κρύφια τῆς σοφίας σου ἐδήλωσάς μοι ובסמור לבא חוכמתא תהודענני
10. עצמות דכית ܓܪ̈ܡܐ ܡܟܝ̈ܟܐ ὀστᾶ τεταπεινωμένα
איבריא דשיפייתא

Psalm lii.

7. וְשֵׁרֶשְׁךָ ܘܥܩܪܟ καὶ τὸ ῥίζωμά σου ויתלשינך

Psalm liii.

5. פעלי ܟܠ ܥܒ̈ܕܝ πάντες οἱ ἐργαζόμενοι כל עבדי
6. כי־אלהים פזר עצמות חנך הבישתה ܡܛܠ ܕܐܠܗܐ ܒܕܪ

l: 10 ס and LXX mistook the numeral for a collective noun "oxen".
l: 23 ס and LXX read שָׁם.
lii: 7 ס and LXX read וְשָׁרְשְׁךָ.
liii: 6 ס and LXX probably read חנף instead of חנך.

ܓܪ̈ܡܝܗܘܢ ܕܐܢܫ̈ܐ ܕܫܦܪܝܢ ὅτι ὁ θεὸς διεσκόρπισεν ὀστᾶ ἀνθρωπαρέσκων ארום אלהא מבדר תקוף משירית חייביא בהיתתא

Psalm liv.

5. ועריצים ܘܥܫܝ̈ܢܐ κραταιοί ועלימין

6. ואדני בסמכי נפשי ܡܪܝܐ ܡܣܡܟܢܗ ܕܢܦܫܝ ὁ κύριος ἀντιλήμπτωρ τῆς ψυχῆς μου יהוה בסמכי נפשי

Psalm lv.

9. אחישה מפלט לי ܘܣܟܝܬ ܠܡܢ ܕܡܦܨܐ ܠܝ προσεδεχόμην τὸν σῴζοντά με ארחיש שזבותא לי

12. הוות בקרבה ܘܥܘܠܬܐ καὶ ἀδικία איתרגושיא במיצעה

15. נמתיק סוד ܠܚܡܢ ܒܪ̈ܘܬܐ ἐδέσματα נתריץ רזא; ibid. ברגש ܒܐܘܝܘܬܐ ἐν ὁμονοίᾳ בסרהוביא

19. מִקְּרָב־לִי ܡܢ ܐܝܠܝܢ ܕܩܪܝܒܝܢ ܠܝ ἀπὸ τῶν ἐγγιζόντων μοι דלא למקרב ביש לי

20. וישב קדם ܗܘ ܕܐܝܬܘܗܝ ܡܢ ܩܕܡ ܥܠܡܐ ὁ ὑπάρχων πρὸ τῶν αἰώνων ויתיב שמיא מלקדמין לעלמין

22. חלקו מחמאת פיו וקרב־לבו ܐܬܦܠܓܘ ܡܢ ܪܘܓܙܐ ܕܐܦ̈ܘܗܝ διεμερίσθησαν ἀπὸ ὀργῆς τοῦ προσώπου αὐτοῦ מילי פומיה והיך זיני קרבא לביה

23. יהבך ܝܨܦܬܟ τὴν μέριμνάν σου סבורך.

Psalm lvi.

2. שְׁאָפַנִי ܕܕܫܘܢܝ κατεπάτησέν με שפייני

7. יגורו ܘܢܬܬܘܬܒܘܢ παροικήσουσιν יכנשון

lv: 9 ס and LXX read אחילה instead of אחישה; and for מִקְּלָם מִקָּלָם. lv: 15 For סוד ס and LXX read צידה or סעוד.
lv: 19 ס and LXX read מִקְּרוֹב לִי.
lv: 22 ס and LXX read מֵחֲמַת.
lvi: 2 ס, LXX and ג read שׁוֹאֲפַי.

9. נדי ספרתה אתה שמה דמעתי בנאדך הלא בספרתך ܐܠܗܐ ܚܝ̈ܝ ܬܢܝܬ ܠܟ ܣܝܡ ܕܡ̈ܥܝ ܩܕܡܝܟ ܘܒܫܘܘܕܝܟ ὁ θεὸς τὴν ζωήν μου ἐξήγγειλά σοι ἔθου τὰ δάκρυά μου ἐνώπιόν σου ὡς καὶ ἐν τῇ ἐπαγγελίᾳ σου הלא יהוה בזיקיך דמעתי בחושבנך

14. הלא רגלי ܘܪ̈ܓܠܝ καὶ τοὺς πόδας μου הלא רגלי

ibid. להתהלך לפני ܕܐܫܦܪ ܩܕܡܝܟ τοῦ εὐαρεστῆσαι ἐνώπιον למהלכא קדם

Psalm lvii.

4. חרף שאפי ܘܝܗܒ ܠܚܣܕܐ ܠܕܝ̈ܫܝ ἔδωκεν εἰς ὄνειδος τοὺς καταπατοῦντάς με חסד שייפי לעלמין

5. נפשי בתוך לבאם אשכבה להטים ܘܦܪܩ ܢܦܫܝ ܡܢ ܓܘܪ̈ܝܐ ܕܐܪ̈ܝܘܬܐ ܟܕ ܕܠܝܚ ܐܢܐ καὶ ἐρύσατο τὴν ψυχήν μου ἐκ μέσου σκύμνων ἐκοιμήθην τεταραγμένος נפשי חיירא כיד במצע שלהובין ארמוך ביני גומרין די מלהטין

8. ואזמרה ܘܐܙܡܪ ܒܐܝܩܪܝ καὶ ψαλῶ ἐν τῇ δόξῃ μου ואזמר

Psalm lviii.

2. האמנם ~ ~ צדיקי

3. חמס ידיכם תפלסון ܘܥܘܠܐ ܡܓ̈ܕܠܢ ܐܝ̈ܕܝܟܘܢ ἀδικίαν αἱ χεῖρες ὑμῶν συνπλέκουσιν חטוף אידיכון יתקנון

9. כמו שבלול ܐܝܟ ܫܥܘܬܐ ὡσεὶ κηρὸς היך זחיל

ib. נְפֶל אֵשׁ ܢܦܠܬ ܢܘܪܐ ἐπέπεσε πῦρ נפולא ואשותא

11. פעמיו ܘܐܝ̈ܕܘܗܝ τὰς χεῖρας αὐτοῦ אפרשורין

lvi : 9 For נֹדִי, ס and LXX probably read נגדי; placing the verb in the first person.

lvii : 4 M. T. might be translated in agreement with ס.

lvii : 8 ψαλω] + σοι εν τη δοξη μου א* (om σοι $א^{ca}$).

lviii : 9 ס and LXX read נָפְלָה אֵשׁ.

Psalm lix.

10. עזו ܚܝܠܝ ܠܘܬܟ τὸ κράτος μου עושני
12. מגננו ܬܘܟܠܢ ὁ ὑπερασπιστής μου תריסנא

Psalm lx.

6. להתנוסס מפני קשט ܕܠܐ ܢܥܪܩܘܢ ܡܢ ܩܕܡ ܩܫܬܐ τοῦ φυγεῖν ἀπὸ προσώπου τόξου לאיתנסאה ביה מן בגלל קושטיה
7. ועננו ܘܥܢܝܢܝ καὶ ἐπάκουσόν μου צלותי
9. מחקקי ܡܠܟܝ βασιλεύς μου אולפני

Psalm lxi.

3. בצור־ירום ממני תנחני ܕܥܠ ܟܐܦܐ ܐܪܝܡܬܢܝ ἐν πέτρᾳ ὕψωσάς με על טינר רם מיני דבר יתי
6. יראי שמך ܠܕܚ̈ܠܝ ܫܡܟ τοῖς φοβουμένοις τὸ ὄνομά σου לדחלי שמך
8. חסד ואמת מן ינצרהו ܠܛܝܒܘܬܐ ܘܩܘܫܬܐ ܕܝܠܗ ܢܛܪܘܗܝ ἔλεος καὶ ἀλήθειαν αὐτοῦ τίς ἐκζητήσει αὐτῶν טיבו וקשוט מן מרי עלמא ינטרון ליה

Psalm lxii.

3, 8. צורי ܐܠܗܝ ὁ θεός μου פורקני
5. ירצו ܪܗܛܘ ἔδραμον יחוון
8. עזי ܘܡܥܕܪܢܝ τῆς βοηθείας μου עושני
10. לעלות ܠܡܥܠ ἀδικῆσαι נשך

lx: 6 ܦ and LXX seem to have mistaken קשט for קשת; and to have derived the verb from נוס, instead of from נסס.

lx: 7 ܦ, LXX and T agree with the Kerê.

lxi: 3 ܦ and LXX possibly read בצור תרוממני תנחמני

lxi: 8 מן is ordinarily regarded as imper. of מנה. ܦ and LXX regarded it as the personal pronoun; which is probably correct, since this reading makes better sense.

11. ובגזל אל־תהבלו ܘܒܚܛܘܦܝܐ ܠܐ ܬܬܪܓܪܓܘܢ καὶ ἐπὶ ἁρπάγματα μὴ ἐπιποθεῖτε ובאונסא לא תקבלון

Psalm lxiii.

11. יגירהו ܢܫܬܠܡܘܢ παραδοθήσονται ידחלוניה

Psalm lxiv.

2. בשיחי ܟܕ ܐܬܟܫܦ ܠܟ ἐν τῷ δέεσθαί με πρὸς σέ בעידן צלותי

7. תמנו ܘܣܦܩܘ ἐξέλιπον וכאין

8. וירם ܢܬܬܪܝܡ ὑψωθήσεται וינרי עילוידהון

9. יתנודדו ܘܢܙܝܥܘܢ ἐταράχθησαν יטלטלון

Psalm lxv.

2. דמיה ܝܐܝܐ πρέπει מתחשבא

3. שמע תפלה ܫܡܥ ܨܠܘܬܝ εἰσάκουσον προσευχῆς μου מקבל צלותא

4. דברי עונת ܡ̈ܠܐ ܕܥ̈ܘܠܐ λόγοι ἀνόμων פתגמי עוין

8. והמון לאמים ܢܬܕܠܚܘܢ ܥ̈ܡܡܐ ταραχθήσονται τὰ ἔθνη וריכפת אומיא

10. דגנם ܡܐܟܘܠܬܗܘܢ τὴν τροφὴν αὐτῶν עיבורידהון

12. עטרת שנת ܒܪܟ ܟܠܝܠܐ ܕܫܢܬܐ εὐλογήσεις τὸν στεφανὸν τοῦ ἐνιαυτοῦ אכלילתא שנת

14. ירעפו ܢܬܡܠܘܢ πληθυνοῦσι יתחפין

lxiv : 7 M. T. will bear the interpretation of ס and LXX.

lxiv : 8 ס and LXX read וַיָּרֻם.

lxv : 8 ס and LXX read יהמו.

lxv : 12 עֲטֶרֶת for עִטַּרְתָּ seems to have been the reading of ס and LXX. תברך may have been supplied from the preceding verse.

Psalm lxvi.

12. לרויה ܠܪܘܝܚܬܐ εἰς ἀναψυχήν לרוותא

Psalm lxvii.

7. יבולה ܦܐܪ̈ܝܗ τὸν καρπὸν αὐτῆς איבה

Psalm lxviii.

5. לרכב בערבות ביה שמו ܠܪܟܒ ܠܡܥܪ̈ܒܐ ܡܪܝܐ ܗܘ
ܫܡܗ τῷ ἐπιβεβηκότι ἐπὶ δυσμῶν Κύριος ὄνομα αὐτῷ ליתיב
על כורסי יקריה בערבות יה שמיה

7. צחיחה ܒܝܬ ܩܒܘܪ̈ܐ ἐν τάφοις צחיחין

10. ונלאה אתה כוננתה ܘܐܬܟܪܗܬ ܘܐܢܬ ܬܩܢܬܗ καὶ
ἠσθένησεν σὺ δὲ κατηρτίσω αὐτήν וכנשתא דאשתלהית את אתקינתא

13. ונות־בית ܘܫܘܦܪܗ ܕܒܝܬܟ καὶ ὡραιότητι τοῦ οἴκου ~

28. רֹדֵם ܒܬܗܪܐ ἐν ἐκστάσει זעיר; ibid. רגמתם ܘܫܠܝܛܢܝܗܘܢ
ἡγεμόνες αὐτῶν רגמו יתהון

32. חשמנים ܐܝܙܓܕ̈ܐ πρέσβεις אוסמנא

35. עז ܬܫܒܘܚܬܐ δόξαν יקר

Psalm lxix.

12. ואתנה לבושי שק ܘܟܦܦܬ ܒܨܘܡܐ ܢܦܫܝ καὶ συνέκαμψα
ἐν νηστείᾳ τὴν ψυχήν μου ובכית בצומא דנפשי

23. ולשלומים ܘܦܘܪܥܢܗܘܢ ἀνταπόδοσιν ונכסתהון

27. יספרו ܘܐܘܣܦܘ προσέθηκαν ישתעיין

Psalm lxx.

4. האמרים ܕܐܡܪܝܢ ܥܠܝ οἱ λέγοντές μοι דאמרין עלי

lxviii: 5 Possibly 𝔖 and LXX read מערבה.
lxviii: 28 𝔖 and LXX derived רֹדֵם from רדם, instead of רדה.
lxix: 23 Possibly the translators read וְשִׁלּוּמִם.
lxix: 27 𝔖 and LXX read יָסִפוּ.

8

Psalm lxxi.

3. לצור ܒܝܬ ܓܘܣܝ ὑπερασπιστήν לסְעַד

6. גוזי ܬܘܟܠܢܝ σκεπαστής מפקי

18. וגם עד־זקנה ܒܣܝܒܐ ܠܩܫܝܫܘܬܐ καὶ ἕως γήρους ולחוד
עד זקנתא

20. תשוב תחיינו ܘܗܦܟܬ ܘܒܝܐܬܢܝ καὶ ἐπιστρέψας παρε-
κάλεσάς με תתוב תסיק יתנא

Psalm lxxii.

12. מְשַׁוֵּעַ ܡܢ ܡܢ ܕܚܣܝܢ ܡܢܗ δυνάστου ממו

14. ומחמס ܘܡܢ ܥܘܠܐ καὶ ἐξ ἀδικίας מאונסא

18. אלהים ~ ~ אלהא

Psalm lxxiii.

6. לכן ענקתמו גאוה יעטף־שית חמס למו ܡܛܠ ܗܢܐ ܐܚܕܬ ܐܢܘܢ
ܫܘܒܗܪܐ ܘܐܬܥܛܦܘ ܥܘܠܗܘܢ ܘܪܘܫܥܗܘܢ διὰ τοῦτο
ἐκράτησεν αὐτοὺς ἡ ὑπερηφανία περιεβάλοντο ἀδικίαν καὶ
ἀσέβειαν αὐτῶν לכך כן עטרתנון ניוותנותא כלילא דמשוין ברישיהון
מן חטוף דילהון

7. עינמו ܥܘܠܗܘܢ ἡ ἀδικία αὐτῶν פרצופיהון. ibid. עברו
משכיות לבב ܘܥܒܪܘ ܐܝܟ ܬܪܥܝܬܐ ܕܠܒܐ διῆλθον εἰς
διάθεσιν καρδίας עברו חושביהון חמורת ליבא

8. וידברו ברע עשק ממרום ידברו ܐܬܚܫܒܘ ܘܡܠܠܘ ܒܒܝܫܬܐ
ܘܒܛܠܘܡܝܐ ܥܠ ܡܪܘܡܐ ܡܠܠܘ διενοήθησαν καὶ ἐλάλησαν

lxxi: 20 ܦ LXX and T agree with the Kerē.
lxxii: 12 ܦ and LXX read מְשׁוּעַ.
lxxiii: 6 Schleusner conjectures that the reading here was שֵׁת.
lxxiii: 7 For עברו, ܦ and LXX read עבדו.
lxxiii: 8 ܦ and LXX במרום; otherwise they agree with the unpointed M. T.

UPON THE PᵉŠIṬṬÂ PSALTER   115

ἐν πονηρίᾳ ἀδικίαν εἰς τὸ ὕψος ἐλάλησαν ܦܘܡܐ ܡܢ ܡܡܩܡܩܝܢ יתממקמקן מן פומא
ܘܡܠܠܘ ܠܐܒܐܫܐ ܘܠܡܠܘܡܐ ܡܢ ܪܘܡ ܠܒܗܢ ܝܡܠܠܘܢ וימללו לאבאשא ולמלומא מן רום לבהן ימללו

10. עמו ܠܗܘܢ ܢܬܡܨܐ ὁ λαός μου ܥܡܐ ܕܝܠܝ. ibid. ומי מלא ימצו למו
ܘܝܘܡܬܐ ܡܠܝܬܐ ܢܫܬܟܚܘܢ ܠܗܘܢ καὶ ἡμέραι πλήρεις εὑρεθήσονται αὐτοῖς
וימחונק במרוופין ודמעין מגיעין מתיק להון

18. למשואות ܠܫܗܘܘܬܐ ܒܪܡ ܥܠ ܢܟܠܐ ܐܬܬܣܝܡܘ ܠܗܘܢ ἐν τῷ ἐπαρθῆναι.
ibid. אך בחלקות תשת למו ܐܠܐ ܒܢܟܠܐ ܣܡܬ ܠܗܘܢ πλὴν διὰ τὰς δολιότητας ἔθου αὐτοῖς
ברם בקבלא שויתא להון

20. בעיר ܒܡܕܝܢܬܐ ἐν τῇ πόλει באתעריתהון

21. אשתונן ܐܫܬܚܠܦܘ ἠλλοιώθησαν בערן כאשא

28. ביהוה ~ יהוה ~

Psalm lxxiv.

1. אפך ישׁן עשׁן ܐܬܪܓܙ ܪܘܓܙܟ ὠργίσθη ὁ θυμός σου יתקף רוגזך

4. מועד בקרב מועדיך ܒܓܘ ܥܐܕܟ τῆς ἑορτῆς σου במצע זמניך

5—6. יודע כמביא למעלה בסבך-עץ קרדמות: ועת פתוחיה יחד בכשיל
ܐܝܟ ܕܠܡܥܠܬܐ ܠܥܠ ܘܐܝܟ ܕܒܥܒܐ ܕܩܝܣܐ ܢܦܠܬ ܣܟܝܢܗܘܢ ܐܟܚܕܐ ܘܒܣܟܐ ὡς εἰς τὴν εἴσοδον ὑπεράνω ὡς ἐν δρυμῷ ξύλων ἀξίναις ἐξέκοψαν τὰς θύρας αὐτῆς ἐπὶ τὸ αὐτὸ ἐν πελέκει καὶ λαξευτηρίῳ κατέρραξαν αὐτήν יגליף בקרדנסא היך גבר דמרים ידיה בסבך קיסא למקטע בכולבא וכדין נליפיתא גרדין כחדא בקופיץ ומיפסלת דיוסמר מחיין כבמרחושין

8. בארץ כל-מועדי-אל שרפו ܐܘܩܕܘ ܥܕܥܐܕܘܗܝ ܕܡܪܝܐ

lxxiii: 10 ܦ and LXX seem to have read ימלאו ימצאו למו.
lxxiii: 18 T + κατεβαλες αυτους εν τω επαρθηναι B^{abmg} אR + κατεβαλας αυτ. εν τω επ. T.
lxxiii: 20 To agree with ܦ and LXX, the M. T. would have to read בהעיר.
lxxiii: 21 ܦ and LXX probably derived this verb from שנה.

8*

ܕܐܠܗܐ ܡܢ ܐܪܥܐ καὶ καταπαύσωμεν τὰς ἑορτὰς Κυρίου
ἀπὸ τῆς γῆς אבהתהון כל מערעיא ראלהא בארעא

19. נפש תורך ܢܦܫܐ ܕܡܘܕܝܐ ܠܟ ψυχὴν ἐξομολογουμένην
σοι נפשת מאלפי אוריתך

Psalm lxxv.

2. הודינו וקרוב שמך ספרו נפלאותיך ܐܘܕܝܢ ܠܟ ܘܩܪܝܒ ܫܡܟ
ܘܐܫܬܥܐ ܟܠܗܝܢ ܬܕܡܪ̈ܬܟ ἐπικαλεσόμεθα τὸ ὄνομά
σου διηγήσομαι πάντα τὰ θαυμάσιά σου אודינן וקריב שמך
אישתעיו פרישותך

3. כי אקח מועד ܡܛܠ ܕܐܣܒ ܙܒܢܐ ὅταν λάβω καιρόν
ארום אירוע זמנא

7. הרים ܕܛܘܪ̈ܐ ὀρέων מורייא

9. ויגר מזה ܐܪܟܢ ܡܢ ܗܢܐ ܠܗܢܐ καὶ ἔκλινεν ἐκ τούτου
εἰς τοῦτο ~

Psalm lxxvi.

6. אשתוללו אבירי לב ܐܬܕܠܚܘ ܟܠܗܘܢ ܣܟܠܝ ܠܒܐ ἐταράχθησαν πάντες οἱ ἀσύνετοι τῇ καρδίᾳ אשלחו מעלידהון זיני
קרבא ניברי ליבא

7. ורכב וסוס ܪ̈ܟܒܝ ܪ̈ܟܫܐ οἱ ἐπιβεβηκότες τοὺς ἵππους
ופרשין איתעקרו

11. כי חמת אדם תודך ܡܛܠ ܕܬܪܥܝܬܗ ܕܒܪܢܫܐ ܬܘܕܐ ܠܟ
ὅτι ἐνθύμιον ἀνθρώπου ἐξομολογήσεταί σοι כד אנת רגו על
עמך אנת מרוים עליהון והינון יודון לשמך

lxxiv: 19 ܦ and LXX read לתתת נפש תורך.
lxxv: 2 The translators probably read קראנו שמך ספרנו נפלאותיך.
lxxv: 3 מועד may mean either "congregation" or "certain time".
lxxv: 7 הרים is commonly derived from רום; but ܦ, LXX and T make it a pl. noun from הר. ερημων] + ορεων ℵRT.
lxxvi: 6 ܦ and LXX perhaps read אבירי לב.

Psalm lxxvii.

5. אחזת שמרות עיני ܘܐܚܕܘܗܝ ܢܛܘܪ̈ܐ ܒܥܝܢ̈ܝ προκατελάβοντο φυλακάς οἱ ἐχθροί μου אחדתא תימורתייא דעייני

11. חלותי היא שנות ימין עליון ܘܫܘܢܝܐ ܗܢܘ ܕܝܡܝܢܗ ܕܥܠܝܐ αὕτη ἡ ἀλλοίωσις τῆς δεξιᾶς τοῦ ὑψίστου מרעותי היא אישתנין גבורת ימין עילאה

12. אזכיר ܕܐܬܕܟܪܬ ἐμνήσθην אדכר

Psalm lxxviii.

13. נֵד ܙܩ̈ܐ ἀσκόν זיקא

25. אבירים ܡ̈ܠܐܟܐ ἀγγέλων מלאכיא

33. ויכל ܥܒܪܘ ἐξέλιπον ושיצי. ibid. בבהלה ܒܣܘܪܗܒܐܝܬ μετὰ σπουδῆς בבהולתא

36. ויפתוהו ܪܚܡܘܗܝ ἠγάπησαν ושדלינון

41. התוו ܐܪܓܙܘ παρώξυναν תיהוא

42. מני־צר ܡܢ ܐܝܕܐ ܕܐܠܘܨܐ ἐκ χειρὸς θλίβοντος מן מעיקא

48. ומקניהם לרשפים ܘܩܢܝܢܗܘܢ ܠܝܩܕܢܐ καὶ τὴν ὕπαρξιν αὐτῶν τῷ πυρί וניתיהון לרישפין

49. מלאכי רעים ܒܝܕ ܡ̈ܠܐܟܐ ܒܝ̈ܫܐ διὰ ἀγγέλων πονηρῶν דאזגרין בישן

50. וחיתם לדבר ܘܒܥܝܪ̈ܗܘܢ ܠܡܘܬܐ καὶ τὰ κτήνη αὐτῶν εἰς θάνατον ובעירהון למותא

53. לבטח ܒܣܒܪܐ ἐν ἐλπίδι לרוחצן

62. ובנחלתו התעבר ܘܐܣܬܡܒ ܡܢ ܝܪܬܘܬܗ τὴν κληρονομίαν αὐτοῦ ὑπερεῖδεν ובאחסנתיה ארגיז

lxxvii: 11 שנות may be either the pl. of the noun שנה, or infin. of the verb. In the latter case, it might explain the rendering of ܦ and LXX.

lxxvii: 12 ܦ, LXX, T have followed the Kerē.

lxxviii: 53 ܦ and LXX read בבטח.

64. לא תבכינה ܠܐ ܐܬܒܟܝ̈ܝ οὐ κλαυσθήσονται לא ספיקן דתבכון

69. כארץ ܐܝܟ ܐܪܥܐ ἐν τῇ γῇ היך ארעא

70. ממכלאת ܡܢ ܓܘܪܐ ܕܥܢܐ ἐκ τῶν ποιμνίων τῶν προ-
βάτων עדריא דענא

71. הביאו לרעות ܠܡܪܥܝܐ ποιμαίνειν אייתיה למשלט

Psalm lxxix.

10. למה יאמרו ܕܠܐ ܢܐܡܪܘܢ μή ποτε εἴπωσιν למה יימרון.
ibid. נקמת .... יודע ܬܬܝܕܥ .... ܬܒܥܬܐ γνωσθήτω ....
ἡ ἐκδίκησις פורענות .... יתגלי

Psalm lxxx.

2. ישב ܕܝܬܒ ܥܠ ὁ καθήμενος ἐπὶ דשכינתיה

5. עמך ܕܥܒܕܟ τοῦ δούλου σου דעבדך

7. ילעגו למו ܡܝܩܘ ܒܢ ἐμυκτήρισαν ἡμᾶς יתלעבון להון

16. ועל בן ܘܥܠ ܒܪܢܫܐ υἱὸν ἀνθρώπου ועל מלכא משחא

Psalm lxxxi.

6. על ארץ ܡܢ ܐܪܥܐ ἐκ γῆς בכל ארעא. ibid. לא ידעתי אשמע
ܕܠܐ ܝܕܥ ܗܘܐ ܫܡܥ ἔγνω ἤκουσεν דלא חכימית אליפית שמעית

9. ~ ܘܐܡܠܠ καὶ λαλήσω ~

16. יכחשו לו ܕܓܠܘ ܠܗ ἐψεύσαντο αὐτῷ יכדבון ליה

17. ויאכילהו .... אשביעך ܘܐܘܟܠܗ .... ܣܒܥܗ ἐψώμισεν...
ἐχόρτασεν ויאכילניה .... אשבעינך

Psalm lxxxii.

3. דל ויתום ܠܝ̈ܬܡܐ ܘܠܡܣ̈ܟܢܐ ὀρφανὸν καὶ πτωχόν מסכינא ויתמא

lxxviii : 69 An example of the carelessness common to ס and, occasionaly found in LXX; both translators undoubtedly read בארץ.

lxxxi : 6 Pa' and Us^m read ܠܐܪܥܐ.

Psalm lxxxiii.

2. ܡܢܘ ܕܢܕܡܐ ܠܟ τίς ὁμοιωθήσεταί σοι לֹא אֵל־דֳּמִי־לָךְ תִּשְׁתּוֹק לְךָ

Psalm lxxxiv.

6. ܡܣܝܥܢܘܬܗ ܠܗ ἀντίλημψις αὐτοῦ עֹז

7. ܡܢ ܒܝܬ ܕܣܡ εἰς τόπον ὃν ἔθετο מַעְיָן ibid. גַּם־בְּרָכוֹת יַעְטֶה מוֹרֶה ܘܐܦ ܒܘܪܟܬܐ ܢܬܠ ܡܢ ܕܝܗܒ ܒܪܟܬܐ καὶ γὰρ εὐλογίας δώσει ὁ νομοθετῶν בֵּירְכֵן יַעֲמֹד לְדַתִּייבִין לְאוּלְמָן אוֹרָיתֵיהּ

8. ܘܢܬܚܙܐ ܐܠܗܐ ܐܠܗܐ ܕܝܠܗܘܢ ὀφθήσεται ὁ θεὸς τῶν θεῶν יֵרָאֶה אֶל־אֱלֹהִים קָדָם יְהוָה

13. ܡܪܝܐ ܐܠܗܐ יְהוָה Κύριε ὁ θεός

Psalm lxxxvi.

11. ܢܚܕܐ ܠܒܝ εὐφρανθήτω ἡ καρδία μου יַחֵד לְבָבִי יִחַד לְבָבִי

Psalm lxxxvii.

4. ܘܥܡܐ ܕܟܘܫܝܐ καὶ λαὸς Αἰθιόπων עִם כּוּשָׁאֵי עַמְכוּשׁ

7. ܘܕܣܠܘܬܐ ܫܪܝܢ ἀρχόντων שָׁרִים

Psalm lxxxviii.

5. ܕܠܝܬ ܠܗ ܡܥܕܪܢܐ ἀβοήθητος דָּלִית לֵיהּ חֵילָא אוּדְרָאֵיל

lxxxiii: 2 ܦ and LXX derived דמי from דמה, and changed the negative into an interrogative.

lxxxiv: 7 ܦ and LXX differ from the usual rendering; but the readings are not mistakes: ירה signifies "to sprinkle" and "to teach", and ברכות can be pl. of either בְּרָכָה "blessing" or בְּרֵכָה "pool".

lxxxiv: 8 ܦ and LXX read אֶל. Κυριε] + ο θεος ℵ^{c.a}RT.

lxxxvi: 11 ܦ and LXX derived יחד from חדה.

lxxxvii: 4 ܦ and LXX read עַם.

lxxxvii: 7 ܦ and LXX read as if the M.T. were יְשָׁרִים חֹלְלִים וְכָל־מַעְיָנַי בָּךְ.

lxxxviii: 5 Another example of a ܦ word similar to the Hebrew in appearance, but having a different signification.

7. במצלות ܘܒܛܠܠܐ ܕܡܘܬܐ ἐν σκιᾷ θανάτου במטולתא

13. בארץ נשיה ܒܐܪܥܐ ܕܐܬܛܥܝܬ ἐν γῇ ἐπιλελησμένῃ
בארע בהותא ובדיא

16. ונער ܘܒܥܡܠܐ ἐν κόποις ועניד. ibid. נשאתי אמיך אפונה
ܐܬܪܝܡܬ ܘܐܬܡܟܟܬ ܘܬܘܪܬ ὑψωθεὶς δὲ ἐταπεινώθην
καὶ ἐξηπορήθην עלי מעינא דחילתך סוברית

Psalm lxxxix.

11. רהב ܠܡܫܬܒܗܪܢܐ ὑπερήφανον רהבא

44. צור חרבו ולא הקמתו במלחמה ܘܠܐ ܥܘܕܪܢܐ ܕܣܦܣܝܪܗ
ܣܡܟܬܝܗܝ ܒܩܪܒܐ τὴν βοήθειαν τῆς ῥομφαίας αὐτοῦ καὶ
οὐκ ἀντελάβου αὐτοῦ ἐν τῷ πολέμῳ לאחורא סיפיה ולא אקימתא
יתיה בקרבא

Psalm xc.

3. עד־דכא ܒܪܢܫܐ ܠܡܘܟܟܐ εἰς ταπείνωσιν עד מותא

5. שָׁנָה ܫܢܬܐ ἔτη ~

6. ימולל ܝܒܫܐ σκληρυνθείη מתמולל

8. עלמנו ܥܠܡܢ ὁ αἰὼν ἡμῶν טליותנא

9. כמו־הגה ܐܝܟ ܥܢܟܒܐ ܗܓܝ ὡς ἀράχνην היך הבל פומא דסתווא

10. ורהבם ܘܣܘܓܐܗܘܢ καὶ τὸ πλεῖον αὐτῶν וסוגעיהון ibid.
ܡܛܠ ܕܐܬܬ ܥܠܝܢ ܡܟܝܟܘܬܐ ܘܐܬܪܕܝܢ כי גז חיש ונעפה
ὅτι ἐπῆλθον πραΰτης ἐφ' ἡμᾶς καὶ παιδευθησόμεθα ארום עדו
בסרהוביא וטייסין לצפרא

11. וכיראתך ܘܕܚܠܬܐ ܕܪܘܓܙܟ τοῦ φόβου τοῦ θυμοῦ σου
דדחלין מינך משדכין רוגזך

Psalm xci.

2. ומצודתי אלהי ܬܘܩܦܝ ܓܘܣܝ ܐܠܗܐ καταφυγή μου ὁ θεός
μου תוקפי

lxxxviii: 7 𝔖 and LXX read בצלמות.
lxxxviii: 16 Possibly 𝔖 and LXX read נשאתי אָמוֹךְ ואפונה.
xc: 5 𝔖 and LXX read שָׁנָה. The T has a paraphrase.

3, 6. מדבר הוות ܘܡܢ ܡܡܠܠܐ ܕܫܘܓܢܝܬܐ καὶ ἀπὸ λόγου ταραχώδους ממותא ואיתרגישתא

4. צנה וסחרה אמתו ܘܙܝܢܐ ܢܚܕܪܟ ܘܩܘܫܬܗ ὅπλῳ κυκλώσει σε ἡ ἀλήθεια αὐτοῦ תריסא ועגילא הימנותיה

13. על־שחל ܥܠ ܚܘܪܡܐ ἐπ' ἀσπίδα על נור

14. כי בי חשק ܡܛܠ ܕܠܝ ܣܟܐ ὅτι ἐπ' ἐμὲ ἤλπισεν מטול די במימרי

Psalm xcii.

15. ינובון ܢܬܪܒܘܢ πληθυνθήσονται כאבהתהון יעבדון

Psalm xciii.

1. תכון ܘܐܬܩܢܗ ἐστερέωσεν תקיף

Psalm xciv.

19. שרעפי בקרבי ܕܟܐܒ̈ܘܗܝ ܕܠܒܐ τῶν ὀδυνῶν μου ἐν τῇ καρδίᾳ μου מחשבתא בגווי

21. יגודו ܘܨܠܡ θηρεύσουσιν יכנשון

Psalm xcv.

1. לצור ישענו ܠܐܠܗܢ ܦܪܘܩܢܐ τῷ θεῷ τῷ σωτῆρι ἡμῶν קדם תקיף פורקננא

4. ותועפות הרים לו ܘܪܘܡܐ ܕܛܘܪ̈ܐ καὶ τὰ ὕψη τῶν ὀρέων רום טוריא די ליה

11. אשר ܕ- ܐܝܟ ὡς ד

Psalm xcvi.

7. עז ܘܐܝܩܪܐ καὶ τιμήν ועושנא

9. בהדרת־קדש ܒܕܪܬܐ ܕܩܘܕܫܗ ἐν αὐλῇ ἁγίᾳ αὐτοῦ בשבהורת קודשא

10. תכון ܘܐܬܩܢܗ κατώρθωσεν תכין

xci: 3 𝔖 and LXX read מְדַבֵּר; in v. 6, the LXX translate it by πράγματος, while 𝔖 again reads ܡܠܬܐ.

xciv: 21 All the translators seem to have read יגודו.

Psalm xcvii.

7. אלהים ܡܠܐܟܘܗܝ οἱ ἄγγελοι αὐτοῦ עמיא פלחי טעותא

11. זָרֻעַ ܕܢܚ ἀνέτειλεν דנח

Psalm xcviii.

7. ירעם ܢܙܘܥ σαλευθήτω יכלי

Psalm xcix.

1. ישב ܝܬܒ ܥܠ ὁ καθήμενος ἐπὶ די שכינתיה שריא ביני

5—6. קָדוֹשׁ הוּא׃ משה ܩܕܝܫ ܗܘ ܡܘܫܐ ἅγιός ἐστιν Μωυσῆς קדיש הוא׃ משה

Psalm ci.

5. אתו לא אוכל ܥܡܗ ܠܐ ܐܟܠ ܗܘܝܬ τούτῳ οὐ συνήσθιον לא אדור בעלמא

Psalm cii.

9. מהוללי ܡܫܒܚܢܝ οἱ ἐπαινοῦντές με מתלעבי

12. נטוי ܐܬܪܟܢܘ ἐκλίθησαν מולא

24—25. קִצַּר יָמָי׃ אֹמַר אֵלִי ܒܘܨܪܢܐ ܕܝܘܡܝ ܐܡܪ ܠܝ τὴν ὀλιγότητα τῶν ἡμερῶν μου ἀνάγγειλόν μοι איתקצרן יומי׃ אימר קדם אלהי

Psalm ciii.

16. ולא־יכירנו עוד מקומו ܘܠܐ ܡܫܬܘܕܥ ܬܘܒ ܐܬܪܗ καὶ οὐκ ἐπιγνώσεται ἔτι τὸν τόπον αὐτοῦ ולא אישתמודעיה תוב אתריה

xcvii: 11 ס, LXX and T read זרח; for which word the M. T. זרע was probably originally intended. (See Baethgen, *Der textkrit. Werth d. alten Uebersetz. zu d. Ps. J. P. T.* No. 4, 1882, p. 652).

xcviii: 7 For ירעם, the translators read ירעם.

cii: 9 ס and LXX read מְהַלְלַי.

cii: 24 ס and LXX read קֹצֶר יָמַי אֱמֹר אֵלַי.

ciii: 16 (See note in Baethgen, *Der textkrit. Werth d. alt. Uebersetz. zu d. Ps. J. P. T.* 1882, No. 4, p. 653).

Psalm civ.

12. עפאים מבין ܡܼܢ ܒܹܝܬ ܠܛܵܘܼܪܹ̈ܐ ἐκ μέσου τῶν πετρῶν מביני זאזיא

15. פנים להצהיל ܠܡܲܗܵܪܘܼ ܐܲܦܹ̈ܐ τοῦ ἱλαρῦναι πρόσωπον לאנהרא אפיא

20. תרמש ܪܲܚܫܝܼܢ διελεύσονται רחשין

35. הללויה ~ הללויה

Psalm cv.

4. ואוריתיה ܘܐܸܬܥܲܫܲܢܘ κραταιώθητε וָעֻזּוֹ

17. לעבד ܠܥܲܒܼܕܘܼܬܼܵܐ εἰς δουλείαν

21. שמו ~ שדר

22. לאסר ܕܲܢܪܲܕܹܐ τοῦ παιδεῦσαι למסר

27. שמו ܣܲܡ ἔθετο שוו

28. ולא־מרו ܘܐܲܡܪܲܡܪܘ καὶ παρεπίκραναν ולא סריבו

45. הללויה ~ הללויה

Psalm cvi.

1. הללויה ~ הללויה

4. וזכרני ܐܸܬܕܲܟܼܪܲܝܢ μνήσθητι ἡμῶν אדכר לי

15. רזון ܣܲܒܼܥܵܐ πλησμονήν פתגנותא

45. להם ויזכר ܘܐܸܬܕܲܟܲܪ καὶ ἐμνήσθη ודכיר להון

48. הללויה אמן ܐܵܡܹܝܢ ܘܐܵܡܹܝܢ γένοιτο γένοιτο אמן הללויה

civ: 12 D and LXX probably read כיפאים. Although the LXX has πετρων, the sense is the same.

cv: 4 D and LXX read וָעֻזּוֹ.

cv: 17 O´ εἰς δουλείαν; Swete εἰς δοῦλον.

cv: 22 D and LXX mistook אסר for יסר.

cv: 28 D and LXX derived מרו from מרר, and dropped the negative.

cvi: 15 D and LXX read רצון.

cvi: 48 γενοιτο] + γενοιτο AR²T.

Psalm cvii.

4. תעו במדבר בישמון דרך עיר מושב לא מצאו ܛܥܘ ܒܡܕܒܪܐ
ܕܐܝܫܝܡܘܢ ܘܐܘܪܚܐ ܕܡܕܝܢܬܐ ܕܥܡܪܐ ܠܐ ܐܫܟܚܘ
ἐπλανήθησαν ἐν τῇ ἐρήμῳ ἐν ἀνύδρῳ ὁδὸν πόλιν κατοικη-
τηρίου οὐχ εὗρον על עמא דבית ישראל איתגבי ואמר עמא בית
ישראל טעו במדברא בצדי אורחא קרתא דמיתבא לא אשכחו

10. עני ܒܡܣܟܢܘܬܐ ἐν πτωχίᾳ בסיגוף

11. המרו ܡܪܡܪܘ παρεπίκραναν סריבו

12. כשלו ܐܬܟܪܗܘ ἠσθένησαν אתקילו

17. משעם מדרך אולים ܣܥܕ ܐܢܘܢ ܡܢ ܐܘܪܚܐ ܕܥܘܠܗܘܢ
ἀντελάβετο αὐτῶν ἐξ ὁδοῦ ἀνομίας αὐτῶν על חוקיה מלך
שבטא דבית יהודה אתגבי

Psalm cviii.

2. ~ ܡܛܝܒ ܗܘ ܠܒܝ ~ ἑτοίμη ἡ καρδία μου ~

9. מחקקי ܡܠܟܝ βασιλεύς μου ספרי

Psalm cix.

8. פקדתו יקח ܘܣܘܥܪܢܗ ܕܟܠܚܕ ܡܢܗܘܢ καὶ τὴν ἐπισκοπὴν αὐτοῦ
מניין שנוי

20. זאת פעלת ܗܢܘ ܥܒܕܐ τοῦτο τὸ ἔργον דא עובדא

22. חלל ܐܬܕܠܚ τετάρακται שפי

Psalm cx.

2. עזך ܕܚܘܣܢܐ δυνάμεως דעושנך

3. יַלְדֻתֶךָ ܝܠܕܬܟ ἐξεγέννησά σε תולדתך

cvii: 4 In M. T. דרך is connected with בישמון by the accent. Olshausen has suggested לא דרך as the reading of ܦ and LXX.

cvii: 17 Hitzig has suggested as the reading of ܦ and LXX או לחם; and Olshausen חולים, from a root אמל.

cix: 22 ܦ and LXX read יחיל.

cx: 3 ܦ and LXX perhaps read ילדתך.

Psalm cxi.

10. ܥܒܕܝܗܘܢ ܠܒܗܘܢ ܥܫܝܢ ποιοῦσιν αὐτήν

Psalm cxii.

5. ܘܡܚܡܣܢ ܡܠܘ̈ܗܝ ܒܕܝܢܐ ܘܡܟܠܟܠ ܕܒܪ̈ܘܗܝ ܒܡܫܦܐ οἰκονομήσει τοὺς λόγους αὐτοῦ ἐν κρίσει יסובב מילי כהלכתא

Psalm cxiii.

6. ܘܫܘܐ ܠܡܚܙܐ ܡܟܝܟܐ̈ ܠܡܫܦܝܠܝ לראות καὶ τὰ ταπεινὰ ἐφορῶν דממיך עייניה למחמי

9. ܗܠܠܘܝܗ ~ ܗܠܠܘܝܗ .9

Psalm cxiv.

7. ܘܕܚܠܝ ܐܬܪܥܥܬ ܐܪܥܐ חולי ארץ ἐσαλεύθη ἡ γῆ אתחלחלי ארעא

Psalm cxv.

2. ܕܠܐ ܢܐܡܪܘܢ ܥܡ̈ܡܐ למה יאמרו μή ποτε εἴπωσιν למא יימרן

4. ܦܬܟܪ̈ܐ ܕܥܡ̈ܡܐ τὰ εἴδωλα τῶν ἐθνῶν עצביהם מעותהן

9. ܕܒܝܬ ܐܝܣܪܐܝܠ οἶκος Ἰσραήλ ישראל

9, 10, 11. ܡܥܕܪܢܗܘܢ ܘܡܣܬܪܢܗܘܢ עזרם ומגנם βοηθὸς αὐτῶν καὶ ὑπερασπιστής αὐτῶν מעידהן ותריסיהון

ibid. ܐܬܬܟܠܘ ܒܡܪܝܐ ἤλπισαν רחיצו בקחו

16. ܫܡܝܐ ܕܫܡܝܐ השמים השמים ὁ οὐρανὸς τοῦ οὐρανοῦ שמי שמיא

17. ܠܩܒܪܐ εἰς ᾅδου בית קבורת אדמתא דומה

18. ܗܠܠܘܝܗ ~ ܗܠܠܘܝܗ

cxii: 5 M. T. will bear the construction of D and LXX.
cxiv: 7 D and LXX read תזיל.
cxv: 10, 11 According to Baethgen (*J. P. T.* 1882, No. 4, p. 657) D and LXX read בָּטְחוּ.
cxv: 17 D, LXX and T agree as to the sense; and give an explanation of the M. T., rather than a translation.

Psalm cxvi.

1. אהבתי כי־ישמע יהוה את־קולי תחנוני ܪܚܡܬ ܕܢܫܡܥ ܡܪܝܐ ܩܠܐ ܕܒܥܘܬܝ Ἠγάπησα ὅτι εἰσακούσεται ὁ θεὸς τῆς φωνῆς τῆς δεήσεώς μου רחימית ארום ישמע יהוה ית קלי בעותי

6. פתאים ܠܫܒܪܐ τὰ νήπια שרנניא

9. אתהלך לפני יהוה ܕܐܫܬܡܪ ܩܕܡܘܗܝ ܐܠܗܐ אתהלך קדם יהוה

11. בחפזי ܒܬܗܝܠܘܬܝ τῇ ἐκστάσει במערקי

16. כי ~ ~ ארום

19. הללויה ~ ~ הללויה

Psalm cxvii.

2. הללויה ~ ~ הללויה

Psalm cxviii.

6. יהוה לי ܡܪܝܐ ܡܥܕܪܢܝ Κύριος ἐμοὶ βοηθὸς מימרא דיהוה בסעדי

7. יהוה לי בעזרי ܡܪܝܐ ܡܥܕܪܢܝ Κύριος ἐμοὶ βοηθός מימרא דיהוה למסעדא

13. דחה דחיתני לנפל ܐܬܕܚܝܬ ܕܐܬܗܦܟܬ ܘܐܦܠ ὠσθεὶς ἀνετράπην τοῦ πεσεῖν מדחי דחיית יתי למנפל

16. רוממה ܐܪܝܡܬܢܝ ὕψωσέν με מרממא

Psalm cxix.

9. לשמר כדברך ܕܢܛܪ ܦܬܓܡܝܟ φυλάσσεσθαι τοὺς λόγους σου למיטר היך דברייך

16. אשתעשע ܪܢܝܬ μελετήσω איתפרנק

24. שעשעי ܪܢܝܬ μελέτη פרנוקי

cxviii: 16 ܦ and LXX read רוממני.
cxix: 9 ܦ and LXX read דבריך.
cxix: 16 ܦ and LXX read אשיחה (Oppenheim, *Die Syr. Uebersetz. des fünft. Buches der Ps.* p. 20).

29. דרך שקר ܐܘܪܚܐ ܕܥܘܠܐ ὁδὸν ἀδικίας אורח דשקרא

34, 145, 69, 58. בכל־לב ܡܢ ܟܠܗ ܠܒܝ ἐν ὅλῃ καρδίᾳ μου בכל לבא

47. ואשתעשע ܘܐܬܪܢܐ ἐμελέτων ואתפרנק

49. דבר ܡܠܬܟ τὸν λόγον σου פתגמא

61. חבלי רשעים עודני ܚ̈ܒܠܐ ܕܥܘ̈ܠܐ ܚܕܪܘܢܝ σχοινία ἁμαρτωλῶν περιεπλάκησάν μοι סיעת רשיעיא אתכנשו

66. טוב טעם ܠܒܣܝܡܐ ܘܠܝܕܥܬܐ χρηστότητα καὶ παιδίαν שפיר טעם

67. ועתה אמרתך שמרתי ܘܡܐܡܪܟ ܢܛܪܬ τὸ λόγιόν σου ἐγὼ ἐφύλαξα מימרך נטרית

68. אתה ܐܢܬ ܡܪܝܐ εἶ σύ Κύριε את

69. טפלו עלי שקר זדים ܣܓܝ ܥܠܝ ܥܘܠܐ ܕܡܫܬܒܗܪ̈ܢܐ ἐπληθύνθη ἐπ' ἐμὲ ἀδικία ὑπερηφάνων חברו עלי שקרא זידונין

70. טפש כַּחֵלֶב ܐܬܥܒܝ ܠܒܗܘܢ ܐܝܟ ܚܠܒܐ ἐτυρώθη ὡς γάλα ἡ καρδία αὐτῶν אטפש היך תרב

83. בקיטור ܒܓܠܝܕܐ ἐν πάχνῃ בקטרא

84. תעשה ܥܒܕ ܐܢܬ ܠܝ ποιήσεις μοι תעביד

96. לכל־תכלה ܣܘܦܐ ܚܙܝܬ πάσης συντελείας לכל מה דאשתרי

109. בכפי ܒܐܝ̈ܕܝܟ ἐν ταῖς χερσίν σου ידי

113. סעפים ܠܥܘ̈ܠܐ παρανόμους דחשבין

114. ומגני ܣܬܪܝ ܐܢܬ ܘܡܣܟܝ ἀντιλήμπτωρ μου ותריסי

118. כי־שקר תרמיתם ܕܥܘܠܐ ܗܘ ܪܥܝܢܗܘܢ ὅτι ἄδικον τὸ ἐνθύμημα αὐτῶν ארום שקרא נכלהון

119. ~ ܒܟܠܙܒܢ διὰ παντός ~

127. ומפז ܡܢ ܕܗܒܐ ܘܛܘܦܐܙܝܢ καὶ τοπάζιον ומן אובריזא

cxix : 29 D and LXX also read ובתורתך for ותורתך.

cxix : 109 D and LXX read בכפיך. χερσι] χερσιν σου ℵ[ca] RT, χερσιν μου A. cxix : 118 D and LXX read תרעיתם.

cxix : 127 cf. Ps. xix : 11 ; xxi : 4.

130. פתיים ܠܫܒܪ̈ܐ νηπίους שרניני

131. ואשאפה ܘܡܫܟܬ ܪܘܚܐ ἥλκυσα πνεῦμα ואלפית

150. רדפי זמה ܪ̈ܕܘܦܝ ܥܘܠܐ οἱ καταδιώκοντές με ἀνομίᾳ רֹדְפַי זנו

163. שקר ܥܘܠܐ ἀδικίαν שקרא

Psalm cxx.

2. משפת־שקר ܡܣܦܘܬܐ ܕܥ̈ܘܠܐ χειλέων ἀδίκων מספיותא דשקרא

5. כי־גרתי מֶשֶׁךְ ܕܬܘܬܒܘܬܝ ܐܪܝܟܬ ὅτι ἡ παροικία μου ἐμακρύνθη ארום איתותבית עם אונאי

7. המה למלחמה ܗܢܘܢ ܡܬܟܬܫܝܢ ܗܘܘ ܡܓܢ ἐπολέμουν με δωρεάν הינון לקרבא

Psalm cxxii.

7. בחילך ܒܚܝܠܟܝ ἐν τῇ δυνάμει σου בחילך

Psalm cxxiv.

7. יוקשים ܕܨܝ̈ܕܐ τῶν θηρευόντων תקליא

Psalm cxxvi.

1. כחלמים ܐܝܟ ܗܢܘܢ ܕܒܝܐܝܢ ὡς παρακεκλημένοι היך מרעיא דאיתסיין

6. משך־הזרע ܙܪ̈ܥܐ τὰ σπέρματα נגדא דבר זרעא

Psalm cxxvii.

3. שכר פרי הבטן ܐܓܪ̈ܐ ܕܦܐܪ̈ܐ ܕܡܥ̈ܘܒܐ ὁ μισθὸς τοῦ καρποῦ τῆς γαστρὸς αὐτῆς כשרין אגר עובדין מבין ולדי מעא

cxix: 150 פ and LXX read רֹדְפַי (see Oppenheim, *Die Syr. Uebers. des fünft. Buches d. Ps.* p. 29).

cxx: 5 פ and LXX seem to have read מָשַׁךְ; thus making גרתי a substantive. (Oliver, *Trans. of the Syr. Ps.* p. 281).

cxxvii: 3 The unpointed M. T. might be rendred as פ and LXX.

Psalm cxxix.

3. הָאֱרִיכוּ לְמַעֲנִיתָם ܘܐܪܟܼܘ ܚܒܼܠܗܘܢ ἐμάκρυναν τὴν ἀνομίαν αὐτῶν אוֹרִיכוּ לְמוֹרְדוּתְהוֹן

7. מְעַמֵּר ܡܥܡܪ ܚܒܼܠܐ ὁ τὰ δράγματα συλλέγων

Psalm cxxx.

5. וּלְאִקָרֵיהּ אוֹרִיכֵית ~ ~ וְלִדְבָרוֹ הוֹחָלְתִּי
6. ܡܣܟܝܐ ܠܡܪܝܐ ܡܢ נַפְשִׁי לַאדֹנָי מִשֹּׁמְרִים לַבֹּקֶר שֹׁמְרִים לַבֹּקֶר ܡܛܪܬܐ ܕܨܦܪܐ ܥܕܡܐ ܕܨܦܪܐ ἤλπισεν ἡ ψυχή μου ἐπὶ τὸν κύριον ἀπὸ φυλακῆς πρωίας μέχρι νυκτός נַפְשִׁי אוֹרִיכָא לֵיהֹוָה מִן נְמוֹרֵי מַטְרַת לְצַפְרָא דְּנַמְרִין לְקַרְבָא קֻרְבַּן צַפְרָא

Psalm cxxxi.

1. לֹא גָבַהּ חֶשּׁוּשׁ οὐχ ܐܬܬܪܝܡ ܠܒܝ לֹא אַתְנַבַּהּ

Psalm cxxxii.

2, 5. לַתַּקִּיפָא ܠܐܠܗܐ לַאֲבִיר τῷ θεῷ
17. אַצְמַח ܐܢܗܪ אַצְמִיחַ ἐξανατελῶ
18. כְּלִילֵיהּ ܢܗܪܗ נִזְרוֹ τὸ ἁγίασμά μου

Psalm cxxxiii.

2. כְּמִשְׁחָא טָב ܡܫܚܐ ܛܒܐ ὡς μύρον כַּשֶּׁמֶן הַטּוֹב

Psalm cxxxiv.

2. קוּדְשָׁא ܠܡܩܕܫܐ εἰς τὰ ἅγια קֹדֶשׁ

Psalm cxxxv.

14. וְעַל־עַבְדַּוְהִי יִתְנַחַם ܡܪܚܡ ܥܠ ܥܒܕܘܗܝ καὶ ἐπὶ τοῖς δούλοις αὐτοῦ παρακληθήσεται וְעַל עַבְדֵי צַדִּיקַיָּא יְתוּב בְּרַחֲמֵי
21. הַלְלוּיָה ~ ~ הַלְלוּיָה

cxxix : 3 ܦ and LXX read עֲנוֹתָם.
cxxxii : 2 ܦ and LXX read לַאדִיר.

9

Psalm cxxxvi.

12. ܡܪܡܐ ὑψηλῷ ܘܕܪܥܐ נטויה

Psalm cxxxvii.

3. ܕܒܝܐ ܘܫܒܝܢ oἱ ἀπαγαγόντες ותוללינו

Psalm cxxxviii.

2. על כל שמך ܥܠ ܟܠ ܥܡ ἐπὶ πᾶν ὄνομα על־כל־שמך

Psalm cxxxix.

4. ממלל ܥܘܠܐ מלה λόγος ἄδικος

4—5. ܥܒܕ ܐܢܐ ܟܠܡܕܡ ܕܥܕ ܡܓܕܡ ידעת כלה: אחור וקדם
ܕܝܠܟ σὺ ἔγνως πάντα τὰ ἔσχατα καὶ τὰ ἀρχαῖα ירעת
מחשבת לבי כולא: מאחוראי ומאפי

6. נשגבה ܐܫܬܥܠܝܬ ἐκραταιώθη איתקפת

8. ואימך ܘܐܢ ܐܚܘܬ ἐὰν καταβῶ ܘܐܦ ܐܢ ܐܨܥܗ

13. כי־אתה קנית כליתי תסכני בבטן אמי ܡܬܠܝܢ ܡܢ ܕܒܝܐ ἀντελάβου
אשתית לי בכריסא דאמי ἐκ γαστρὸς μητρός μου

15. נעצמי ܓܪܡܝ τὸ ὀστοῦν μου

ibid. אשר־עשיתי ܕܥܒܕܬ ὃ ἐποίησας די אתעבידת

16. גלמי ראו עיניך ועל־ספרך כלם יכתבו ימים יצרו ולא אחד בהם
ܓܘܫܡܝ ܚܙܝ ܥܝܢܝܟ ܘܥܠ ܣܦܪ ܕܒܪܢܟ ܟܠܗܘܢ ܝܘܡܝ ܡܬܟܬܒܝܢ ܘܐܦ ܠܐ ܚܕ ܡܢܗܘܢ
τὸ ἀκατέργαστόν
σου εἴδοσαν οἱ ὀφθαλμοί μου καὶ ἐπὶ τὸ βιβλίον σου πάντες
γραφήσονται ἡμέρας πλασθήσονται καὶ οὐδεὶς ἐν αὐτοῖς
גושמי חמיין עיניך ועל ספר דברנך כולהון יומי מכתבן ביומא דאתברי
עלמא מן שירויא איתבריין כולהון ביריתא ולית בחד חד ביניהון

cxxxix: 4 Symmachus translates οὐκ ἔστιν ἐν ἐμοὶ ἑτερολογία.
cxxxix: 15 ⅅ and LXX read אשר־עשיתָ.
cxxxix: 16 ⅅ and LXX possibly read גמולי for גלמי. The verb יצר may mean either "to create" or "to shorten".

17. ראשהם עצמו מה אל רעיך מה־יקרו ולי ܠܝ ܕܝܢ ܛܒ ܝܩܪܘ
ܪ̈ܚܡܝܟ ܐܠܗܐ ܘܛܒ ܚܣܢܘ ܘܫܠܝ̈ܛܢܝܗܘܢ ἐμοὶ δὲ λίαν
ἐτιμήθησαν οἱ φίλοι σου ὁ θεὸς λίαν ἐκραταιώθησαν αἱ
ἀρχαὶ αὐτῶν ולי כמה יקירין רחמיך צדיקיא אלהא איתחיילו רבניהון
20. ܡܛܠ ܕܡܠܠܟ ܘܢܣܒܘ אשר ימרוך למזמה נשוא לשוא עריך
ܠܣܪܝܩܘܬܐ ܡܕ̈ܝܢܬܟ ὅτι ἐρεῖς εἰς διαλογισμὸν λήμψον-
ται εἰς ματαιότητα τὰς πόλεις σου די יימון בשמך על ניכלא
משתבעין על מגן בעלי דבבך
23. ܫܒ̈ܝܠܝ שרעפי τὰς τρίβους μου הירהורי

Psalm cxli.

1. ܐܨܬ ܒܥܓܠ חושה לי εἰσάκουσόν με חיש לי
4. ܐܬܡܠܟܘܢ אלחם συνδοιάσω אסעוד
5. יהלמני צדיק חסד ויוכיחני שמן ראש אל־יני ראש כי עוד ותפלתי
ܢܠܦܢܝ ܙܕܝܩܐ ܘܢܟܣܢܝ ܡܫܚܐ ܕܚ̈ܛܝܐ ܠܪܫܝ ברעותיהם
ܠܐ ܢܕܗܢ παιδεύσει με δίκαιος ἐν ἐλέει καὶ ἐλέγξει με
ἔλαιον δὲ ἁμαρτωλοῦ μὴ λιπανάτω τὴν κεφαλήν μου ימסחינני
צדיקא מטול חסדא ויכסינני משח רבות קודשא לא יבטל מן רישי ארום
עד כדון צלותי מסתדרא בבישתהון
7. ܐܝܟ ܦܠܚܐ ܕܒܙܥܐ ܐܪܥܐ כמו פלח ובקע בארץ ὡσεὶ
πάχος γῆς διερράγη ἐπὶ τῆς γῆς די כמתגבר דפלח וסבוע
במרדיא בארעא

cxxxix: 20 עריך may mean "thine enemies" or "thy cities".

cxli: 4 ܦ and LXX read יחלמני. It has been conjectured however that the reading of the syriac should be ܐܬܠܚܡ (Oliver, *Trans. of the Syr. Ps.* p. 311). συνδοιασω | συνδυασω ℵ^{ca} A^{a} (?R). T] ενδυασω ℵ*.

cxli: 5 ܦ and LXX read שמךרשע. The resemblance between the ܦ and LXX is very marked. By some translators the ܦ is made interrogative. (Oliver, *Trans. of the Syr. Ps.* p. 319).

Psalm cxliii.

3. דכא ܘܡܟܟ ἐταπείνωσεν דכייך
4. ישתומם ܘܙܥ ἐταράχθη ישתעמם
8. ~ ܡܪܝܐ Κύριε ~

Psalm cxliv.

9. אזמרה־לך עשור בנבל ܘܒܟܢܪܐ ܕܥܣܪ ܡܢ̈ܝܢ ἐν ψαλτηρίῳ
δεκαχόρδῳ בנבלא עסרתי
12. 13. 14. אשר בנינו כנטעים מגדלים בנעוריהם בנותינו כזוית מחטבות
תבנית היכל: מזוינו מלאים מפיקים מזן אל זן צאננו מאליפות מרבבות
בחוצותינו: אלופינו מסבלים אין פרץ ואין יוצאת ואין צוחה ברחבתינו
ܒܢ̈ܝܗܘܢ ܐܝܟ ܢܨܒܬܐ ܡܫܬܪ̈ܪܝܢ ܡܢ ܛܠܝܘܬܗܘܢ
ܘܒܢ̈ܬܗܘܢ ܐܝܟ ܟܠ̈ܠܬܐ ܕܡܨܒ̈ܬܢ ܒܕܡܘܬܐ ܕܗܝܟܠܐ
ܬܘ̈ܣܝܗܘܢ ܡܠܝܢ ܘܡܬܐܣܦܝܢ ܙܢ ܠܙܢ ܥܢ̈ܗܘܢ ܡܠ̈ܕܢ
ܘܡܪ̈ܒܝܢ ܒܫܘܩ̈ܝܗܘܢ ܒܡܪ̈ܥܝܗܘܢ ܒܥܢ̈ܝܢ ܘܠܝܬ ܒܗܘܢ
ܕܒܩܪ̈ܐ ܠܝܬ ܬܘܪܥܬܐ ܐܦܠܐ ܠܠܬܐ ܒܫܘܩ̈ܝܗܘܢ
ὧν οἱ υἱοὶ ὡς νεόφυτα ἡδρυμμένα ἐν τῇ νηότητι αὐτῶν
αἱ θυγατέρες αὐτῶν κεκαλλωπισμέναι περικεκοσμημέναι
ὁμοίωμα ναοῦ τὰ ταμεῖα αὐτῶν πλήρη ἐξερευγόμενα ἐκ
τούτου εἰς τοῦτο τὰ πρόβατα αὐτῶν πολύτοκα πληθύνοντα
ἐν ταῖς ἐξόδοις αὐτῶν οἱ βόες αὐτῶν παχεῖς οὐκ ἔστιν
κατάπτωμα φραγμοῦ οὐδὲ διέξοδος οὐδὲ κραυγὴ ἐν ταῖς
ἐπαύλεσιν αὐτῶν דבננא כנציבין דדקלין באולפן אוריתא רביין מן.
טליותהון בנתנא זוותגין וכשרין לכהניא דמשמשין במצע היכלא:
תוסברינא מליין מספקן מן שתא לשתא ענגא מילדן אלפיא מפשן ריבבותא
באשקקנא: תורינא מרי מטול לית תקוף ולא מפקא בישא ולית צווחת
בכייתא בפלטיתנא

Psalm cxlv.

4. וגבורתיך ܘܓܢܒܪܘܬܟ τὴν δύναμίν σου וגבורתך
5. אשיחה ܢܫܬܥܘܢ λαλήσουσιν ישתעון
12. גבורתיו ܓܢܒܪܘܬܟ τὴν δυναστείαν σου גבורתי

12. מלכותו ܕܡܠܟܘܬܟ τῆς βασιλείας σου מלכתיה

14. ~ ܡܗܝܡܢ ܗܘ ܡܪܝܐ ܒܡܠܘܗܝ. ܘܙܕܝܩ ܒܟܠܗܘܢ ~
ܥܒܕܘܗܝ. πιστὸς Κύριος ἐν τοῖς λόγοις αὐτοῦ καὶ ὅσιος ἐν πᾶσι τοῖς ἔργοις αὐτοῦ ~

Psalm cxlvi.

10. הללויה ~ ~ הללויה

Psalm cxlvii.

16. כפור ܥܪܦܠܐ ὁμίχλην גליד

20. בל־ידעום ܠܐ ܚܘܝ ܐܢܘܢ οὐκ ἐδήλωσεν αὐτοῖς לא הודעינון

ibid. הללויה ~ ~ הללויה

Psalm cxlviii.

3. כוכבי אור ܟܘܟܒܐ ܘܢܘܗܪܐ τὰ ἄστρα καὶ τὸ φῶς כוכבי נהרא

5. ~ ܡܛܠ ܕܗܘ ܐܡܪ ܘܗܘܘ ܦܩܕ ܘܐܬܒܪܝܘ ὅτι αὐτὸς εἶπεν καὶ ἐγενήθησαν αὐτὸς ἐνετείλατο καὶ ἐκτίσθησαν ~

8. קיטור ܓܠܝܕܐ κρύσταλλος קטרא

13. הללויה ~ ~ שבחו ית יהוה

Psalm cxlix.

9. הללויה ~ ~ הללויה

cxlv : 14 This reading is not in M. T. If translated, it would be נאמן יהוה בכל דבריו וחסיד בכל מעשיו (see Baethgen, *J. P. T.* 1892, No. iv, p. 667).

cxlviii : 5 Perhaps repeated from Ps. xxxiii : 9.

cxlviii : 10 ܣ and LXX read יצפור.

§ 4. *Summary of Part II—The internal evidence of a LXX influence upon the Pˤšittâ Psalter*

A. The relation of the Pˤšittâ to the Massoretic text.

While it is not perfectly obvious what was the original text of every book in the Syriac canon,[1] there can be no doubt that the basis of the Syriac Psalter was the Massoretic text. This is evident, not from the division of the Psalms themselves, which follows neither the Massoretic text nor the Septuagint, but from the faithfulness of the Syriac to the Hebrew not only in general, but in particular instances, where extreme divergences in the Greek would have necessitated corresponding variants in the Pˤšittâ had the LXX been the basis of the translation. Thus, ψ v: 10 and xiv: 3 are found in all the Greek Mss. but in none of the Syriac. The Syriac translator would, also, have unwittingly incorporated many of the smaller additions found in that version, had he been translating from the Septuagint text.[2] That the Targum could have been the basis, or even the medium[3], between the Greek and the Syriac versions, is still more impossible. Traces of Aramaic influence are easily discernible in the Pˤšittâ[4], but they extend no further than to the interpretation of words, seldom of sentences.

[1] Cf. Dathe's reply to Semler in *Psalterium Syriacum*, praef. p. xi seq.; also Tregelles, *Biblical Dictionary* in loco and W. R. Smith, *Encyc. Brit.* in loco. G. H. Gwilliam, *The Materials for the Criticism of the Pesh. N. T. Studia Biblica* vol. iii, p. 48.

[2] xvii: 21; xxiii: 4; xxxii: 10; lxx: 8; lxxxii: 2; lxxxix: 11; cvii: 2; cxviii: 104; cxxxi: 4 et al.

[3] Buhl, *Canon and Text of the O. T.* p. 190. Gwilliam, *The Materials for the Crit. of the Pesh. N. T. Stud. Bib.* iii, 48.

[4] Baethgen, *Der textkrit. Werth d. alten Uebersets. zu d. Ps. J. P. T.* 1882, No. 3, p. 433 seq. and *Untersuchungen über die Psalmen nach der Pesch.* p. 25.

B. The relation of the Pešiṭtâ to the LXX

That the Septuagint played an important part in the work of translating the Syriac Psalter, can no longer be denied. An examination of the preceding variants reveals the fact, that of 450 Greek and Syriac variants from the Massoretic text only 31 [1], agreeing with the Targum, can possibly be ascribed to Aramaic influence. If the reading of some of the other Syriac Mss. be substituted for the text of Lee, twenty-five or thirty more variants may be added agreeing with the Septuagint against both Targum and Massoretic text.[2] This Septuagint influence displays itself in two ways:

1) in the interpretation of words and
2) in the translation of sentences.

A few illustrations will suffice to make both these uses clear.

1) ψ viii: 2 [עז] ܬܫܒܘܚܬܐ αἶνον; ψ xv: 3 [לרעהו] ܠܩܪܝܒܗ τῷ πλησίον αὐτοῦ; ψ xviii: 26 [עם־גבר] ܥܡ ܓܒܝܐ μετὰ ἐκλεκτοῦ; ψ xx: 8 [נזכיר] ܢܬܪܘܪܒ μεγαλυνθησόμεθα; ψ xxii: 1 [שאגתי] ܣܟܠܘܬܝ τῶν παραπτωμάτων μου; ψ xxxiii: 7 [כנד] ܐܝܟ ܙܩܐ ὡσεὶ ἀσκόν; ψ xlvi: 4 [בגאותו] ܒܚܣܢܗ ἐν τῇ κραταιότητι αὐτοῦ; V. 7 [תמוג] ܘܐܬܬܙܝܥܬ ἐσαλεύθη; ψ lxviii: 6 [צחיחה] ܒܩܒܪܐ ἐν τάφοις; ψ lxviii: 28 [רגמתם] ܘܫܠܝܛܢܝܗܘܢ ἡγεμόνες αὐτῶν; ψ lxxviii: 33 [כבהלה] ܒܣܪܗܒܘܬܐ μετὰ σπουδῆς; ψ lxxxvi: 11 [יחד] ܢܚܕܐ εὐφρανθήτω; ψ xciv: 19 [בקרבי] ܒܠܒܝ ἐν τῇ καρδίᾳ μου;

---

[1] v. 10; vii: 7; xi: 1; xviii: 18; xix: 8; xxii: 14; xxiii: 6; xxvii: 2; xxxiii: 7; xliv: 27; li: 9; lv: 12; lix: 10; lxvi: 12; lxxi: 20; lxxviii: 72; lxxix: 7; xc: 10; xcvii: 11; cv: 22; cvi: 3; cxv: 16; cxviii: 14; V. 15; cxix: 9, 17; ci: 16, 42, 103; cxxxix: 17; cxl: 12.

[2] Ch. iv, § 2, p. 69—95.

ψ xcviii:7 ירעם] ܢܙܘܥ σαλευθήτω; ψ cv:22 לאסר] ܕܢܪܕܐ τοῦ παιδεῦσαι; ψ cvi:15 רזון] ܣܒܥܬܐ πλησμονήν; ψ cxvi:6 פתאים] ܠܛܠܝ̈ܐ τὰ νήπια; ψ cxix:131 ואשאפה] ܘܡܫܟܬ ܪܘܚܐ καὶ ἥλκυσα πνεῦμα; ψ cxxxii:17 אצמיח] ܐܕܢܚ ἐξανατελῶ.

2) Just as frequently is LXX influence observable in the rendering of phrases and sentences. A few instances are ψ ix:7 האויב תמו חרבות לנצח] ܕܒܥܠܕܒ̈ܒܐ ܚܣܪ ܣܝܦܐ ܠܥܠܡ τοῦ ἐχθροῦ ἐξέλιπον αἱ ῥομφαῖαι εἰς τέλος; ψ xxx:8 העמדתה להררי עז] ܐܘܣܦܬ ܥܠ ܫܘܦܪܝ ܚܝܠܐ παράσχου τῷ κάλλει μου δύναμιν; ψ liii:6 כי־אלהים פזר עצמות חנך הבישתה] ܡܛܠ ܕܐܠܗܐ ܒܕܪ ܓܪ̈ܡܝܗܘܢ ܕܐܝܠܝܢ ܕܫܦܪܝܢ ܠܒܢܝ̈ܢܫܐ ܒܗܬܘ ὁ θεὸς διεσκόρπισεν ὀστᾶ ἀνθρωπαρέσκων; ψ lvii:5 נפשי בתוך לבאם אשכבה להטים] ܘܦܪܩܗ ܢܦܫܝ ܡܢ ܒܝܬ̈ ܕܕܡܟܒܬ ܟܕ ܕܠܝܚ ܐܢܐ καὶ ἐρύσατο τὴν ψυχήν μου ἐκ μέσου σκύμνων ἐκοιμήθη τεταραγμένος; ψ lxxviii:48 ומקניהם לרשפים] ܘܩܢܝܢܗܘܢ ܠܢܘܪ̈ܐ καὶ τὴν ὕπαρξιν αὐτῶν τῷ πυρί; ψ cvii:17 אולים מדרך פשעם] ܥܕܪ ܐܢܘܢ ܐܘܪܚܐ ܕܥܘ̈ܠܗܘܢ ἀντελάβετο αὐτῶν ἐξ ὁδοῦ ἀνομίας αὐτῶν; ψ cxxxix:4 כי אין מלה בלשוני] ܐܢ ܐܝܬ ܥܘܠܬܐ ܒܠܫܢܝ ὅτι οὐκ ἔστιν λόγος ἄδικος ἐν γλώσσῃ μου. Symmachus reads, more in accord with the Syriac, οὐκ ἔστιν ἐν ἐμοὶ ἑτερολογία.

APPENDIX I

QUOTATIONS IN THE SYRIAC NEW TESTAMENT FROM THE PᴇŠIṬṬÂ OLD TESTAMENT[1]

Math. xii: 19. 20;[2] *Is.* xlii: 3. 4.

P. ܠܐ ܢܬܚܪܐ ܘܠܐ ܢܙܥܩ ܘܠܐ ܐܢܫ ܢܫܡܥ ܒܫܘܩܐ ܩܠܗ
ܩܢܝܐ ܪܥܝܥܐ ܠܐ ܢܬܒܪ ܘܫܪܓܐ ܕܕܥܝܟ ܠܐ ܢܕܥܟ
ܥܕܡܐ ܕܢܦܩ ܕܝܢܐ.

H. לא יצעק ולא ישא ולא־ישמיע בחוץ קולו קנה רצוץ לא ישבור
ופשתה כהה לא יכבנה לאמת יוציא משפט:

LXX. Οὐ κράξεται οὐδὲ ἀνήσει οὐδὲ ἀκουσθήσεται ἔξω
ἡ φωνὴ αὐτοῦ. Κάλαμον συντεθλασμένον οὐ συντρίψει καὶ
λίνον καπνιζόμενον οὐ σβέσει ἀλλὰ εἰς ἀλήθειαν ἐξοίσει
κρίσιν.

[1] cf. Prager, *De Veteris Testamenti Versione Syriaca quam Peschitto vocant, quaestiones criticae* p. 69.

[2] The order followed is 1. Pᵉšiṭṭâ O. T. (P); 2. Massoretic Text (H); 3. Septuagint (LXX); 4. Pᵉšiṭṭâ N. T. (S); 5. Greek New Testament (G). The text used for the Syriac N. T. is the edition of Samuel Bagster (ܟܬܒܐ ܕܕܝܬܩܐ) London 1829. The Septuagint and Greek N. T. have been added, since it is of importance as well as of interest to note, that while in the passages cited, the Syriac N. T. does not always quote the Pᵉšiṭṭâ verbatim, yet it does so with sufficient accuracy to place its source beyond doubt.

S. ܠܐ ܢܬܚܪܐ ܘܠܐ ܢܩܥܐ ܘܠܐ ܐܢܫ ܢܫܡܥ ܒܫܘܩܐ ܩܠܗ܂ ܩܢܝܐ ܪܥܝܥܐ ܠܐ ܢܬܒܪ ܘܫܪܓܐ ܕܡܛܦܛܦ ܠܐ ܢܕܥܟ܂ ܥܕܡܐ ܕܢܦܩ ܕܝܢܐ ܠܙܟܘܬܐ܂

G. Οὐκ ἐρίσει οὐδὲ κραυγάσει οὐδὲ ἀκούσει τις ἐν ταῖς πλατείαις τὴν φωνὴν αὐτοῦ, κάλαμον συντετριμμένον οὐ κατεάξει καὶ λίνον τυφόμενον οὐ σβέσει ἕως ἂν ἐκβάλῃ εἰς νῖκος τὴν κρίσιν καὶ τῷ ὀνόματι αὐτοῦ ἔθνη ἐλπιοῦσιν.

Math. xiii: 14. 15; *Is.* vi: 9. 10.

P. ܘܠܐ ܬܣܬܟܠܘܢ ܘܬܚܙܘܢ ܘܠܐ ܬܕܥܘܢ܂ ܐܥܒܝ ܓܝܪ ܠܒܗ ܕܥܡܐ ܗܢܐ ܘܒܐܕܢܘܗܝ ܝܩܝܪܐܝܬ ܫܡܥ ܘܥܝܢܘܗܝ ܥܡܨ ܕܠܐ ܢܚܙܐ ܒܥܝܢܘܗܝ ܘܢܫܡܥ ܒܐܕܢܘܗܝ ܘܢܣܬܟܠ ܒܠܒܗ ܘܢܬܘܒ ܘܐܣܐ ܠܗ܂

H. שִׁמְעוּ שָׁמוֹעַ וְאַל־תָּבִינוּ וּרְאוּ רָאוֹ וְאַל־תֵּדָעוּ הַשְׁמֵן לֵב־הָעָם הַזֶּה וְאָזְנָיו הַכְבֵּד וְעֵינָיו הָשַׁע פֶּן־יִרְאֶה בְעֵינָיו וּבְאָזְנָיו יִשְׁמָע וּלְבָבוֹ יָבִין וָשָׁב וְרָפָא לוֹ׃

LXX. Ἀκοῇ ἀκούσετε καὶ οὐ μὴ συνῆτε καὶ βλέποντες βλέψετε καὶ οὐ μὴ ἴδητε ἐπαχύνθη γὰρ ἡ καρδία τοῦ λαοῦ τούτου καὶ τοῖς ὠσὶν αὐτῶν βαρέως ἤκουσαν καὶ τοὺς ὀφθαλμοὺς αὐτῶν ἐκάμμυσαν μήποτε ἴδωσιν τοῖς ὀφθαλμοῖς καὶ τοῖς ὠσὶν ἀκούσωσιν καὶ τῇ καρδίᾳ συνῶσιν καὶ ἐπιστρέψωσιν καὶ ἰάσομαι αὐτούς.

S. ܕܬܫܡܥܘܢ ܘܠܐ ܬܣܬܟܠܘܢ ܘܬܚܙܘܢ ܘܠܐ ܬܕܥܘܢ܂ ܐܬܥܒܝ ܓܝܪ ܠܗ ܕܥܡܐ ܗܢܐ ܘܒܐܕܢܝܗܘܢ ܝܩܝܪܐܝܬ ܫܡܥܘ ܘܥܝܢܝܗܘܢ ܥܡܨܘ ܕܠܐ ܢܚܙܘܢ ܒܥܝܢܝܗܘܢ ܘܢܫܡܥܘܢ ܒܐܕܢܝܗܘܢ ܘܢܣܬܟܠܘܢ ܒܠܒܗܘܢ ܘܢܬܘܒܘܢ ܘܐܣܐ ܐܢܘܢ܂

G. Ἀκοῇ ἀκούσετε καὶ οὐ μὴ συνῆτε καὶ βλέποντες βλέψετε καὶ οὐ μὴ ἴδητε ἐπαχύνθη γὰρ ἡ καρδία τοῦ λαοῦ τούτου καὶ τοῖς ὠσὶν βαρέως ἤκουσαν καὶ τοὺς ὀφθαλμοὺς αὐτῶν ἐκάμμυσαν μήποτε ἴδωσιν τοῖς ὀφθαλμοῖς καὶ τοῖς ὠσὶν

ἀκούσωσιν καὶ τῇ καρδίᾳ συνῶσιν καὶ ἐπιστρέψωσιν καὶ
ἰάσομαι αὐτούς.

Math. xix: 5; *Gen.* ii: 24.

P. ܡܛܠ ܗܢܐ ܢܫܒܘܩ ܓܒܪܐ ܠܐܒܘܗܝ ܘܠܐܡܗ
ܘܢܩܦ ܠܐܢܬܬܗ ܘܢܗܘܘܢ ܬܪܝܗܘܢ ܚܕ ܒܣܪ.

H. עַל־כֵּן יַעֲזָב־אִישׁ אֶת־אָבִיו וְאֶת־אִמּוֹ וְדָבַק בְּאִשְׁתּוֹ וְהָיוּ לְבָשָׂר אֶחָד:

LXX. Ἕνεκεν τούτου καταλείψει ἄνθρωπος τὸν πατέρα
αὐτοῦ καὶ τὴν μητέρα αὐτοῦ καὶ προσκολληθήσεται πρὸς
τὴν γυναῖκα αὐτοῦ καὶ ἔσονται οἱ δύο εἰς σάρκα μίαν.

S. ܡܛܠ ܗܢܐ ܢܫܒܘܩ ܓܒܪܐ ܠܐܒܘܗܝ ܘܠܐܡܗ
ܘܢܩܦ ܠܐܢܬܬܗ ܘܢܗܘܘܢ ܬܪܝܗܘܢ ܚܕ ܒܣܪ.

G. Ἕνεκα τούτου καταλείψει ἄνθρωπος τὸν πατέρα
αὐτοῦ καὶ τὴν μητέρα αὐτοῦ καὶ κολληθήσεται τῇ γυναικὶ
αὐτοῦ καὶ ἔσονται οἱ δύο εἰς σάρκα μίαν.[1]

Math. xxi: 5; *Zach.* ix: 9.

P and S. ܗܐ ܡܠܟܟܝ ܐܬܐ ܠܟܝ ܘܙܕܝܩܐ ܘܦܪܘܩܐ
ܘܡܟܝܟܐ ܘܪܟܝܒ ܥܠ ܚܡܪܐ ܘܥܠ ܥܝܠܐ ܒܪ ܐܬܢܐ.

H. הִנֵּה מַלְכֵּךְ יָבוֹא לָךְ צַדִּיק וְנוֹשָׁע הוּא עָנִי וְרֹכֵב עַל־חֲמוֹר וְעַל־
עַיִר בֶּן־אֲתֹנוֹת.

LXX and G. Ἰδοὺ ὁ βασιλεύς σου ἔρχεταί σοι δίκαιος
καὶ σώζων αὐτὸς πραΰς καὶ ἐπιβεβηκὼς ἐπὶ ὑποζύγιον καὶ
πῶλον νέον.

---

[1] In this passage it is uncertain whether both Pᵉšiṭṭâ Old and New Testaments are not following the Septuagint. To claim that such is the case, is to concede that there is an influence of the Septuagint on the Pᵉšiṭṭâ in the Book of Genesis.

[2] S omits ܘܦܪܘܩܐ ܘܙܕܝܩܐ. G also omits δίκαιος καὶ σώζων. S seems to be a compromise between P and G.

Math. xxi: 13; *Is.* lvi: 7.

P and S. ܒܝܬܝ. ܒܝܬ ܨܠܘܬܐ ܢܬܩܪܐ.
H. ביתי בית־תפלה יקרא:
LXX and G. οἶκός μου οἶκος προσευχῆς κληθήσεται.[1]

Mark. xi: 17; *Is.* lvi: 7.

P and S. ܒܝܬܝ. ܒܝܬ ܨܠܘܬܐ ܢܬܩܪܐ ܠܟܠܗܘܢ ܥܡ̈ܡܐ.
H. ביתי בית־תפלה יקרא לכל־העמים:
LXX and G. Οἶκός[1] μου οἶκος προσευχῆς κληθήσεται πᾶσιν τοῖς ἔθνεσιν.

Mark. xii: 36; *Ps.* cx: 1.

P and S. ܐܡܪ ܡܪܝܐ ܠܡܪܝ. ܕܬܒ ܠܟ ܡܢ ܝܡܝܢܝ. ܥܕܡܐ ܕܐܣܝܡ ܒܥܠܕܒ̈ܒܝܟ ܟܘܒܫܐ ܠܪ̈ܓܠܝܟ.[2]
H. נאם יהוה לאדני שב לימיני עד־אשית איבך הדם לרגליך:
LXX and G. Εἶπεν ὁ κύριος τῷ κυρίῳ μου κάθου ἐκ δεξιῶν μου ἕως ἂν θῶ τοὺς ἐχθρούς σου ὑποπόδιον τῶν ποδῶν σου.[3]

Mark. xv: 34; *Ps.* xxii: 2.

P. and S. ܐܠܗܝ ܐܠܗܝ. ܠܡܢܐ ܫܒܩܬܢܝ.[4]
H. אלי אלי למה עזבתני:

[1] G. has ὁ οἶκός. The reading is the same in all the Mss.

[2] S. only differs in reading ܬܒ for ܕܬܒ and ܬܚܝܬ ܪ̈ܓܠܝܟ for ܠܪ̈ܓܠܝܟ.

[3] G reads simply κύριος; and for ὑποπόδιον, ὑποκάτω.

[4] This quotation seems to be directly from the Syriac. Had the quotation been made in Aramaic (see Neubauer, *On the Dialects spoken in Palestine in the time of Christ:* Studia Biblica vol I, p. 39, Oxford 1885) it would read אלי אלי מטול מה שבקתני.

LXX. Ὁ θεὸς ὁ θεός μου πρόσχες μοι ἱνατί ἐγκατέλιπές με.
G. Ἐλωί ἐλωί λαμά σαβαχθανεί.

Luke iv: 11;[1] *Ps.* xci: 11.

P. and S. ܕܠܡܠܐܟܘܗܝ. ܢܦܩܘܕ ܥܠܝܟ ܕܢܛܪܘܢܟ ܒܟܠܗܘܢ ܐܘܪܚܬܟ ܘܥܠ ܕܪ̈ܥܝܗܘܢ ܢܫܩܠܘܢܟ ܕܠܐ ܬܬܩܠ ܪܓܠܟ ܥܠ ܟܐܦܐ.[2]

H. כי מלאכיו יצוה־לך לשמרך בכל־דרכך על כפים ישאונך פן־תגף באבן רגלך׃

LXX and G. Ὅτι τοῖς ἀγγέλοις αὐτοῦ ἐντελεῖται περὶ σοῦ τοῦ διαφυλάξαι σε ἐν πάσαις ταῖς ὁδοῖς σου ἐπὶ χειρῶν ἀροῦσίν σε μήποτε προσκόψῃς πρὸς λίθον τὸν πόδα σου.[3]

John ii: 17; *Ps.* lxix: 10.

P. and S. ܕܛܢܢܗ ܕܒܝܬܟ ܐܟܠܢܝ.
H. כי־קנאת ביתך אכלתני׃
LXX and G. Ὅτι ὁ ζῆλος τοῦ οἴκου σου κατέφαγέν με.[4]

John xix: 24; *Ps.* xxii: 19.

P. and S. ܘܦܠܓܘ ܢܚܬܝ. ܒܝܢܬܗܘܢ ܘܥܠ ܠܒܘܫܝ ܐܪܡܝܘ ܦܣܐ:

H. יחלקו בגדי להם ועל־לבושי יפילו גורל׃
LXX and G. Διεμερίσαντο τὰ ἱμάτιά μου ἑαυτοῖς καὶ ἐπὶ τὸν ἱματισμόν μου ἔβαλον κλῆρον.

[1] Prager adds Luke xiii: 35 from Ps. cxviii: 25; this is evidently a mistake since the passage in Luke is not a quotation, nor does it resemble Ps. cxviii: 25 (Prager, *De Veteris Testamenti Versione Syriaca* p. 69).

[2] S. omits ܒܟܠܗܘܢ ܐܘܪܚܬܟ; and renders ܪܓܠܟ ܥܠ ܟܐܦܐ by ܪܓܠܟ ܒܟܐܦܐ.

[3] G. omits ἐν πάσαις ταῖς ὁδοῖς σου.

[4] G. reads καταφάγεταί με.

Acts iv: 25—27; *Ps.* ii: 1—2

P. and S. ܠܚܢܐ ܐܪܓܫܘ ܥܡܡܐ ܘܫܘ̈ܒܐ ܪܢܘ ܣܪ̈ܝܩܬܐ ܩܡܘ ܡܠܟ̈ܐ ܕܐܪܥܐ ܘܫܠܝ̈ܛܢܐ ܘܐܬܡܠܟܘ ܐܟܚܕܐ ܥܠ ܡܪܝܐ ܘܥܠ ܡܫܝܚܗ.

H. לָמָּה רָגְשׁוּ גוֹיִם וּלְאֻמִּים יֶהְגּוּ־רִיק יִתְיַצְּבוּ מַלְכֵי־אֶרֶץ וְרוֹזְנִים נוֹסְדוּ־יָחַד עַל־יְהוָה וְעַל־מְשִׁיחוֹ:

LXX and G. Ἱνατί ἐφρύαξαν ἔθνη καὶ λαοὶ ἐμελέτησαν κενά; παρέστησαν οἱ βασιλεῖς τῆς γῆς καὶ οἱ ἄρχοντες συνήχθησαν ἐπὶ τὸ αὐτὸ κατὰ τοῦ Κυρίου καὶ κατὰ τοῦ χριστοῦ αὐτοῦ.

Acts viii: 32; *Is.* liii: 7.

P. and S. ܐܝܟ ܐܡܪܐ ܕܠܢܟܣܬܐ ܐܬܕܒܪ ܘܐܝܟ ܢܩܝܐ ܩܕܡ ܓܙܘܙܗ ܫܬܝܩ ܗܘܐ ܗܟܢܐ ܘܠܐ ܦܬܚ ܦܘܡܗ.[2]

H. כַּשֶּׂה לַטֶּבַח יוּבָל וּכְרָחֵל לִפְנֵי גֹזְזֶיהָ נֶאֱלָמָה וְלֹא יִפְתַּח פִּיו:

LXX and G. ὡς πρόβατον ἐπὶ σφαγὴν ἤχθη καὶ ὡς ἀμνὸς ἐναντίον τοῦ κείραντος αὐτὸν ἄφωνος οὕτως οὐκ ἀνοίγει τὸ στόμα αὐτοῦ.

Acts xiv: 15; *Ps.* cxlv: 6.

P. and S. ܥܒܕ ܫܡܝܐ ܘܐܪܥܐ ܘܝܡ̈ܡܐ ܘܟܠ ܕܐܝܬ ܒܗܘܢ.

H. עֹשֵׂה שָׁמַיִם וָאָרֶץ אֶת־הַיָּם וְאֶת־כָּל־אֲשֶׁר־בָּם:

LXX and G. τὸν ποιήσαντα τὸν οὐρανὸν καὶ τὴν γῆν τὴν θάλασσαν καὶ πάντα τὰ ἐν αὐτοῖς.[3]

---

[1] S. reads ܡܬܚܫܒܝܢ for ܘܐܬܡܠܟܘ, as do also the editions of Ceriani and Urmia.

[2] S. varies but slightly; reading ܠܐ ܦܬܚ, and at the end ܦܘܡܗ̇.

[3] G. differs slightly; reading ὃς ἐποίησεν, and καὶ τὴν θάλασσαν.

Rom. iv: 18;[1] *Gen.* xv: 5.

P. and S. ܗܟܢܐ ܢܗܘܐ ܙܪܥܟ

H. כה יהיה זרעך

LXX and G. Οὕτως ἔσται τὸ σπέρμα σου.

Rom. ix: 17; *Ex.* ix: 16.

P. ܡܛܠ ܗܕܐ ܗܘ ܐܩܝܡܬܟ ܡܛܠ ܕܐܚܘܝܟ ܚܝܠܝ
ܘܡܛܠ ܕܢܬܟܪܙ ܫܡܝ ܒܟܠܗ ܐܪܥܐ.

H. בעבור זאת העמדתיך בעבור הראתך את כחי ולמען ספר שמי בכל־הארץ

LXX. Καὶ ἕνεκεν τούτου διετηρήθης ἵνα ἐνδείξωμαι ἐν σοὶ τὴν ἰχσύν μου καὶ ὅπως διαγγελῇ τὸ ὄνομά μου ἐν πάσῃ τῇ γῇ.

S. ܠܗܕܐ ܐܩܝܡܬܟ ܕܐܚܘܐ ܒܟ ܚܝܠܝ ܘܕܢܬܟܪܙ
ܫܡܝ ܒܐܪܥܐ ܟܠܗ.

G. Εἰς αὐτὸ τοῦτο ἐξήγειρά σε ὅπως ἐνδείξωμαι ἐν σοὶ τὴν δύναμίν μου καὶ ὅπως διαγγελῇ τὸ ὄνομά μου ἐν πάσῃ τῇ γῇ.

Rom. ix: 29; *Is.* i: 9.

P. and S. ܐܠܘܠܐ ܡܪܝܐ ܨܒܐܘܬ ܐܘܬܪ ܠܢ ܣܪܝܕܐ
ܐܝܟ ܣܕܘܡ ܗܘܝܢ ܗܘܝܢ ܘܠܥܡܘܪܐ ܡܬܕܡܝܢ ܗܘܝܢ.

H. לולי יהוה צבאות הותיר לנו שריד כמעט כסדם היינו לעמרה דמינו:

LXX and G. Καὶ εἰ μὴ κύριος σαβαὼθ ἐγκατέλιπεν ἡμῖν σπέρμα ὡς Σόδομα ἂν ἐγενήθημεν καὶ ὡς Γόμοῤῥα ἂν ὡμοιώθημεν.

[1] Prager (*De Vet. Test. Ver. Syr.* p. 69) adds Rom iii: 13 from Ps. cxl: 4; but the quotation is untoubtedly from LXX Ps. v: 10, or Ps. xiii: 3. There is not the slightest connection between this passage and Ps. cxl: 4.

[2] Both S and G follow P more closely than either H or LXX.

Rom. x: 18; *Ps.* xix: 5.

P. and S. ܒܟܠܗ ܐܪܥܐ ܢܦܩܬ ܣܒܪܬܗܘܢ ܘܒܣ̈ܘܦܝܐ
ܕܬܐܒܝܠ ܡܠ̈ܝܗܘܢ.[1]

H. בכל־הארץ יצא קום ובקצה תבל מליהם׃

LXX and G. εἰς πᾶσαν τὴν γῆν ἐξῆλθεν ὁ φθόγγος αὐτῶν καὶ εἰς τὰ πέρατα τῆς οἰκουμένης τὰ ῥήματα αὐτῶν.

Rom. xi: 9—10; *Ps.* lxix: 23—24.

P. and S. ܢܗܘܐ ܦܬܘܪܗܘܢ ܩܕܡܝܗܘܢ ܦܚܐ
ܘܦܘܪܥܢܗܘܢ ܠܬܘܩܠܬܐ ܢܚܫܟܢ ܥܝ̈ܢܝܗܘܢ ܕܠܐ ܢܚܙܘܢ
ܘܚܨܗܘܢ ܒܟܠܙܒܢ ܢܗܘܐ ܟܦܝܦ.[2]

H. יהי־שלחנם לפניהם לפח ולשלומים למוקש תחשכנה עיניהם מראות ומתניהם תמיד המעד׃

LXX and G. Γενηθήτω ἡ τράπεζα αὐτῶν ἐνώπιον αὐτῶν εἰς παγίδα καὶ εἰς ἀνταπόδοσιν καὶ εἰς σκάνδαλον. Σκοτισθήτωσαν οἱ ὀφθαλμοὶ αὐτῶν τοῦ μὴ βλέπειν καὶ τὸν νῶτον αὐτῶν διαπαντὸς σύγκαμψον.[3]

Rom. xv: 3; *Ps.* lxix: 10.

P. and S. ܘܚܣܕܐ ܕܡܚܣܕܢܝܟ ܢܦܠ ܥܠܝ.

H. חרפות חורפיך נפלו עלי׃

LXX and G. Οἱ ὀνειδισμοὶ τῶν ὀνειδιζόντων σὲ ἐπέπεσον ἐπ' ἐμέ.

[1] S. reads ܣܒܪܬܗܘܢ in place of ܒܪܬ ܩܠܗܘܢ, and also reads ܘܒܣ̈ܘܦܝܗ.

[2] S. reads ܠܦܚܐ, which does not affect the sense.

[3] G. omits ἐνώπιον αὐτῶν, adds καὶ εἰς θήραν after εἰς παγίδα, and inverts the order of the words εἰς σκάνδαλον καὶ εἰς ἀνταπόδομα. cf. Ps. xxxv: 8 (LXX, xxxiv: 9).

Rom. xv: 11; *Ps.* cxvi: 1.

P. and S. ܫܒܚܘ ܠܡܪܝܐ ܟܠܟܘܢ ܥܡܡܐ܂ ܫܒܚܝܗܝ ܟܠܟܝܢ ܐܡܘܬܐ.

H. הללו את־יהוה כל־גוים שבחוהו כל־האמים:

LXX and G. Αἰνεῖτε τὸν κύριον πάντα τὰ ἔϑνη ἐπαινέσατε αὐτὸν πάντες οἱ λαοί.[1]

Eph. iv: 8; *Ps.* lxviii: 19.

P. and S. ܣܠܩܬ ܠܡܪܘܡܐ ܘܫܒܝܬ ܫܒܝܬܐ ܘܝܗܒܬ ܡܘܗܒܬܐ ܠܒܢܝܢܫܐ.[2]

H. עלית למרום שבית שבי לקחת מתנות באדם:

LXX. Ἀναβὰς εἰς ὕψος ᾐχμαλώτευσας αἰχμαλωσίαν ἔλαβες δόματα ἐν ἀνϑρώπῳ.

G. Ἀναβὰς εἰς ὕψος ᾐχμαλώτευσεν αἰχμαλωσίαν καὶ ἔδωκεν δόματα τοῖς ἀνϑρώποις.[3]

Eph. iv: 26; *Ps.* iv: 5.

P. and S. ܪܓܙܘ ܘܠܐ ܬܚܛܘܢ

H. רגזו ואל־תחטאו:

LXX and G. Ὀργίζεσϑε καὶ μὴ ἁμαρτάνετε.

---

[1] G. omits τὸν κύριον; and for ἐπαινέσατε, reads ἐπαινεσάτωσαν; with this reading the Alexandrian and Sinaitic Mss. agree.

[2] S. ܣܠܩ for ܣܠܩܬ; and ܘܝܗܒ for ܘܝܗܒܬ.

[3] The fact that in this passage the Greek follows the Syriac has caused much speculation. It has been suggested that the Hebrew לקחת is transposed from חלקת; which is ingenious but improbable (cf. Toy, *Quotations in the N. T.* p. 198). Another suggestion is that both are following the Targum, which here agrees with S. The only other possibility seems to be that Paul is quoting the Pᵉšiṭṭâ.

i *Pet.* iii: 10—12; *Ps.* xxxiv: 13—17.

P. ܐܝܢܐ ܗܘ ܓܒܪܐ ܕܨܒܐ ܚܝܐ ܘܪܚܡ ܝܘܡܬܐ ܛܒܐ܂ ܠܫܢܟ ܛܪ ܡܢ ܒܝܫܬܐ ܘܣܦܘܬܟ ܠܐ ܢܡܠܠܢ ܢܟܠܐ܂ ܥܢܕ ܡܢ ܒܝܫܬܐ ܘܥܒܕ ܛܒܬܐ ܒܥܝ ܫܠܡܐ ܘܗܪܛ ܒܬܪܗ ܕܥܝܢܘܗܝ ܕܡܪܝܐ ܥܠ ܙܕܝܩܐ ܘܐܕܢܘܗܝ ܠܡܫܡܥ ܐܢܘܢ ܐܦܘܗܝ ܕܝܢ ܕܡܪܝܐ ܥܠ ܒܝܫܐ܂

H. מי־האיש החפץ חיים אהב ימים לראות טוב נצר לשונך מרע ושפתיך
מדבר מרמה סור מרע ועשה טוב בקש שלום ורדפהו עיני יהוה אל־
צדיקים ואזניו אל־שועתם פני יהוה בעשי רע:

LXX. Τίς ἐστιν ἄνθρωπος ὁ θέλων ζωὴν ἀγαπῶν ἰδεῖν ἡμέρας ἀγαθάς; παῦσον τὴν γλῶσσάν σου ἀπὸ κακοῦ καὶ χείλη τοῦ μὴ λαλῆσαι δόλον ἔκκλινον ἀπὸ κακοῦ καὶ ποίησον ἀγαθόν ζήτησον εἰρήνην καὶ δίωξον αὐτήν ὅτι ὀφθαλμοὶ κυρίου ἐπὶ δικαίους καὶ ὦτα αὐτοῦ εἰς δέησιν αὐτῶν πρόσωπον δὲ κυρίου ἐπὶ ποιοῦντας κακά.

S. ܡܢ ܗܘ ܓܒܪܐ ܕܨܒܐ ܚܝܐ ܘܪܚܡ ܝܘܡܬܐ ܛܒܐ܂ ܠܫܢܗ ܢܛܪ ܡܢ ܒܝܫܬܐ ܘܣܦܘܬܗ ܕܠܐ ܢܡܠܠܢ ܢܟܠܐ܂ ܢܥܢܕ ܡܢ ܒܝܫܬܐ ܘܢܥܒܕ ܛܒܬܐ ܢܒܥܐ ܫܠܡܐ ܘܢܪܗܛ ܒܬܪܗ ܕܥܝܢܘܗܝ ܕܡܪܝܐ ܥܠ ܙܕܝܩܐ ܘܐܕܢܘܗܝ ܠܡܫܡܥ ܐܢܘܢ ܐܦܘܗܝ ܕܡܪܝܐ ܥܠ ܒܝܫܐ[1].

G. Ὁ γὰρ θέλων ζωὴν ἀγαπᾶν καὶ ἰδεῖν ἡμέρας ἀγαθάς παυσάτω τὴν γλῶσσαν ἀπὸ κακοῦ καὶ χείλη τοῦ μὴ λαλῆσαι δόλον ἐκκλινάτω δὲ ἀπὸ κακοῦ καὶ ποιησάτω ἀγαθόν ζητησάτω εἰρήνην καὶ διωξάτω αὐτήν ὅτι ὀφθαλμοὶ κυρίου ἐπὶ δικαίους καὶ ὦτα αὐτοῦ εἰς δέησιν αὐτῶν πρόσωπον δὲ κυρίου ἐπὶ ποιοῦντας κακά.

[1] The difference between S. and P. is simply that the former has changed a command into an exhortation; the verb being in the third instead of the second person. G., on the contrary, seems to be a very free quotation from the LXX. But here too the third person is substituted for the second.

Heb. i: 5; *Ps.* ii: 7; ii *Sam.* vii: 14.

P. and S. (ii *Sam.*) ... ܒܪܝ ܐܢܬ ܘܐܢܐ ܝܘܡܢܐ ܝܠܕܬܟ ... ܐܢܐ ܐܗܘܐ ܠܗ ܠܐܒܐ ܘܗܘ ܢܗܘܐ ܠܝ ܠܒܪܐ.

H. בני אתה אני היום ילדתיך ... (ii *Sam.* vii: 14) אני אהיה־לו לאב והוא יהיה־לי לבן:

LXX and G. Υἱός μου εἶ σὺ ἐγὼ σήμερον γεγέννηκά σε ... (ii *Sam.* vii: 14) καὶ ἐγὼ ἔσομαι αὐτῷ εἰς πατέρα καὶ αὐτὸς ἔσται μοι εἰς υἱόν.

Heb. i: 7; *Ps.* civ: 4.[1]

P. and S. ܥܒܕ ܡ̈ܠܐܟܘܗܝ ܪܘܚܐ ܘܡܫ̈ܡܫܢܘܗܝ ܢܘܪܐ ܝܩܕܐ.[2]

H. עשה מלאכיו רוחות משרתיו אש להט

LXX and G. Ὁ ποιῶν τοὺς ἀγγέλους αὐτοῦ πνεύματα καὶ τοὺς λειτουργοὺς αὐτοῦ πῦρ φλέγον.[3]

Heb. i: 8; *Ps.* xlv: 6.

P. and S. ܟܘܪܣܝܟ ܐܠܗܐ ܠܥܠܡ ܥܠܡܝܢ ܫܒܛܐ ܦܫܝܛܐ ܫܒܛܐ ܕܡܠܟܘܬܟ.[4]

H. כסאך אלהים עולם ועד שבט מישר שבט מלכותך:

LXX and G. Ὁ θρόνος σου ὁ θεὸς εἰς αἰῶνα αἰῶνος ῥάβδος εὐθύτητος ἡ ῥάβδος τῆς βασιλείας σου.[5]

[1] Prager wrongly refers in this connection to Ps. 107: 4: *De Vet. Test. Ver. Syr.* p. 70.

[2] S. reads ܢܘܪ with which the text of the Urmia edition agrees.

[3] G. reads πυρὸς φλόγα (thus A[a]).

[4] S. reads ܕܟܘܪܣܝܟ ܕܠܟ.

[5] G. reads εἰς τὸν αἰῶνα τοῦ αἰῶνος καὶ ... (thus also ℵART).

Heb. ii: 12; *Ps.* xxii: 22.

P. and S. [Syriac]
H. אספרה שמך לאחי בתוך קהל אהללך:
LXX and G. Διηγήσομαι τὸ ὄνομά σου τοῖς ἀδελφοῖς μου ἐν μέσῳ ἐκκλησίας ὑμνήσω σε.[2]

Heb. ii: 13; *Is.* viii: 18.

P. and S. [Syriac][3]
H. הנה אנכי והילדים אשר נתן לי יהוה:
LXX and G. Ἰδοὺ ἐγὼ καὶ τὰ παιδία ἅ μοι ἔδωκεν ὁ θεός.

Heb. iii: 15; iv: 7; *Ps.* xcv: 7—8.

P. and S. [Syriac][4]
H. היום אם־בקלו תשמעו אל־תקשו לבבכם כמריבה:
LXX and G. Σήμερον ἐὰν τῆς φωνῆς αὐτοῦ ἀκούσητε μὴ σκληρύνητε τὰς καρδίας ὑμῶν ὡς ἐν τῷ παραπικρασμῷ.

Heb. x: 5—7;[5] *Ps.* xl: 7—9.

P. [Syriac]

---

[1] S. reads [Syriac]; and [Syriac] for [Syriac].
[2] G. reads Ἀπαγγελῶ.
[3] S. reads [Syriac].
[4] In iii: 15 S. reads [Syriac]; in iv: 7 it omits [Syriac].
[5] Some include Heb. viii: 8 and seq. from Jer xxxi: 31 and seq.; but it is difficult to find any more evident dependence of S. upon P., than upon LXX or H.

H. זבח ומנחה לא חפצת אזנים כרית לי עולה וחטאה לא שאלת או
אמרתי הנה־באתי במגלת־ספר כתוב עלי לעשות־רצונך אלהי חפצתי:

LXX and G. Θυσίαν καὶ προσφορὰν οὐκ ἠθέλησας σῶμα δὲ κατηρτίσω μοι ὁλοκαύτωμα καὶ περὶ ἁμαρτίας οὐκ ᾔτησας τότε εἶπον Ἰδοὺ ἥκω ἐν κεφαλίδι βιβλίου γέγραπται περὶ ἐμοῦ τοῦ ποιῆσαι τὸ θέλημά σου ὁ θεός μου ἐβουλήθην.[1]

S. ܕܒܚܐ ܘܩܘܪܒܢܐ ܠܐ ܨܒܝܬ ܓܘܫܡܐ ܕܝܢ ܐܬܩܢܬ ܠܝ ܝܩܕܐ ܫܠܡܐ ܘܥܠ ܚܛܗܐ ܠܐ ܫܐܠܬ ܗܝܕܝܢ ܐܡܪܬ ܕܗܐ ܐܢܐ ܐܬܐ ܐܢܐ ܕܒܪܫ ܟܬܒܐ ܟܬܝܒ ܥܠܝ ܕܐܥܒܕ ܨܒܝܢܟ ܐܠܗܐ.

Heb. xiii:6; *Ps.* cxvii:6.

P. and S. ܡܪܝܐ ܡܥܕܪܢܝ ܠܐ ܐܕܚܠ ܡܢܐ ܢܥܒܕ ܠܝ ܒܪܢܫܐ[2].

H. יהוה לי לא אירא מה יעשה לי אדם:

LXX and G. Κύριος ἐμοὶ βοηθὸς καὶ οὐ φοβηθήσομαι τί ποιήσει μοι ἄνθρωπος.

While the number of the quotations in the Syriac New Testament which agree with the Peshittâ Old Testament, is not so very large in comparison with the entire number of quotations in the New Testament, yet they are sufficient to give strong evidence that the Peshittâ Old Testament was consulted, if not always directly quoted, by the authors of the Syriac New Testament.

How many more agreements between the Peshittâ Old and New Testaments we should find if the original texts were more fully restored, must at present remain an open question.

---

[1] G. differs slightly, reading for ᾔτησας—εὐδόκησας; inverting the order of τὸ θέλημα and ὁ θεός; and omitting ἐβουλήθην. The variations of S. from P. are not important.

[2] S. reads ܒܪܢܫܐ.

Work is now being done along the line of textual criticism of the Syriac New Testament. Possibly the quotations of Ephrem Syrus, who certainly quoted the Pᵉšiṭtâ to a large extent¹, and perhaps those of Aphrates² as well may throw some light upon this subject in the near future. There are several excellent articles bearing directly upon this very question in the Studia Biblica series.³

[1] *Studia Biblica*, vol. iii: p. 107. F. H. Woods, *An examination of the N. T. quotations by Ephrem Syrus* says, "Roughly speaking, out of 168 quotations from the N. T. 43 agree exactly with that Version" (Pᵉšiṭtâ O. T.).

[2] *Studia Biblica* vol. iii: p. 118. It is generally thought that the quotations of Aphrates approximate more nearly to the Curetonian than to the Pᵉšiṭtâ.

[3] Vol. 1, p. 113 *The Corbey St. James (ff.) and its relation to other Latin Versions and to the original language of the Epistle*—by J. Wordsworth; also *Some further remarks on the Corbey St. Jas*—by W. Sanday (p. 233); vol. ii: p. 195. *The Evidence of the early Versions and Patristic quotations on the text of the Books of the New Testament*, by Ll. J. M. Bebb; and vol. iii: p. 105 et seq. *An examination of the New Testament quotations of Ephrem Syrus* by F. H. Woods— also Ibid., p. 47. *The Materials for the Criticism of the Peshitto New Testament, with specimens of the Syriac Massorah* by G. H. Gwilliam.

APPENDIX II

TABULATION OF THE VARIANTS OF THE SEVERAL MSS. FROM THE TEXT OF LEE[1]

Wau omitted

g. 41:10; 149:9.

U. 17:7; 19:7; 22:14; 31:18; 34:8, 20; 35:3; 36:7, 11; 38:9; 39:8; 41:10; 43:1; 44:1; 50:3; 55:12; 57:4; 58:11; 59:8; 60:7; 85:10; 88:3; 89:8, 20; 91:8; 93:5; 95:10; 96:5; 98:7; 102:18; 104:15; 105:17, 20, 23; 106:9, 31, 45, 46; 107:29, 39; 109:3, 16; 122:2; 140:6; 142:8; 149:9.

P. 20:6; 22:14; 25:10; 34:8, 20; 35:19; 36:11; 41:10; 43:1; 44:1; 46:9; 50:23; 55:12; 58:8, 11; 60:7, 8; 68:21; 71:18; 72:18; 75:4, 5; 78:14; 85:10; 89:8; 93:5; 96:5; 98:7; 102:18; 105:23; 106:9, 45; 107:39; 109:16; 115:19; 118:45; 124:5; 149:9.

C. 1:3, 6; 2:11; 3:4; 5:3, 6; 6:2; 11:6; 16:9; 17:11; 18:10; 19:7, 12; 21:8; 25:3; 26:3; 36:25; 38:1; 39:8; 40:4, 11; 44:1, 3, 13; 45:4; 46:9; 49:17; 50:23; 51:16; 55:6, 12; 58:11; 60:8; 63:9; 64:3; 68:18; 69:17; 72:15, 18; 74:8; 75:6; 78:14, 21; 84:3, 6; 86:17; 89:8, 20, 21, 27; 91:8, 15; 98:7; 102:15, 18; 103:5, 10; 104:15; 105:17, 20, 23, 44; 106:9, 16; 107:14, 18; 108:4; 109:22; 114:11; 115:19; 118:159; 124:5; 128:6, 7; 131:12; 134:30; 141:7; 146:10; 148:13; 149:9.

a. 3:3, 4; 5:5; 7:13; 10:5, 7; 17:5, 7; 18:3, 10, 21, 33; 19:5, 12; 21:8; 22:25; 26:10; 31:9; 35:28; 37:11; 38:13; 39:8; 40:11; 42:7; 45:8, 15; 47:5; 50:16; 51:16; 52:9; 53:3, 4; 59:16; 66:6; 69:6, 8, 15; 71:5, 9, 13, 22; 72:17; 75:5; 78:14, 18, 64; 79:1; 84:3, 5; 85:10, 12; 88:9; 89:20,

---

[1] The References are to the Pˢšiṭtâ Psalter.

33, 43, 44; 91:8, 15; 92:2; 96:5; 97:10; 101:2; 102:11; 104:7, 16; 105:17, 33, 44; 106:9, 16, 26; 107:14, 17, 18; 108:13; 111:8; 112:10; 114:7, 9, 10; 118:42, 159; 120:3; 123:3; 128:6; 129:8; 131:12; 134:3; 139:11; 141:7; 146:9, 10; 148:4, 13.

β. 5:5; 8:7; 18:16; 19:12; 26:3; 29:6; 30:9; 35:12; 37:25; 38:2; 40:12; 41:13; 42:7; 43:1; 45:14; 47:5; 50:3, 9; 51:7, 16; 56:5, 9; 64:9; 67:6; 69:3, 8; 72:17; 74:22, 75:6; 77:18; 78:14, 34, 64; 79:1, 4; 84:3, 5; 85:12; 88:15; 89:43; 91:8, 14; 92:2; 96:5; 102:11; 106:31, 32; 109:16; 112:10; 120:3; 126:1; 128:7; 129:6; 134:7; 138:17; 141:7; 148:4.

Wau added
g. 19:5.

U. 8:16; 18:7; 36:1, 7, 12, 30; 38:6; 39:13; 40:3; 50:1; 55:6; 58:8; 59:13; 64:5; 68:27; 69:28; 71:6, 9, 12; 78:70; 79:3; 86:16; 91:2, 5; 93:4; 95:9; 101:7; 104:34; 106:43; 107:12; 108:9; 111:8; 114:7, 17; 118:43; 147:20.

P. 9:3; 36:7, 30; 44:21; 55:6; 58:8; 64:5; 68:12, 27; 71:6; 78:70; 91:2; 93:4; 101:7; 104:34; 107:12; 111:8; 114:7, 17; 122:2.

C. 2:12; 4:2; 5:6, 12; 6:3; 7:13; 8:6; 9:4; 17:1; 18:5, 6, 7; 19:5, 12; 21:12; 22:27; 25:18; 26:4; 28:9; 30:7; 31:23; 32:6; 35:19; 36:8, 19; 38:6; 45:13; 48:6; 50:1; 56:2; 58:8, 11; 68:2, 8; 69:28; 71:6, 18, 19; 72:11, 18; 78:25; 85:3; 89:45, 52; 96:11; 97:3; 101:7; 104:10, 11, 12, 34; 106:4, 43; 107:1, 12; 108:9; 111:8; 134:6; 136:6; 138:6, 10; 139:10; 145:7, 10.

α. 4:4; 9:4; 10:14; 13:6; 16:3, 6, 7; 17:1; 18:6, 17, 37, 44, 48; 19:12; 21:13; 22:14, 27; 25:12; 29:4; 30:7, 8, 10; 31:4; 32:8; 33:3, 16, 19; 35:19; 36:6, 8, 12; 37:19; 38:6; 39:4; 41:6, 10; 44:2, 6; 48:7, 14; 50:2, 23; 56:2; 58:7, 8; 64:5; 68:8, 12; 70:2; 71:21; 73:8; 77:17; 78:25, 51, 70; 81:11; 83:18; 85:3; 89:52; 92:10, 12; 94:3, 20; 96:12;

97:1; 98:7; 101:7; 104:12, 21; 105:5; 106:4, 5, 8; 107:13, 23; 108:8, 9; 109:12; 111:8; 113:4; 114:6, 7, 17; 131:4; 138:16; 139:10; 142:3, 5, 11; 143:15; 144:11; 145:7.

β. 7:13; 8:3; 16:2, 3, 6, 7; 17:1; 18:19; 19:5; 21:13; 25:18; 31:8; 35:16, 19; 36:6; 44:2; 58:8; 68:8, 27; 77:10; 90:9; 108:9; 114:17; 138:1, 16; 142:5.

Dâladh omitted

U. 2:3; 57:3; 60:4; 61:2, 7; 68:24; 71:15; 78:19; 87:5; 99:7; 105:15; 115:8.

P. 18:31; 56:1; 57:3; 61:2; 63:3; 78:19; 87:5; 105:15; 115:8.

C. 3:2; 8:4; 17:12; 29:6; 78:5, 19; 87:5.

α. 3:3; 8:4; 17:12; 29:6; 33:18; 41:1; 61:7; 71:5; 78:19; 87:5; 94:18.

β. 2:4; 42:9; 71:5; 81:16; 87:5; 105:15; 117:20; 128:6.

Dâladh added

U. 35:19; 40:5; 41:19; 48:14; 56:8; 59:4; 62:11; 66:2, 4; 73:9, 10; 80:8; 94:13; 105:41; 121:1; 148:10.

P. 73:10; 121:1.

C. 40:5; 45:2; 58:4.

α. 36:7; 90:116; 102:23; 131:11.

β. 49:7; 57:4; 58:4; 91:10; 96:5.

Different Spelling of the Same Word

g. 50:7; 118:109.

U. 56:13; 78:42; 83:16; 102:3, 8; 115:4; 120:5, 6; 144:14.

P. 2:1; 5:2, 4; 6:7; 78:42; 102:3, 8; 144:14.

C. 4:7; 5:4; 6:7; 13:3; 18:26; 19:3; 31:8; 32:6; 34:8; 40:2; 47:3; 48:10; 50:7; 56:13; 58:1; 69:3; 72:6; 74:12; 78:20; 80:12; 81:11; 93:1; 94:2; 106:17, 42; 109:25; 118:104, 106, 109; 143:13, 14.

α. 3:5; 4:5; 5:4; 7:17; 8:5; 8:7; 9:9; 10:7, 14; 16:5; 18:10, 39; 21:4; 22:4, 8, 24; 23:5; 24:2, 7, 9; 25:19, 21;

26:6; 29:9; 32:2; 33:9, 21; 35:24; 36:5; 38:4; 40:8, 12, 16; 41:13; 43:2; 44:4, 7, 14; 45:8; 50:7; 53:6; 54:1, 3; 59:5, 7, 9; 60:7; 66:11; 68:8, 21, 26, 27, 34, 35; 69:6, 33; 71:21; 72:10, 13, 14, 15, 17; 73:1; 74:12; 76:1; 78:5, 21, 31, 41, 51, 56, 60, 72; 80:3, 4, 8, 11, 12, 13; 83:2, 5; 84:5; 86:14; 87:3; 89:11, 44; 90:2; 91:8; 93:1; 96:10, 13; 98:3, 7, 9; 103:7; 104:14; 105:10, 23, 36; 106:42; 107:1, 31, 38, 40; 108:8; 110:6, 7; 111:10; 114:1, 12, 3, 5, 9; 115:15; 117:2, 9, 22; 118:109, 160; 120:4; 121:4; 123:1, 6; 124:5; 127:6; 128:1; 129, 7, 8; 130:3; 132:2; 134:3, 12, 19, 21; 135:8, 11, 14, 22; 136:1, 4; 139:3, 7, 8, 11; 140:5; 143:15; 144:18; 145:3; 146:3, 5; 147:19; 148:12; 149:2, 8.

β. 4:5; 8:5; 9:9; 10:17; 11:1; 14:7; 18:10; 19:5; 21:4; 22:4, 7, 24; 24:2, 7, 9; 25:21; 29:9; 35:3, 12; 38:4; 40:8, 12; 44:14; 45:8; 49:2, 12; 50:7, 12; 55:13; 56:4; 58:11; 59:7; 60:7; 66:11; 68:16, 21, 26, 34; 70:1; 72:10; 73:1; 74:12; 76:1; 78:24, 41, 51; 80:1; 81:3, 4, 6; 82:7; 89:11, 44; 90:3; 93:1; 94:12; 96:10; 105:23, 36; 108:8; 110:6, 7; 111:10; 114:1; 117:22; 118:109, 160; 121:4; 127:2; 128:1; 134:3; 136:6; 139:3, 7, 11; 149:2.

Prepositions omitted, added or interchanged

U. 65:12; 66:5; 68:34; 69:2; 78:18; 79:8; 86:13; 89:4; 90:17; 93:5; 94:10; 104:20; 105:16, 22, 42; 118:120; 124:2, 5.

P. 68:34; 69:2; 83:16; 90:17; 93:5; 105:16, 22; 124:2.

C. 16:10; 17:7; 18:24, 34, 47; 27:4; 40:5; 66:1, 5; 68:16, 34; 69:27; 73:13; 77:1; 90:15; 93:5; 105:22; 117:17; 118:133, 145, 146; 135:15, 18; 136:1.

α. 10:5, 6, 17; 16:4; 20:7; 28:8; 30:8; 39:7; 40:1, 6; 44:16; 49:9; 62:8; 69:15, 21, 26; 70:2, 14; 78:5, 6; 80:18; 81:5; 82:15; 106:16; 117:17; 118:122, 133, 146; 128:3; 150:5.

β. 6:7; 10:5, 6, 17; 16:4, 5; 30:8; 41:10; 49:9; 57:4; 62:8; 66:6; 69:35; 80:18; 81:3; 82:5; 118:120, 122, 133; 137:2; 148:13.

Singular for Plural

g. 114:13; 118:123.

U. 2:8, 10; 11:4; 19:4, 13; 50:8; 55:20; 90:10; 104:17; 107:12.

P. 2:8, 10; 16:6; 18:24; 31:19; 35:19; 47:9; 55:20; 75:3; 78:45; 84:2; 90:10.

C. 2:8, 10; 4:3; 5:6, 9; 6:7, 9; 8:8; 10:16; 17:10; 18:9; 21:5, 7; 22:5; 25:19; 27:6; 31:19; 33:7, 11; 36:6; 38:4; 45:17; 48:14; 50:6; 51:14; 52:8; 55:20; 61:4, 8; 65:13; 68:25; 76:12; 77:5; 78:33, 45; 79:3; 83:15, 17; 89:5, 11; 90:1; 92:7; 95:5; 96:11; 100:5; 102:22, 24; 104:5, 24, 25; 105:18; 106:31; 107:41; 111:8; 112:9; 118:44, 82, 90, 123, 151; 131:12, 14; 134:13; 144:1, 13; 145:10; 148:4, 6.

α. 5:6; 7:6; 9:2, 6; 18:9; 21:5, 7; 22:27; 25:10, 17; 33:7; 34:3, 6; 36:7; 37:35; 38:4, 5; 40:17; 41:13; 42:7; 44:12; 45:6, 17; 46:6; 48:14; 49:9; 50:6; 52:9; 61:4, 8; 66:4; 68:21; 74:12; 76:5, 8; 77:6, 17, 20; 78:28, 42; 82:5; 83:5, 18; 87:6; 89:5, 11, 49; 92:7; 94:18; 95:5; 96:10; 97:6; 102:25; 103:11; 104:5, 8, 17; 105:18; 107:41; 111:8; 112:9; 118:44, 82; 131:12, 14; 140:6; 144:2, 13, 21; 148:4, 6, 10, 11.

β. 21:13; 33:7; 34:6; 57:6; 74:12; 78:1, 35; 82:5; 109:16.

Plural for Singular

U. 11:6; 12:9; 22:6; 48:14; 63:3; 81:16; 118:35, 96.

P. 5.2; 23:5; 118:35, 96; 143:2.

C. 1:3; 2:1; 6:7; 7:5; 8:9; 10:9; 19:10; 33:9; 36:3, 4, 9; 45:14; 50:4; 78:27; 80:4; 86:2; 94:2; 104:24; 106:11; 108:1; 114:16; 118:133; 127:2; 128:3; 149:6.

α. 8:9; 10:11; 35:27; 61:8; 78:28, 42, 44; 104:25; 106:26; 107:30; 114:16; 143:13.

β. 107:14.

Different Readings, consisting chiefly in omitted or inserted pronominal suffixes, and different verbal forms

g. 7:10; 35:22; 68:26; 86:6; 102:22; 105:3; 106:37; 109:16; 118:97, 162.

U. 1:4; 4:9; 7:10; 10:13; 12:3; 18:46; 21:4; 23:4; 30:11; 33:4; 36:30; 40:1; 44:21; 45:4; 58:6; 63:7; 65:1; 68:4, 26; 70:6; 73:5; 76:1; 77:16; 78:5; 79:10; 81:5, 9; 84:2; 86:1, 4, 8; 88:13; 89:2; 91:9; 95:1, 3; 100:3; 102:16, 23; 103:24; 104:8, 17; 105:21; 106:5, 21; 107:40; 111:5, 9; 115:6, 9; 117:25; 118:18, 46, 57, 141; 134:12; 142:2, 10; 144:8.

P. 5:6, 11; 7:7; 10:3; 11:6; 15:4; 16:4; 17:7; 18:41; 19:7; 20:4, 7; 23:4; 33:4; 36:30; 41:10; 45:4; 63:7; 65:1; 68:4, 2; 69:3; 70:6; 73:15; 77:16; 79:10; 81:5, 9; 86:8; 88:13; 89:2; 91:9; 100:3; 102:16, 23; 103:24; 104:8, 30; 105:21; 111:5; 117:25; 118:18, 146, 157; 142:14.

C. 1:6; 2:2, 10; 3:5; 4:5, 6; 5:11; 7:10; 8:9; 10:5, 15; 14:4, 5; 15:4; 16:4, 5; 19:13; 20:7; 21:10, 11; 22:2, 3, 8, 20; 23:4; 26:1; 27:9; 30:5; 31:7; 33:8; 35:24; 38:4; 39:10; 42:8; 44:21; 45:6; 46:5; 50:3, 8; 51:5; 52:8; 55:6; 57:7; 60:1, 10; 66:7; 68:4, 26; 69:3, 24; 71:19; 72:10; 73:24; 74:2, 6; 76:8; 77:16; 79:10; 80:18; 81:5, 9; 84:7; 85:6, 7, 10, 12; 86:5, 8; 88:8, 12, 18; 89:2; 90:5, 10; 92:15; 94:23; 97:3; 100:3; 102:16; 103:24, 26; 104:1, 25, 30; 105:31, 34; 106:4, 37, 47; 107:40; 108:12; 109:16, 23, 26; 110:2, 6; 111:9; 112:3; 115:9; 117:23; 118:18, 57, 141, 162, 170; 134:12, 21; 137:1; 138:2; 139:3; 140:6; 141:4; 142:10; 147:13.

a. 1:6; 2:2, 5, 10; 6:7; 7:10; 8:7, 9; 12:7; 14:5; 17:7; 18:7, 21, 26; 19:11; 20:2; 21:9, 10; 22:3, 7, 11, 15; 25:3, 5; 26:9; 28:6; 29:6; 31:5, 21; 32:2; 33:8; 34:2, 9; 35:9; 38:13, 18; 39:10; 42:8, 10; 44:6, 24; 45:12, 13, 16; 46:4, 5;

48:1, 8; 49:9, 19; 50:3, 8; 51:9, 10; 52:5; 54:4, 10; 55:20; 57:7; 58:5, 11; 59:12; 60:8; 62:6; 63:5; 65:5, 11; 66:1, 13; 68:5, 7, 14, 18, 23, 31; 69:3, 15, 25; 70:4, 6; 72:1, 13; 73:23; 74:2, 16, 18; 75:13; 76:10; 77:8, 16; 78:46, 64; 79:10, 11; 85:2; 86:8, 11; 88:2, 8, 12, 13, 14; 89:2, 3, 13, 17; 90:2, 4, 5; 92:15; 94:1, 23; 96:4; 97:3, 8, 10; 98:7; 99:1; 100:3; 101:3; 102:2, 3, 16, 18, 19; 103:3, 11; 104:1, 2, 4, 5, 18, 34; 105:4; 106:3, 17, 37, 48; 108:4, 12; 109:18, 23, 25, 26; 110:2; 111:9; 112:3, 9; 113:8; 114:7; 115:4, 8, 9, 19; 117:23, 26, 27; 118:4, 8, 18, 43, 57, 72, 98, 121, 123, 125, 137, 141, 148, 149, 162, 169, 175, 176; 120:5; 121:2, 46; 127:3; 130:2; 132:3; 134, 14, 16; 136:4, 6; 138:2, 6; 139:6, 8; 141:5, 8; 142:10, 11; 143:2, 8, 11; 145:1; 147:13, 19; 150:4, 5.

β. 2:1; 5:4; 7;16; 7:17; 10:17; 19:5; 22:20; 26:12; 33:8; 36:8; 38:13; 39:4; 44:23; 48:8; 49:18, 19; 50:8; 51:10; 52:8; 53:2; 55:20; 56:5; 57:1; 59:10; 60:1, 8; 66:1; 67:1, 4; 68:7; 72:9; 73:24; 74:1; 79:10; 83:3; 86:8; 90:5, 8, 17; 95:6; 96:10; 104:4, 33; 106:17, 47; 108:11; 111:9; 113:8; 115:9; 118:57, 175; 120:5; 131:8; 132:3; 134:14; 137:1.

Variants suggesting a possible reconstruction of the text of Lee

g. 43:5; 50:23; 51:1; 73:7.
U. 10:9; 38:19; 104:35.
P. 9:16; 31:4; 38:19; 51:17.
C. 2:11; 7:15; 29:6; 33:3; 35:8; 104. 4; 106:26; 111:9; 118:162; 139:3.
α. 7:10; 9:16; 17:13; 19:4; 31:4, 19; 35:8; 38:13; 39:3; 43:5; 44:23; 45:4; 51:2, 4, 15; 66:5; 68:22; 90:13.
β. 7:10; 12:6; 19:4; 21:10; 31:4, 15; 38:13; 39:3; 40:14; 48:1; 49:7; 51:2, 4, 15; 52:15; 53:1; 66:5; 68:22; 76:10; 90:13.

———

APPENDIX III

LITERATURE CONSULTED

Assemani, Bibliotheca Orientalis, vol. ii.

Baethgen, Friedrich, Untersuchungen über die Psalmen nach der Peschitta, Kiel, 1878. — Der textkritische Werth der alten Uebersetzungen zu den Psalmen. Jahrbücher für Protestantische Theologie. 1882, Nos. 3, 4. See also Deutsche Literatur Zeitung, Oct. 13, 1894, col. N. 84.

Bleek, Einleitung in das alte Testament, Berlin, 1878.

Bloch, Die Quellen des Flavius Josephus, 1892.

Buhl, Canon and Text of the Old Testament, Edinburgh, 1892.

Capellus, Critica Sacra, lib. iv, ch. ii—v.

Cheyne, The Historical origin and Religious Ideas of the Psalter. Bampton Lectures, 1891.

Chwolson, The Quiescent letters וה. Hebraica, vol. vi.

Cornill, Das Buch des Propheten Ezechiel, Leipzig, 1886. — Einleitung in das alte Testament, Bonn, 1893.

Credner, De Prophetarum minorum Versionis Syr. quam Peschito vocant indole, 1827.

De Sacy, Notices et extraits des Mss. de la bibl. nation. iv.

De Wette-Schrader, Einleitung in das Alte Testament, Berlin, 1869.

Driver, Notes on the Hebrew text of the books of Samuel. Oxford, 1890. — A treatise on the Use of the Tenses in Hebrew; 3rd ed. Oxford, 1892.

Eichhorn, Einleitung in das Alte Testament, 1823, 24.

Field, Originis Hexaplorum quae supersunt; sive veterum interpretum Graecorum in totum Vetus Testamentum fragmenta, Oxford, 1875.

Frankel, Vorstudien zu der Septuaginta, Leipzig, 1841.

Freudenthal, Alexander Polyhistor, Breslau, 1875.

Gesenius, Der Prophet Jesaia, Leipzig, 1820.

Gottheil, Dr. R. J. H., Zur Textkritik der Pᵉšiṭṭâ, Mittheilungen

d. Akad. Oriental. Ver. ii. Berlin, 1889; Syriac Literature, Johnson's Universal Cyclopaedia, vol. vii.

Grätz, Exegetische Studien zum Propheten Jeremiah. Zeitschrift 1882.

Gray, Quotations in the New Testament, Journ. of Sacred Lit. No. iv, Oct. 1848.

Harnack, Die Ueberlieferung der Griech. Apolog. d. 11. Jahrh. in d. alten Kirche u. im Mittelalter, Leipzig, 1882.

Hatch, Essays in Biblical Greek, Oxford, 1889.

Hirtzel, De Pentateuchi Ver. Syr. quam Peschitta vocant indole commentatio, 1825.

Hody, De Bibliorum textibus originalibus, Oxford, 1705.

Howorth, The True Septuagint Version of Chronicles, Ezra and Nehemiah; Academy, July 22, 1893, p. 73.

Jacob, Das Buch Esther bei dem Septuagint. ZAW. 1890.

Janichs, Animadversiones Criticae in Ver. Syr. Pesch. librorum Koheleth et Ruth, 1871.

Josephus, Antiquities of the Jews.

Kautzsch, De Veteris Testamenti locis a Paulo Apostolo allegatis, Lipsiae, 1809.

Keil, Lehrbuch der hist. krit. Einleitung in d. A. T., 1859.

König, Einleitung in das Alte Testament, Bonn, 1893.

Lagarde, Anmerkungen zur Griech. Uebersetzung der Proverbien, Leipzig, 1863.

Levy, Syriac Versions, Mc Clintock and Strong, Cyclopaedia, vol. x, p. 113.

Lightfoot, Horae hebr. in Epist. ad Cor. addenda ad Cap. xiv.

Löhr, Textkritsche Vorarbeiten zu einer Erklärung des Buches Daniel. ZAW. 1895.

Maybaum, Die Anthropomorphien und Anthropopathien bei Onkelos und den späteren Targumim mit besonderer Berücksichtigung der Ausdrücke Mimra, Jᵉkura und Schechintho, 1870.

Merx, Das Gedicht von Hiob, Vorbemerk. lxxiii. Jena, 1871.

Niese, Flavii Josephi opera edidit et Apparata Crit., Berol., 1887.

Nestle, Untersuchungen über die Psalmen nach der Peschitta. Theol. Lit. Zeit. 1880. See also Hertzog's Real-Encycl. xv, 192.

Neubauer, The Authorship and the Titles of the Psalms according to early Jewish Authorities. Studia Biblica, vol. ii. The Dialects spoken in Palestine in the time of Christ. Studia Biblica, vol. i.

Oppenheim, Die Syrische Uebersetzung des fünften Buches der Psalmen und ihr Verhältnis zu dem Massorethischen Texte u. den älteren Uebersetzungen, namentlich dem LXX. Targ., Leipzig, 1890.

Perles, Meletemata Peschitthoniana, Prague, 1859.

Prager, De Veteris Testamenti Versione Syriaca quam Peschittho vocant. Questiones Criticae, Gottingae, 1871.

Ryssel, Untersuchungen über die Textgestalt u. die Echtheit des Buches Micha, Leipzig, 1887.

Schürer, The Jewish People in the time of Jesus Christ, New York, 1891.

Schönfelder, Onkelos et Peschittho, 1865.

Sebök, Die syrische Uebersetzung der zwölf kleinen Propheten, Breslau, 1887.

Simon, Histoire Critique du vieux Test., Paris, 1678.

Staerk, Zur Kritik der Psalmen Ueberschriften, Z.A.W. 1892, p. 91.

Stenij, De Syriaca libri Yobi interpretatione, Helsingfors, 1887.

Tholuck, Die Psalmen. Voranmerk. xxiv.

Toy, Quotations in the New Testament, New York, 1884.

Turpie, The Old Testament in the New.

Waehner, Antiquitates Ebraeorum § 253.

Wescott, Epistle to the Hebrews, New York, 1892.

Wiegand, Der Gottesname Zur. ZAW. x : 85; cf. Article by Sayce Academy, Aug. 23, 1890.

Wisemann, Horae Syriacae, Romae, 1829.

Woods, An Examination of the New Testament Quotations of Ephrem Syrus. Studia Bibl. vol. iii.

Wright, Syriac Literature. Encycl. Brit. in loco. (Reprinted: A short history of Syriac Literature, London, 1894.)

ABBREVIATIONS.

א Sinaitic Ms.
A Codex Alexandrinus.
a Urmia Text.
B Vatican Ms.
β Scholia of Bar ʿEbrayâ.
C Ceriani Text.
G Greek New Testament.
g Paris Polyglot.
LXX Septuagint.
M. T. Massoretic Text.
N. T. New Testament.
O. T. Old Testament.
P Ms. of Pocock.
p¹ Pĕšiṭtâ Old Testament.
R. Psalterium Graeco-Latinum Veronese.
R. T. Verona and Zurich Psalters.
S Syriac New Testament.
ܚ Pĕšiṭtâ Psalter.
T Targum.
U Ms. of Usher.

¹ This is only used in Appendix L.

H.G.

www.ingramcontent.com/pod-product-compliance
Lightning Source LLC
Chambersburg PA
CBHW022116160426
43197CB00009B/1047